CLOSED: 99 WAYS TO STOP ABORTION

CLOSED: 99 Ways to Stop Abortion

Joseph M. Scheidler

Foreword by
Franky Schaeffer

Distributed to the bookstore trade by
CROSSWAY BOOKS • WESTCHESTER, IL
A DIVISION OF GOOD NEWS PUBLISHERS

NOTE TO THE READER: Because the methods advocated in this book have potential for abuse, the author and publisher wish to make clear to the reader that it is not their intention to motivate, encourage or advocate illegal conduct or behavior. The author and publisher do respect the moral courage of those in the pro-life cause who engage in non-violent and peaceful protest to the point of civil disobedience after obtaining legal advice, and when they are prepared to suffer the legal consequences of their action.

The author and publisher advise that wherever there is any question concerning the legal right of any person potentially affected by anything stated or implied in this book, the reader should consult legal counsel. The author has set forth his experiences and opinions in the sincere hope that the reader (if not already so persuaded) will support the pro-life movement by direct action to stop the abortion industry's perpetuation of the tragic death of innocent, unborn babies.

Regnery Books is an imprint of Regnery Gateway, Inc. All inquiries concerning this book should be directed to Regnery Gateway, Inc., 940 North Shore Drive, Lake Bluff, IL 60044.

Distributed to the religious and general bookstore trade by Crossway Books, a division of Good News Publishers, 9825 West Roosevelt Road, Westchester, IL 60153.

ISBN 0-89107-346-9
Library of Congress Catalog Card Number 85-042646

Cover design by Cioni Artworks.
Photo on back cover by Ken Buck.

CONTENTS

ACKNOWLEDGMENTS

Many people are responsible for this book. Some of them are listed in the Index for their contributions to the kind of pro-life activism that made it possible to put together ninety-nine chapters on how to close down the abortion industry. I am grateful to them all for their ideas and their valiant efforts.

But special thanks go to my wife, Ann, for encouraging me to put these methods together in book form and coming up with the idea for the title.

Gratitude goes also to Marie Rivera who doggedly transcribed every one of the ninety-nine chapters from my sometimes incoherent tapes. And thanks also to Barbara Menes for typing, to Dick O'Connor for the art work and proofreading, and to attorney John Jakubczyk, for his legal advice.

Others who offered valuable suggestions and took the time to correct copy were Thomas Chadwick, Sandra Jones, and Virginia Reuter. And a special thanks to Franky Schaeffer who encouraged the writing of this book, served as my agent, and wrote the inspiring foreword that gives the book exactly the right send-off.

I would like to dedicate this book to my mother, Kathleen Scheidler, who first taught me to respect the life of the innocent unborn and whose last words to me on her deathbed at the age of eighty-two were, ''Joe, I'm so proud of your pro-life work. Keep it up.''

FOREWORD

As the last chapters of the twentieth century unfold, we Americans find ourselves being led into the 1990s by leaders who, for the most part, have abandoned belief in moral absolutes. Lamentably few genuine heroes ever appear on the modern scene for us to emulate, and it is unlikely that they would be recognized should they appear. True leadership and selfless heroism in our time must come in unexpected forms from unexpected people and in unexpected places. Contrast the pre-packaged heroism of our astronauts with the spiritual beauty, love, and strength of Mother Teresa. In giving her life for "the least of these", she does not rest on her laurels, but dares to speak out with courage, as she did at Harvard University, for the virtues of virginity and chastity, and against murder through abortion. Instead of mouthing empty platitudes in her Nobel Prize acceptance speech, Mother Teresa used the occasion of receiving the Peace Prize to defend the rights of the unborn. Disregarding the pressure to "fit in" with society's mainstream, she strives with courage and conviction, eyes fixed steadily on the Master, to do what is right, pure, and lovely.

Another unexpected and less recognized hero of the late twentieth century is Father Bruce Ritter of New York City. Through his homes for runaway teenagers who have been lured or coerced into prostitution and child pornography, Father Ritter has demonstrated the love of Christ. While the American Civil Liberties Union (ACLU) and the New York Supreme Court busy themselves defending the "civil liberty" of child pornography, Father Ritter proclaims the gospel and reaches out to provide food, shelter, and love for homeless and abused children.

Ponder the courage of Archbishop John J. O'Connor of New York and Archbishop Bernard Law of Boston who speak out—and are attacked for doing so—on the subject of abortion. Their outspokenness has put many of their more reticent colleagues to shame, has antagonized the pro-abortion media, and has angered political leaders who detest "interference" from those such as Bernard Law and John O'Connor. Yet they speak on undaunted.

The history of the Church is paved with acts of mercy and compassion. While there are myriads of hospitals named St. Mary's, St. Luke's, St. John's, St. Theresa's, St. Francis', there are very few

11

hospitals named St. Darwin, St. Jean-Jacques Rousseau, or St. Voltaire. The Church has not achieved perfection in this world nor has it made the world good. But imagine the untrammelled savagery of our world if there were no Mother Teresas, no Father Ritters, no Salvation Armies, no missionary doctors, no pennies saved to buy blankets for the huddled refugees from Afghanistan. Even the barbarity and excesses of the Soviet Union have been moderated by the Soviet desire to curry favor with Western public opinion which, because of Judeo-Christian influence, professes protection of human rights. A world without the mitigating influence of Christianity would perhaps be like the Soviet Union under Stalin, but without the pretense of protecting human rights.

George Orwell has accurately described such a godless world in his book *1984*. We hear its echoes in Aldous Huxley's book *Brave New World*, and we learn exactly how such a society is organized from reading *Animal Farm*. Visually one thinks of the mean streets in Ridley Stott's brilliant film *Blade Runner* or the societal structures of Federico Fellini's ancient Rome as portrayed in *Satyricon*.

The holocaust carried on against the Jews by the Nazis during World War II was a dark and dastardly act, but through this fortress of evil, light poured through certain chinks in the wall. Christ's love was carried by Corrie Ten Boom to the few she was able to hide in her attic. Dietrich Bonhoeffer staunchly defended truth and goodness against the forces of wickedness. Nameless saints known only to God Himself and recorded only in the Book of Life, shared their last loaves, gave a blanket to someone colder than they, took someone's place in line for the gas chamber. Without such redemptive acts of heroism, pity, and compassion even the twentieth century, known primarily as the century of genocide and holocaust, would be much worse. The boat people fleeing Communist Vietnam were a tragedy, but the tragedy would have been even greater if there had been no agencies of compassion, no families that would open their homes to take these people in. Perhaps an image of hell would be a world in which man remains unredeemed and eternally plays out his wicked desires unfettered by Christian compassion or charity.

C. S. Lewis understood well that inhuman ideas masquerading as human are the most dangerous of all. In *The Lion, the Witch and the Wardrobe* he wrote: "But in general, take my advice, when you meet anything that's going to be human and isn't yet, or used to be human once and isn't now, or ought to be human and isn't, keep your eyes on it and feel for your hatchet.'' The rhetoric of the abortion movement has set a new high in the use of euphemisms, dressing up murder of one's child as ''choice'' and demanding abortion rights on the basis of ''compassion''. Such euphemisms pervert the mind and deform the heart into something that ''used to be human once and isn't now''.

Thank God that in our day of inhumanity and spiritual lifelessness, the Lord has raised up heroes, leaders, and saints to step forward into the breach. Joseph Scheidler is such a man. Like Dietrich Bonhoeffer who was unwilling to let the merciless rule of Nazism roll on unopposed, Joseph Scheidler has seen the sorrow, suffering, and wickedness of abortion and has accepted the challenge to stop this evil trade in human flesh, this resurrection of the spirit of Nazism, this ''liberal'' fascism. Joseph Scheidler has been unwilling, in this age of genocide and eugenics, to sit back and wait either for changing political climates or Supreme Court reversals. Every day that passes more babies are murdered within their mother's wombs. These babies suffer agonizing deaths, and their mothers are scarred psychologically, spiritually, and often physically for the rest of their lives. The abortion business is a soul-destroying evil paralleled only in the darkest moments of history, and Joseph Scheidler has stepped forward to lead the fight against abortion, not by word alone but also by deed.

A growing number of courageous and believing Christians are beginning to understand that abortion will not simply go away for the wishing. Something must be done *now*! Joseph Scheidler provides in this book the method and the means, step by step, for shutting down abortion clinics through the exercise of our constitutional rights and freedoms. As Mother Teresa surveyed the sadness and death of India, she, too, must have realized that she could not solve every problem. And yet she started somewhere; she began to make a dent. She did not wait for political solutions or government programs but went out into the streets herself to bring the love of Christ to the outcasts.

Many attempt to avoid the reality and truth presented by Joe Scheidler. Some say that to advocate direct action through peaceful demonstrations, picketing, and non-violent civil disobedience against abortion clinics is to incite violence. But such an argument is as absurd as to accuse Mother Teresa of inciting violence because she has taken direct action on behalf of the poor in Calcutta. Others argue that to take direct action is ''uncompassionate'', ''unloving'', or even ''un-Christlike''. Yet Christ took direct action against the hypocrisy and wickedness of the age in which he lived. He drove the money changers out of the

Temple. He took direct action against disease by healing the sick. He accused the Pharisees and the Sanhedrin, to their faces, of wickedness and deceit. Love must not be confused with timidity and compromise. True compassionate, loving, Christlike behavior is often tough. Just as it is not loving to pat on the head a child who has run into the street, neglecting to teach him the dangers of playing in the street, so it is also unloving to mumble platitudes about forgiveness and acceptance in the face of the villainous abortion industry. To remain silent in the midst of evil is to side with that evil. To do nothing, to say nothing, is to allow the dead and the dying to lie unattended on the roadside.

From time to time we have seen some unfortunate episodes of violence against the abortion industry. However, the case can be made that this violence has often been instigated by the abortion industry itself, because the very violence of abortion, *the cruel dismembering piece by piece of unborn children*, sparks a violent antagonism which, though not excusable, is understandable. The abortion industry and organizations such as Planned Parenthood create a feeling of tremendous frustration within many pro-life activist groups by the systematic attempt to strip pro-life activists of their constitutional rights of free assembly and free speech. In case after case abortion clinics are bringing lawsuits against pro-life activists in an attempt to intimidate them into silence. Court injunctions by pro-abortion judges against pro-life demonstrations strip pro-life activists of the peaceable means to protest. In Boston recently a crisis pregnancy clinic was closed because of a suit brought against it by Planned Parenthood. Regrettably, some pro-lifers mistakenly, out of anger and frustration, are driven toward non-peaceful methods.

Abortionists who take thousands of lives for pay cannot expect the Christian community simply to turn away as if nothing was happening. If abortionists and their organizations attempt to protect their trade in human flesh by stripping others of their constitutional rights through court injunctions against picketing, they have then deprived the pro-life movement of constitutional, peaceable means of action. Unfortunately, violence begets violence.

The bigotry of the pro-abortion forces has produced frustration. As Cal Thomas wrote in a column in the *Boston Globe* (November 30, 1984),

> . . . Tactically, as well as politically, the bombing of abortion clinics is
> probably not a good idea. It allows the pro-choicers to shift the debate

from what is taking place inside the buildings to what is taking place outside.

Pro-life groups, however, continue to be denied access to the media with their most compelling argument against abortion. That argument is rooted in pictures of the unborn and of what actually takes place during an abortion. Once the word (or in this case, the picture) is out, the argument between "product of conception" and "baby" will quickly be brought to an end.

Until then, we are likely to see more of these bombing incidents, just as we did during the 1960s when blacks, frustrated by peaceful attempts to win their civil rights, decided to take matters into their own hands and direct the attention of the country to their plight.

A national debate on abortion is long overdue. It is only when that debate is allowed to take place that we can expect the bombings to stop.

Joseph Scheidler's book shows the practical ways that each of us can take the love of Christ forcefully, but peaceably, and with purpose, into the streets. We cannot wait for the "abortion problem" to be solved for us. Street by street, neighborhood by neighborhood, we must fight this necessary battle until legalized abortion is relegated to the barbaric past along with slavery and cannibalism! This street by street approach is the only method that really works; first, because it puts pressure on politicians, judges, and the media elite in a way that mere talk will never do; and second, because it actually saves *babies' lives*. We may not be able to shut every abortion clinic in the country, but we can shut the abortion clinic in our neighborhood. We may not be able to save every baby, but we can save many.

Laws against rape, murder, and theft manage only to stop some rapes, some murders, and some thefts, but they are seen as necessary laws because they curb evil that would otherwise be rampant. So, too, the pro-life movement must adopt the methods outlined in Joe Scheidler's book which will stop some abortions, some murders, some infanticide, some destruction of women's souls. The fact that Christ died for all mankind but only some believe does not negate the efficacy of His sacrifice. In a fallen world we cannot create perfection. But as Christians understanding man's fallen nature we can make things *much better*. People are not statistics. Every baby saved is a warm, breathing, human dearly loved by God, with its own individual destiny and name.

With deep gratitude, therefore, I commend Joe Scheidler for the personal price he has paid, as evident in this moving and inspiring book. In a misguided generation, God raises up shepherds to do the work of those leaders who have abdicated their responsibility to lead His people. When apparent shepherds show themselves to be hirelings fleeing before the wolves (as the evangelical leaders have fled before the wolf of the eugenics movement) the Lord raises up men like Joe Scheidler to show us the way. Hear him.

Franky Schaeffer, 1985

INTRODUCTION

This book is based on the equation that abortion equals murder. It will make sense only to those who believe without question that abortion is the unjust, premeditated taking of an innocent human life. *Closed: 99 Ways to Stop Abortion* is a collection of methods that can be used, and that have been used successfully, to stop abortions.

In America, a violent death from abortion takes place every twenty seconds. That is a total of 4,500 deaths every day, 1.7 million abortions each year. Slaughter of a nation's posterity will destroy that nation both physically and spiritually. America is being destroyed by the killing of its children before they are born.

Those who understand abortion and want to stop it have an obligation to recruit others into the pro-life movement and to pass on to them their experience and expertise so that, in time, the injustice of abortion will end. Pro-life activists cannot wait for the legislative and judicial process that will make abortion illegal. The activist has to save lives now.

We wonder at intelligent people passing laws and making rulings to justify the barbaric destruction of human beings in the name of privacy. We marvel also at the broad acceptance of this travesty as a solution to the personal problem of unplanned pregnancy.

But not all Americans were mesmerized by the abortion rulings. From the beginning, small groups of pro-life people fought the trend to make the killing of the unborn acceptable. They have been succeeding in their efforts to bring society back to its senses, and they are convinced that in time they will win.

No social movement in the history of this country has succeeded without activists taking to the streets. Activism, including demonstrations, pickets, protests, and sit-ins, is necessary not only to save lives but to garner public attention, bring the media into the struggle, and shake politicians into recognizing the determination of anti-abortion supporters. Anyone who misses this purpose of activism is a poor student of history.

This book is about acting on the conviction that every unborn human life is of inestimable value, of itself, to society, and in the eyes of God. This book says it is not enough to believe in the value of that life and

17

condemn abortion. It says that unless we act on our hatred of abortion we are little better than those who support it.

This book is based on an act of faith. It takes the belief in defenseless human life seriously, and proposes ways to save those lives through suffering, sacrifice, prayer, and action. It is a response to the command to go and teach, and it teaches that we shall not kill.

Since the activities and methods proposed in this book are *intended* to interfere with and even stop the business of abortion, when you use them clinic personnel may file complaints against you or call the police and have you arrested. Cases resulting from these actions will often be dismissed. But they may also result in some form of penalty, fines, or supervision. If you have any questions about the legality or advisability of any of the methods of protest discussed in this book, we suggest that you consult a competent attorney before you engage in them. We do not intend to suggest or recommend any activities that the reader would consider immoral or unethical. Whatever you decide to do must conform to your rightly formed conscience. But if you are willing to suffer and be ridiculed for the sake of small and helpless human beings whom you will never know and who will never know what you did for them, this book is for you. Read it and learn.

If you are an abortionist and favor the killing of the unborn and you want to know what pro-life activists have in store for you and the abortion industry, this book is also for you. Read it and weep.

1 SIDEWALK COUNSELING

Sidewalk counseling is a method of saving babies by talking to their parents in front of the abortion clinic. It is probably the single most valuable activity that a pro-life person can engage in. When pro-lifers counsel in front of an abortion clinic, they are coming between the woman and the doctor, between the baby who is scheduled to be killed and the doctor who will do the killing.

Counseling goes to the very heart of the abortion problem. The problem of abortion is a problem of killing babies. They are killed in abortion clinics or hospitals or doctors' offices, and pro-lifers go there to intercede for the baby's life. The aim of the Pro-Life Action League and other activist groups is to get more people out on the streets to stand between the killers and the victims.

There is no one way to do sidewalk counseling. The counselor has to know something about human nature and must be able to understand the crisis the woman is facing. The counselor must understand what has driven her to this unnatural, inhuman solution to a problem pregnancy. The counselor must understand why she wants to kill her baby. Surely the worst solution to *any* problem is to kill an innocent human being. Yet, that is the solution a woman chooses in having an abortion. Something drove her to that. Some people think it is such a difficult decision to make that once it is made there is no way to turn back.

But women *can* be turned back. In Chicago, in one thirty day period, half a dozen sidewalk counselors at only a few clinics were able to stop ninety women from having abortions. Seventeen were stopped in a single morning at a clinic on Michigan Avenue. While a few of these women may have gone back to have their abortions later, more than ninety percent did not return and they kept in touch with the pro-life counseling center. All because there were sidewalk counselors present.

An analogy sometimes used to bring home the reality of abortion is formed by the question: If someone came into your living room and grabbed your three-year-old and rushed out of the house, threw the child into an automobile and drove off, what would you do? Would you write a letter to the editor? Would you complain to your congressman?

Would you notify the police to give better protection to your neighborhood? No, you would not do any of those things. You would rush out of the house, jump into your car, and pursue the kidnapper in order to rescue your child. If you saw him take the child into a building, *you would go into that building*. No one could keep you out. You would go where the child is. You would try to save him.

That is what we do when we go to an abortion clinic. We believe in the total humanity of the unborn child. We believe in it so firmly that we put ourselves between the child and the abortionist. But we must be armed with knowledge and skill so that we will actually save the child. We have to do the saving through words, actions, a right attitude, and prayer.

Some people go to the clinics just to pray. That can be very effective. People at prayer are an impressive sight to people going in to kill their child. Prayer has its own special power. It is always necessary. But pro-lifers at the clinic also must talk to the woman, the boyfriend, the parent who is with the young girl, or the girlfriend who is accompanying her. Frequently, the woman accompanying the patient will have had an abortion. Often the patient herself will have had a previous abortion. There are many obstacles to overcome.

The counselor can gently ask the woman if she wants to talk. Some counselors will take "no" for an answer and not pursue the matter. Others will continue their efforts. Some try to win the woman over by a cheerful greeting and then offer her literature that will not be repugnant to her, literature with a picture of a baby or a pregnant woman. Others will simply get down to basics and ask, "Have you thought about the baby?" "Have you thought about what an abortion does?" "Have you thought about your own health and your own body?" Counselors who have been going to the clinics for years do not become discouraged by rejection. They realize that most attempts will end in rejection. At least nine out of ten women approached will have the abortion anyway. Counselors will be called names. People strike out at pro-life counselors or brush past them. But whatever the reaction, the attempt itself is something positive and in many cases is probably the only effort that has been made to save the baby's life. A peaceful presence and the presentation of a positive alternative to this tragic situation can be a blessing in itself.

One method that has been effective in dissuading women from having abortions is to broadcast the malpractice suits that have been brought against the particular clinic. As you get to know more and more women who have visited a particular abortion clinic and suffered physical and psychological traumas there as a result of their abortions, you can approach other women with a genuine concern for their health and show them an example from an actual court case. One Chicago clinic, considered to be among the best in town, once had twenty-two outstanding malpractice suits against it. Counselors who have worked outside this clinic on at least three occasions saw an ambulance pulling up to take away an injured woman who had gone there for an abortion.

Malpractice suits are kept on file at the courthouse and you can check these, along with the cases coming up for hearings. The charges, doctor's names, clinic's names, dates, and many more facts are available to the public.

We have discovered that often a young woman does not realize just how well developed the life inside her is at her stage of pregnancy. The clinic personnel have told her that it is not even a baby, but is only tissue. They have lied to her to make her feel at ease about having an abortion. Once pro-life counselors talk to her about fetal development, show her pictures of what her baby looks like and how well developed it is, she may very well change her mind. Sometimes all it takes is to have someone there with the facts of fetal development and the facts of abortion. She is not going to get any of these facts inside the clinic.

The counselor should encourage the woman to talk or get her boyfriend to talk to her if he's against the abortion. Sometimes a friend comes with the woman, not so much to accompany her, as to try to talk her out of the abortion. The pro-life counselor should use all the help he or she can get. The counselor should try to take the woman somewhere where they can sit down and talk about the problem.

If the woman is willing to talk, it is extremely helpful if there is a pregnancy help agency nearby to which she can be taken or referred. Pro-life leadership has been trying to set up pregnancy help offices near every abortion clinic. There, women can have pregnancy tests and talk with counselors immediately. In Chicago, most abortions are stopped at clinics where there is a pregnancy help agency nearby and where women can get help quickly. It is not enough to give a woman a phone number and tell her to call in a few days. The more immediate the alternative is, the better chance there is of stopping the abortion.

It may be necessary for the sidewalk counselor to follow through, get the woman's name and phone number, and help her during her pregnancy. It is not always enough to talk a woman out of an abortion. The counselor may need to follow up to make certain the woman doesn't waver in her decision to carry the baby to term. A counselor may even help secure a good doctor, find a place for her to stay, or get financial help. Perhaps it is a matter of talking to her parents, husband, or boyfriend. Whatever the problem is that is causing her to contemplate abortion, it must be solved. The counselor must help make this as comfortable a decision as possible. Abortion seems like a quick, easy solution. But it is a solution many women, in the long run, cannot live with.

Listed at the end of this chapter are some resources on sidewalk counseling. Remember, sidewalk counseling is probably the single most valuable pro-life activity. If done successfully, it may prove to be one of the main means of permanently stopping abortion. After all, if abortion clinics do not have customers they will go out of business. If there were two or three counselors, on a regular basis, at each of the three thousand or more abortion clinics in the United States, over one hundred thousand lives could be saved every year and many clinics would be forced to close down.

Catholics United for Life says that the main requirements for effective counseling are an interest in other people and their problems, compassion and empathy. You must always be able to put yourself in the other person's place. The best counselors are good listeners, because often people will find their own solutions if they only have someone to listen while they talk out their problems. Counseling is nine-tenths listening and one-tenth advising.

Another essential requirement for sidewalk counselors is a solid morality. You need a good sense of ethics and a concern for the other person's future. The trouble with abortion clinic counselors is that they give women short-term solutions, without considering the long-term consequences.

The decision to abort stops a life that would otherwise go on for the duration of the mother's life and beyond, leading into other lives and families. An abortion actually involves thousands of lives. A woman who ends a pregnancy ends generations. A good counselor would understand the magnitude of a decision to abort and would never counsel an abortion.

There are thousands of successful sidewalk counselors saving babies every day of the year, all over the country, and they do not all follow the same method. Each person approaches the challenge differently. If you want to learn more from those who have perfected the special talent of counseling, we suggest you write for information from the following:

PRO-LIFE ACTION LEAGUE
   6160 N. Cicero
   Chicago, IL 60646
Ask for *The Chicago Method*, by
Richard Freeman, one of the country's most successful sidewalk counselors. Include $2.50 for postage
and handling.

CATHOLICS UNITED FOR LIFE
   New Hope, KY 40052
A detailed guide for those who have
never counseled before.

THE POCKET-PAC PRO-LIFE PRESENTATION

All pro-life activists, and especially sidewalk counselors, should carry with them a set
of color prints showing fetal development and the methods of abortion. Their use is not
restricted to sidewalk counseling. You never know when someone will bring up the subject
of abortion, on a bus or airplane, at work, at the beauty parlor or in the barber shop. With a
set of these eight basic pictures you can educate and convince people on the spot. You have
the basics of a right-to-life presentation in your pocket book or wallet.

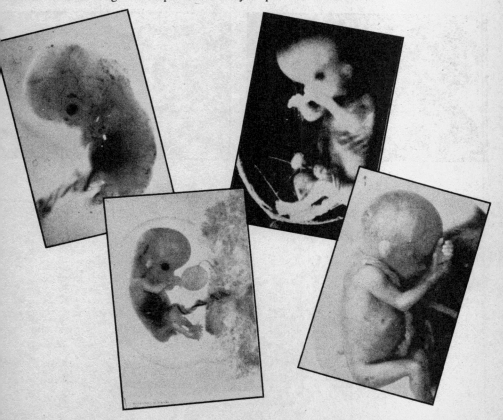

Each set contains four glossy color 3 1/4 x 4 1/2 in. prints of fetal development at 6 weeks, 8 weeks, 12 weeks and 16-18 weeks, and four prints showing the major abortion techniques: suction; D & E; saline; and hysterotomy. Sets are $5 each. Order from the Pro-Life Action League, Suite 210, 6160 N. Cicero Ave., Chicago, IL 60646. Price includes postage and handling.

2 TRUTH TEAMS

In its most basic form, the truth team is a couple, usually a young man and woman, posing as clients for an abortion, who station themselves in the waiting room area of an abortion clinic in order to discuss a "proposed" abortion with genuine clients in order to change their decision about having an abortion. The team can also be two young women, or a young woman and her "mother". A "team" of one is possible—a young woman alone or young man "waiting" for his girl—but this arrangement should be discouraged. One person truth teams are difficult and unsafe. The person must strike up a conversation directly with a genuine client, which is more difficult to do. Also, there will be no friendly witness in case of trouble.

The two member team usually has taken literature from a pro-life counselor outside and begins the conversation by discussing some statement in the literature or something the pro-lifers outside said about the humanity of the baby, the dangers of abortion, or the legal issues involved. While discussing this matter with each other, the pending abortion is addressed in such a way as to draw in any interested listeners. The conversation must remain sufficiently low-key, so that clinic personnel will not become suspicious too soon. The objective is, of course, to plant in the minds of the clients in the waiting room serious doubts about the advisability of having an abortion.

Most clinic directors have made provisions for preventing truth teams from accomplishing their goals, but it is impossible for them to be 100 percent effective in their efforts without driving away genuine customers. While clinics have a variety of pre-abortion procedures, it is often possible to find a way to get into an area of the clinic and talk to customers contemplating abortions.

Truth teams can be very effective. One team says in a single morning it has dissuaded six couples from going through with abortions. A thorough knowledge of the biological and medical facts is essential, but a good sense of timing and a bit of acting talent is also an asset.

It can be effective for two or three teams to be present in a waiting room on a given occasion. One team begins the conversation and a second team "enters in". After discussing abortion in a convincing way, the first team gets up and walks out. The second team follows a few minutes later. A third team, which has not entered into the discussion, can stay behind, to encourage others and suggest that perhaps the two couples who left had the right idea. Teams can also report later on the reaction their leaving and subsequent defections by genuine clients had on clinic personnel. They leave the clinic when their turn comes for the abortion or when it is time to pay. If early payment is required, coverts should use whatever time is available to present their various misgivings.

Truth teaming takes courage, but is extremely rewarding. Arrangements should be made in advance to have pro-life street counselors outside to give assistance to women who elect to leave. Successful truth teams may well be a *team*, having rehearsed their dialogue well before engaging in this mission. They are in an enviable position, reaching the young woman at the very last moment when she may be most susceptible to their arguments.

In Chicago, a truth team, Bob and Gloria, became so effective that they were not only able to work their way into the clinics to talk to the young people, but frequently asked to talk to the clinic counselor or were asked by the counselor if they needed help. On several occasions they went into the counselor's office to discuss what the clinic was doing.

Gloria would tell Bob that she was convinced that abortion destroys a human life, and that the pamphlet given them by the pro-lifers indicated that the "product of conception" (as clinic personnel called it) actually is a baby with a heart-beat, brain-waves, hands, and feet. Frequently others waiting in the room would join the conversation. On one occasion they got the counselor to promise that she would look into the matter of fetal life. Bob and Gloria said they would come back the following Saturday to discuss the issue.

A week later Bob and Gloria returned to the clinic with a book that showed pictures of fetal development. The book they used was *A Child is Born, The Drama of Life Before Birth*, a Dell Publication with photographs by Lennart Nillson. They also described to the counselor the Chicago Museum of Science and Industry exhibit on fetal development. They told her it was obvious to anyone who saw the exhibit that a little human being exists in the womb. They said that they were concerned about women who have abortions and then find out these facts later on. It could cause them a great emotional suffering. This seemed to have a profound effect on the counselor, who appeared to have a conscience.

Bob and Gloria wrote up their experiences. We have their reports on file at our office. They make interesting reading, and when we are training other counselors we sometimes use these accounts to help them understand how a good truth team works.

3 THE PICKET AND DEMONSTRATION

The peaceful demonstration or picket is one of the most effective tools pro-lifers have to stop abortions and eventually close down the abortion industry. During one full year in Chicago, a senior citizen picketed a State Street abortion clinic every day, despite rain, heat, or freezing temperatures, and literally closed the clinic. The old gentleman, Philip de Filipo, is dead now but the clinic remains closed. Despite jeers from passersby as well as threats by the clinic owners and their attorneys, Phil continued passing out literature, talking to clients, and carrying a picket sign telling of the value of unborn human life. He remained at his post until the clinic closed a few days before he died.

More effective than a small picket is the massive demonstration in front of a clinic entry. Many potential clients do not want to pass through a moving picket line, or risk being photographed if the media are present, which it is likely to be when the crowd is large.

Pickets must be well-planned, well-organized, and, above all, orderly. Signs should be carefully checked beforehand. Anything crude, insulting, or off the subject should be rejected. Wording on picket signs should be large, concise, uncomplicated, and to the point. Names of clinic owners, operators, and doctors may be used on the signs. ABORTION KILLS BABIES, ABORTION IS MURDER, DON'T ABORT YOUR BABY, GIVE LIFE A CHANCE, LIFE YES—ABORTION NO, ADOPTION NOT ABORTION are examples of slogans that zero in on the subject and the attitude. Lengthy quotes may be effective when they are photographed for a newspaper or magazine article, in which case they will be read in full, but in general, they are unsuitable, especially for television. Large, single-subject photographs of live babies or aborted babies are useful, but small cutout pictures cannot be seen.

While colored lettering such as red, blue, and green are effective, black is always best, and paper should be light, preferably white. Yellow, cream, or tan are tolerable. Black lettering on a white background is the best arrangement. White lettering on a black background, while a good contrast, is often more difficult to read but is becoming popular. Always use paints rather than markers or crayons. If water-base paint is used make sure it is water-proofed by using an acrylic spray or covering the sign with thin cellophane, such as the cheap, thin polyethylene dropcloth available in discount and hardware stores.

Mounting signs on sticks not only increases their visibility, but makes them easy to carry. In some demonstrations, however, police will outlaw sticks, in which case they must be easy to remove. Make sure signs are firm enough not to flop or tear, and write the same message on both sides. A blank back on a sign tells nothing.

Every picket should have appointed marshals who indicate the parameters of the march, keep the picket moving, watch the spacing, prevent bunching up, and maintain order and discipline. Marshals should wear a distinctive badge or armband.

Name-calling or any behavior that may give the picket a bad image or reflect negatively on the pro-life movement must be avoided. Carrying signs, praying, chanting informative slogans, and singing are proper activities during the picket.

The marshal who gives directions and leads songs and chants should use a megaphone or bullhorn. He should welcome suggestions from the group, but not allow conflicting messages, songs, or slogans to be called out simultaneously. Generally, simple slogans, songs, and prayers, led alternatively with occasional periods of complete silence, will occupy the group. It is impressive to see a crowd of a hundred or more pickets walking in complete silence before an abortion clinic.

A picket held on a public sidewalk will be directed by police to keep moving, usually in single file and in a long oval. It should move slowly enough that children, adults carrying children or pushing babies, and elderly members do not tire. Demonstrations, especially if arrangements have been made for speakers, do not have to keep moving.

During the picket the sidewalk must not be blocked, and access to entrances and exits must remain free if your group wants to avoid problems with the police.

Police should be notified of the picket in advance, and when they arrive, a representative of the group should introduce himself to the officer in charge, give his name, the name and purpose of his group, and indicate how long the picket is expected to last. Cooperation with the police is important, and it is best not to argue with them or ignore their orders. If, on occasion, they ask the picket to move back, tighten up, keep moving, or even move across the street, it is generally better to comply than to argue. As a rule, police restrictions will not harm the effectiveness of the picket, whereas disobeying their orders might lead to difficulties. The police almost always win.

Pickets are an old American tradition, one with wide acceptance. Recent court rulings have been favorable towards pickets and public demonstrations, allowing them to be carried out even in some shopping centers. Rather than becoming outmoded or obsolete, the picket is more in vogue today than ever before, and it is one of the pro-life movement's most effective tools. It is protected under the First Amendment rights of free speech and assembly.

In many cities, pickets have effectively cut down on abortions, have led to valuable discussions with clinic management and personnel, and have reminded the community and press of the gravity of the abortion controversy. It is difficult to ignore the presence of two or three hundred picketers at a clinic every week, vociferously claiming that human lives are being destroyed. A picket is a necessary means of bringing attention to the evil it is trying to curb. Nearly anyone can join in a picket—old, young, children, couples, religious groups. Even those not in full agreement with the pro-life philosophy have joined our pickets to protest payment for abortion with tax money, although generally it is better for group morale for all members to be strong pro-lifers.

Promptness is vital to a good picket. Picketers must be advised to arrive on time. All directions and directives must be clear. If a picket is to begin at a certain time, all leaders, marshals, and sign carriers should meet at a designated point beforehand so that they will arive at the picket site exactly on time. Nothing is more devastating to a picket than for picketers to arrive and find no leadership present. Some pickets have dissolved for this reason. In Chicago, some years ago, several dozen picketers arrived at various times for a scheduled event, but since the leader was away making phone calls trying to persuade more groups to come, none of the groups stayed, and the picket dissolved. Wait long enough for all the participants to gather.

In preparing for the picket it is a good idea to have individuals in charge of every facet of the picket. For instance, always try to have someone skilled at carpentry to set up a small platform. We use a one foot high, five by four foot platform at pickets so that the director can stand above the crowd. The platform has three sockets, one for a a pole to hold the loudspeaker, one for an American flag, and one for a cross. American flags should be carried in all pickets, since the pro-life movement represents the true spirit of America, guaranteeing an inalienable right to life.

It is important to have someone in charge of handling the press. This individual carries a set of press packets and hands them out to all media representatives. He also makes the calls to the media and should be prepared to answer their questions.

Also, have someone take down the names, addresses, and phone numbers of all picketers. This serves several purposes: it provides a list of reliable people to call on in the future; it gives you names and addresses of those you may want to send thank-you letters and press clippings; and also it gives picketers the feeling that their participation is not taken for granted and that they are important to the cause. You should have no trouble getting people to give their names. Have someone with a clipboard walk with each picketer until all names and addresses have been recorded. This may take time, but afterwards it will prove useful.

Several things can be done during the picket to keep it from getting tedious. Reverse the direction of the picket occasionally. Have a wide selection of songs, chants, and slogans. Break up the slogans so that the men say one part and the women say another, alternately. Teach the group a new song while they are marching. Use recorded music to accompany the singing.

Have someone with a good voice lead songs and chants, and invite speakers from religious or civic groups to address the picket from the director's platform.

As a rule, if someone has been designated to speak on behalf of the picketers, discourage others in the group from talking to the press. If you cannot direct the press to the spokesman you have selected, make certain everyone in the picket has a clear idea of what the picket is all about. Before any picket or demonstration begins, the director should explain, from the platform, the precise nature of the picket and indicate what should be relayed to the press, should anyone in the group be asked to make a statement.

Over the years we have learned the psychology of picket lines and have developed it. As soon as we get participants moving with their signs, we start a vigorous chant and let the picketers put all their energy into it. We have found that it gets the adrenalin flowing, lets people express their anger at abortion, starts the picket off with a strong pace, builds confidence, presents an image of strength and decisiveness, and startles those inside the clinic.

As the picket progresses, there will be some picketers who call out to patients going into the clinic and to the clinic personnel. It is better not to try to stop this because picketers have strong feelings that are difficult to curb, and usually their shouting is not derogatory. It is the only way they have while they are in the picket line of reaching those entering the clinic. Even if you have counselors on the edges of the picket, there are still going to be people heading into the clinic who will not be reached by the counselors. They may, however, be reached by someone in the picket line telling them not to kill their baby, or reminding them that Jesus loves them and their baby.

These are not bad things to have going on. They may look bad to a disinterested passerby, and the media may try to color them as sinister, but the important thing is that the message is relayed that abortion is a terrible thing. The shouted message even reaches into the clinic. The people inside will hear it and may reflect on what they are about to do. People have a right to express the outrage they feel, so long as they are not abusive.

After a period of animated chants, the picket becomes more pensive and meditative and it slows down its pace a bit. The picketers have spent their initial energy in singing and chanting slogans, and now begin to think more seriously about the reality of abortion and of the children who are dying. The picketers become more subdued. This is a good time to sing songs like "Let Me Live" or "All We Are Saying Is Give Life a Chance" and other songs that create a prayerful mood. It might even be time to recite some prayers.

By the time the police and press arrive, the picket is an image of control and reflection. It is inevitable that if it starts out boisterous and raucous it will, after a while, become calm, quiet, and easy to manage. It also becomes easier for the counselors to work on a one-to-one basis with clients. The mood will indicate to the police that they have nothing to worry about.

Inevitably, there will be those in the picket who will try to direct it by complaining to the leader or telling other marchers what they should do. This should be discouraged. The person who organized the picket is the one who leads it, and those who disagree should express their concerns privately, rather than argue them out in front of the public.

On occasion I have taken aside those who wanted to make some change. I have told them that my organization worked hard to put this picket together, and that I am in charge of it. If they want to have a picket of their own, they have a perfect right to organize one and run it their way. This is usually effective. I have sometimes taken the advice of those who call me aside, and I have changed things, but I have not done this often. There will always be people who complain that the signs are too harsh, that people are calling out things they shouldn't, and that the picketers are not compassionate. Others will say the picket is too tame and is not accomplishing what it set out to do. You may take these well-intended suggestions under consideration, but in the final analysis the individual conducting the picket should decide how it is run. And this arrangement should be made clear from the start. Don't show disagreement in front of the enemy.

A large and well-organized picket will sometimes attract passersby who will join it when they learn the reason for the picket. In a well-remembered picket in Indianapolis, early media coverage prompted some pro-lifers to drive all the way across town to join in, swelling the number of protestors to nearly three hundred, where only one hundred picketers were anticipated. It is imperative to have counselors present at every abortion clinic picket. Picketing alone is effective, but it is more positive and helpful when you have counselors on hand.

In every talk I give, I challenge pro-lifers to search their consciences and ask themselves why they don't spend at least two hours a month on a picket line, handing out literature, or doing sidewalk counseling in front of an abortion clinic. I offer two exceptions to this demanding work: cloistered nuns and federal prisoners serving life sentences. The challenge is open to everyone, from cardinal to judge, from governor to pro-life author. I tell them to ask themselves if they are too important to do sidewalk work, to be a foot soldier in the battle for the unborn. I remind them that I know a cardinal who has picketed, an archbishop who has come to the clinics, a Greek Orthodox priest, a judge, a doctor, a police captain, and even a pro-life lawyer. Are they superior to these busy people?

Franky Schaeffer has said that if there is an abortion clinic in your neighborhood and it isn't picketed every time abortions are performed there, that community has accepted abortion. If this is the case in your community, you too have accepted abortion unless you organize to picket it.

CHECKLIST FOR CLINIC PICKET

Before the Picket:

1. Print handouts explaining the purpose of the picket.
2. Have your attorney review the state and city laws governing pickets.
3. Have phone numbers of the media—TV, radio, newspapers—to be contacted the morning of the picket.

4. Check out the clinic for possible problems. Is it in a shopping mall? How is the parking?
5. Gather facts about the clinic personnel. Have they been or are they being sued? Stress this in your leaflet. Warn prospective clinics of these facts and inform the public of them.
6. Make signs, using simple statements and large letters.
7. Have camera and film ready and appoint a photographer.
8. Notify the police prior to the picket. Obtain a permit if necessary.
9. Appoint a spokesman to the press.
10. Explain the do's and don'ts to the participants.
11. Write and mail releases to the press.

During the Picket:

1. Avoid arguing with passersby. Step out of the picket line to discuss the issues with them.
2. Always be courteous. Don't shout back at hecklers.
3. Obey the police as much as possible.
4. Take pictures of the event for your files, newsletter, and follow-up stories.
5. Use a bullhorn for keeping order.
6. Alert the media by phone from the scene of the picket.
7. Do not block pedestrian or auto traffic.
8. Do not litter. Clean up the area afterwards. If the public drops papers, they are littering, not you. The police cannot stop you from distributing materials.
9. If anyone is arrested, take pictures and make a tape recording of the procedure.

Sources:

There have been some good articles written about the picket. We recommend further reading on this vital tool for shutting down the abortion industry. The following are available either directly from the publisher, or from our office:

CROSSWAY BOOKS
  9825 W. Roosevelt Road
  Westchester, IL 60153
The Right to Picket and the Freedom of Public Discourse, by John W. Whitehead (See chap. 36 for chants and songs to be used during the picket.)

CARLAN PUBLISHING CO.
  P.O. Box 1064
  Jefferson City, MO 65102
Organizing for Community Pro-Life Action, by Carl J. Landwehr (chap. 3, "Protest Objectives", p. 155)

4 LEAFLETING

The leaflet, or handout, has been an effective means of getting information about the pro-life movement to the public. We shouldn't consider leafleting simply a stop-gap measure, but an essential form of communication.

During the American Revolution, the colonists were expert in the use of the leaflet; people like Tom Paine and Paul Revere regularly printed articles and handed them out to the people. Since the press at that time was under the sway of England, it was generally hostile to the colonists' ideas. If the colonists wanted to express their views on independence or some other facet of English oppression, they had to resort to the leaflet.

We have a similar problem in this country today, with media hostile to the pro-life movement. In fact, it has been estimated that the press is ninety percent against the pro-life position. Consequently, if we want to tell our side of the story we often have to write it and present it to the public ourselves.

The leaflet or pro-life tract has been a powerful force in promoting our views and is becoming an even more important educational tool as the movement grows.

The first thing to do when you are planning a leaflet is to decide exactly what you want to say, the point of view you wish to express, and the particular information you want to impart. Perhaps you will need a committee to discuss an informative, attractive leaflet and to decide such things as whether you want it to be printed, hand lettered, or typed and whether to include illustrations. All of these things are important, for the leaflet should look as professional as possible. Since a committee can't design a professional leaflet, find a professional artist to prepare a layout and artwork for the printer once preliminary details such as color and size have been agreed on. The leaflet should not look as though it was done in a hurry, with little thought and less talent. People today are accustomed to professional-looking material.

Also, you need to decide how much money you want to put into the leaflet. Leaflets can run as low as two or three cents a copy, or you can design more expensive ones, using color and high-grade paper. Scout around to find a printer who can give you the best price. It is important to know how many leaflets you want to distribute. If you are going to repeat distribution of the same leaflet, it is cheaper in the long run to print a large quantity than to reprint several times. Once a printer begins a press run he likes to keep rolling, and he will give you a better price on a large single run.

When you have the leaflet printed and ready for distribution, select places where people gather in large numbers, such as train stations, bus stops, shopping centers, school campuses. Go to churches on Sunday morning and hand the leaflets directly to worshipers or put them under the windshield wipers or in the car's door handles. None of these methods is illegal. You can go to homes and put a leaflet in the screen door. In apartment buildings you can slip them under the door. Don't put them in mailboxes; that is illegal.

There are few laws restricting leafleting. You are handing people something that is free. They are free to accept or reject it. If there is any question about legality, it is usually safest to follow whatever directives you have been given. For instance, if you have been warned by police not to leaflet in a certain place, you can move to another area. If you want to direct your leaflets at a specific group, such as a high school or college, or a newspaper office, you may have to get special permission or challenge the order.

Some people see leafleting as a poor man's way to disseminate information; but as I said, it has been used successfully by many groups throughout the country, throughout history.

In fact, I was brought into the pro-life movement by a leaflet handed me in October 1972, just before the Supreme Court ruling on abortion was handed down. I was at a pro-life rally in downtown Chicago when someone handed me a "Life and Death" leaflet. The first thing I saw was the "basket babies" picture on the back page. It showed a black plastic bag full of the bodies of dead babies. When I saw it, I went into a kind of shock. I was even more horrified when I noticed that one of the babies looked like my own son. I felt a searing anger. It was the picture on that leaflet that made me resolve to fight abortion. Through the years that I have been in the pro-life movement, I have found that frequently it is a leaflet or picture that gets a person involved. Whenever we distribute leaflets in the Chicago area, people follow through with donations and memberships. When we distributed 100,000 leaflets on January 22, the contributions received in response more than paid the printing bill.

Organizing a good leaflet team is important. You should select outgoing people. Leafleting is something people can do even though they may not want to join a picket line, a demonstration, or sit-in. They may be very willing to stand on a corner and pass out literature. Four or five people at a session on a street corner can pass out three or four thousand leaflets.

It is advisable to have a team of eight to twelve, and the more leafleters you have, the better. Do not let them spread out too much. When we first began leafleting, there were eight of us. We thought it would be best to cover four blocks, so we put two people on a block. But each team reported, when we gathered for more leaflets, that many people were rejecting our leaflets, throwing them on the ground and making rude remarks. So we decided to stay together in one area.

After that our reception was much better. Since there were eight of us in sight of each other, and each handing out the identical leaflet, people were more willing to accept them. They even seemed friendlier. They must have realized that if they didn't take a leaflet from one of us they would have to face several others. They needed a leaflet in hand to get through the group. They were also less hostile when they saw several of us. So, stick together.

Always be courteous. Thank people for taking the leaflets. Smile even if they tear the leaflet up and throw it back at you. Keep a pleasant demeanor. You can't assume that everyone who rejects a leaflet is pro-abortion. Some people will not take a leaflet from *anyone*. You can't force them to change their habits.

Be not only cheerful, but aggressive. Comment on what is in the leaflet: "Did you know abortion is now allowed right up until birth?" Pick something that gets attention.

When you are leafleting, avoid getting into arguments. If someone wants to discuss the issue, be polite, but don't stop leafleting. You are there to disseminate information. If someone persists, point to the phone number on the leaflet and tell them to give the office a call.

There are some tricks to passing out leaflets rapidly. Shuffle them so that you can easily grasp a single leaflet. Fan the stack so that the edges form a kind of stairs. Each leaflet can then be grabbed easily from the bottom, one after the other. Some people like to hand out the leaflets folded. You will soon find the method of distribution that suits you best.

When the leafleting is over, pick up any leaflets lying around and salvage those in waste bins. Then, unless your volunteers are in a hurry to get home, meet somewhere to discuss peoples' reactions. It is conducive to a strong esprit de corps to discuss the leaflet over coffee and doughnuts. Discuss how people were hostile and shouted at you, or threw the leaflet back or came back and thanked you. We have had people stuff money into our pockets and tell us to keep up the good work. We have even had people ask if they can join our leafleting. And several have.

The leaflet committee can be an interesting group to belong to. It develops a team spirit. It can also be fun. Anyone with an outgoing personality can be a good leafleter. People of any age can do it. The handicapped are good helpers. People are less likely to refuse something offered by a person in a wheelchair or on crutches.

There are many pro-life groups that print excellent leaflets. Or you may want to design your own. Below is a list of organizations that have leaflets available. One problem with some of these is that they don't leave room for your name and address, and as a rule you should give people a local organization to contact. Some printers leave space for you to rubber stamp your organization's name, address, and phone number.

RIGHT TO LIFE CRUSADE, INC.
  P.O. Box 2703
  Tulsa, OK 74101
"Questions and Answers" (3-5/8 x 8-1/2 in. flyer)

KNIGHTS OF COLUMBUS
Supply Department
  P.O. Box 1670
  New Haven, CT 06507
"Diary of an Unborn Child" (8-1/2 x 11 in.), "Five Ways to Kill an Unborn Child"

HAYES PUBLISHING CO., INC.
  6304 Hamilton Ave.
  Cincinnati, OH 45224
"Did You Know?", "Life or Death"

PRO-LIFE ACTION LEAGUE
  6160 N. Cicero Ave.
  Chicago, IL 60646
"Face the American Holocaust", "Does the Fetus Feel Pain?", "Hospitals Are for Healing"

RIGHT TO LIFE OF GREATER CINCINNATI, INC.
  P.O. Box 24073
  Cincinnati, OH 45224
"The U.S. Supreme Court Has Ruled It's Legal to Kill a Baby. . . ."

LIFE CYCLE BOOKS
  2205 Danforth Ave.
  Toronto, Ontario M4C 1K4
"Vote", "Language of Illusion", "Before You Were Born", "The Pain That Follows"

NRL EDUCATIONAL TRUST FUND
  419 7th St., NW, Suite 402
  Washington, D.C. 20004
"Abortion: Some Medical Facts"

WEBA (WOMEN EXPLOITED BY ABORTION)
  P.O. Box 267
  Schoolcraft, MI 49087
"Surviving Abortion"

CENTER FOR DOCUMENTING THE
AMERICAN HOLOCAUST
  P.O. Box 99
  Palm Springs, CA 92263
"The American Holocaust"

ALL ABOUT ISSUES
  P.O. Box 490
  Stafford, VA 22554
"Facts About Planned Parenthood",
"Planned Parenthood Must Be
Stopped"

CHRISTIAN FAMILY RENEWAL
  Box 73
  Clovis, CA 93612
"Who Killed Junior?"

CATHOLICS UNITED FOR LIFE
  New Hope, KY 40052
"The Birth Control Pill Kills Babies"

NEBRASKA COALITION FOR LIFE
Educational Trust Fund
  P.O. Box 6501
  Omaha, NE 68106
"When Lightning Strikes", (A young
girl's journey to the grief of abortion)

NYPLC
  P.O. BOX 67
  Newport, KY 41071
"Can They Defend Themselves?",
by Ken Kesey, author of *One Flew
Over the Cuckoo's Nest*

HERITAGE HOUSE '76, INC.
  P.O. Box 730
  Taylor, AZ 85939
"The Right to Enslave, the Right to
Kill", "What Can I Do to Help Stop
Abortion?"

Most of these publishers offer a broad range of pro-life literature. We
have listed mostly one-page, inexpensive items for mass distribution.
Ask for catalogues when you write.

Hundreds of thousands of these brochures have been handed out at train stations, on street corners and in neighborhoods to alert the American public to the horror of abortion. They have also served as a source of new membership in the pro-life activist movement.

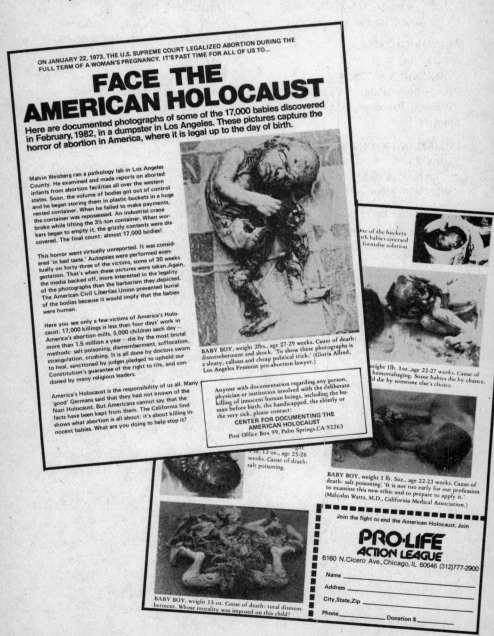

ON JANUARY 22, 1973, THE U.S. SUPREME COURT LEGALIZED ABORTION DURING THE FULL TERM OF A WOMAN'S PREGNANCY. IT'S PAST TIME FOR ALL OF US TO...

FACE THE AMERICAN HOLOCAUST

Here are documented photographs of some of the 17,000 babies discovered in February, 1982, in a dumpster in Los Angeles. These pictures capture the horror of abortion in America, where it is legal up to the day of birth.

Malvin Weisberg ran a pathology lab in Los Angeles County. He examined and made reports on aborted infants from abortion facilities all over the western states. Soon, the volume of bodies got out of control and he began storing them in plastic buckets in a huge rented container. When he failed to make payments, the container was repossessed. An industrial crane broke while lifting the 3½-ton container. When workers began to empty it, the grizzly contents were discovered. The final count: almost 17,000 bodies!

This horror went virtually unreported. It was considered 'in bad taste.' Autopsies were performed eventually on forty-three of the victims, some of 30 weeks gestation. That's when these pictures were taken. Again, the media backed off, more interested in the legality of the photographs than the barbarism they depicted. The American Civil Liberties Union prevented burial of the bodies because it would imply that the babies were human.

Here you see only a few victims of America's Holocaust. 17,000 killings is less than four days' work in America's abortion mills. 5,000 children each day -- more than 1.5 million a year -- die by the most brutal methods: salt poisoning, dismemberment, suffocation, strangulation, crushing. It is all done by doctors sworn to heal, sanctioned by judges pledged to uphold our Constitution's guarantee of the right to life, and condoned by many religious leaders.

America's Holocaust is the responsibility of us all. Many 'good' Germans said that they had not known of the Nazi Holocaust. But Americans cannot say that the facts have been kept from them. The California find shows what abortion is all about: it's about killing innocent babies. What are you doing to help stop it?

One of the buckets with babies emersed in formalin solution

weight 1lb. 1oz.,age 22-27 weeks. Cause of hemorrhaging. Some babies die by chance, d die by someone else's choice.

BABY BOY, weight 2lbs., age 27-29 weeks. Cause of death: dismemberment and shock. 'To show these photographs is a sleazy, callous and cheap political trick.' (Gloria Allred, Los Angeles Feminist pro-abortion lawyer.)

Anyone with documentation regarding any person, physician or institution involved with the deliberate killing of innocent human beings, including the human before birth, the handicapped, the elderly or the very sick, please contact:
CENTER FOR DOCUMENTING THE AMERICAN HOLOCAUST
Post Office Box 99, Palm Springs,CA 92263

1 lb. 13 oz., age 25-26 weeks. Cause of death: salt poisoning.

BABY BOY, weight 1 lb. 5oz., age 22-23 weeks. Cause of death: salt poisoning. 'It is not too early for our profession to examine this new ethic and to prepare to apply it.' (Malcolm Watts, M.D., California Medical Association.)

Join the fight to end the American Holocaust. Join

PRO-LIFE ACTION LEAGUE
6160 N.Cicero Ave.,Chicago, IL 60646 (312)777-2900

Name _____

Address _____

City,State,Zip _____

Phone _____ Donation $ _____

BABY BOY, weight 15 oz. Cause of death: total dismemberment. Whose morality was imposed on this child?

5 RALLIES AND MARCHES

While the pro-life picket takes considerable planning, it can be a small gathering of half a dozen people and still be successful. But a demonstration, rally, or march must be large, and it will take even more planning than the picket.

Demonstrations, rallies, and marches are staged to call attention to some special facet of the pro-life movement, such as the atrocities committed in abortion hospitals and clinics, the opening of a new abortion facility, the commemoration of a special event, or the anniversary of the Supreme Court abortion ruling. The demonstration consists of a large gathering of people carefully organized and called together in an orderly program of protest or commemoration.

Alerting people to the demonstration is best done by sending invitations, phoning, running ads in newspapers, placing notices in church bulletins, and using all available media outlets. Sufficient lead time to announce the event is necessary because the demonstration should be covered by the media. Time, place, and statement of purpose must be announced at least a month in advance so that people can plan to attend.

The demonstration, rally, or march should have a theme with an appropriate slogan that is repeated throughout the activity, on signs, chants, and in press statements: *Project Save Our Babies* or *Action— Because It Saves Lives*. Nellie Gray's *March for Life* has become a national symbol as it assembles each January 22 in Washington, D.C., and has extended itself beyond the march to lobbying, publications, and other educational activities. Her annual *Rose Dinner* has become a sit-down rally honoring pro-life activists from across the country.

One or more speakers should be invited to address the crowd. A platform should be set up for them to speak from, along with appropriate sound equipment, podium, banners, and other accessories. It is sometimes advisable to have entertainment in the form of a singer or musicians to add to the spirit of the event and prevent the crowd from becoming restless.

If the demonstration moves, it becomes a march. In a march there is a gathering point, a line of march, perimeters or limits to the line of

41

march, and a rallying point at the end of the march. All of this must be carefully planned, and that may necessitate the formation of a number of committees: sign committee, platform committee, transportation committee, guests committee, press committee, entertainment committee.

Care must be taken about both what the signs say and their readability. When demonstrators make their own signs, they often put too much material on them. They may use unsuitable materials, like crayon or pencil. Signs must be readable from both the front and back, and have the same message on each side. It is advisable to have signs printed professionally and fixed to a piece of wood (picket) so that they can be held high above the head. Consistency of size and design and repeated statements are good.

The program committee will design and print a program to hand out to the crowd attending. If there is going to be singing, it will be necessary to have the lyrics printed up and distributed. The song leader, possibly someone who can play the guitar or some other instrument, will get participants involved.

If the crowd is going to march, there should be a grand marshal: someone to give instructions from the podium and to explain plans for the march. The march needs marshals, drums, and people carrying banners. Make the front of the march colorful. If it is a long march, there should be a leadoff car or truck, colorfully decorated.

The main speakers may ride in the lead car to increase their visibility. The lead car should proceed slowly so that all participants, young and old, can keep up without difficulty.

The beginning of the march is the best time to pass out signs. As the people leave to form the march, they are handed signs. It is also a good idea to hand out flags or balloons to attract attention. Arrangements should be made beforehand with the police to have someone direct traffic as the march takes to the street. If the weather is cold, consider having coffee urns set up along the way to dispense free coffee to participants. In hot weather, cold punch or juice can be handed out instead. At a march I attended in Ft. Lauderdale, Florida, one very hot day, tables had been set up with cups of cold drinks on them. People were stationed to hand cups to the marchers as they passed. It was a nice gesture, a break in the action, and it made everyone feel good about the event. It is also good to provide for people who can't march, by having cars for pregnant women, people with small children, or older people.

It is also good to plan chants and sing them through the whole course of the march. If the group is large, it should sing or chant by segments.

Leaders along the way with bullhorns can start chants such as:

Life Yes, Abortion No; All we are saying is give life a chance; Stop the killing now

or cheers such as:

Give me an "L"; Give me an "I"; Give me an "F"; Give me an "E". What does it spell? "LIFE!" What do we want? "LIFE!" Louder! "LIFE!"

Chants keep it lively, let the public know you are coming, and generate a good spirit.

If the march is heading to an abortion clinic, participants should be told that. When they arrive, a statement should be read to the group. It is effective, when the group arrives at the clinic, to have the people lower their signs and pound the sticks on the sidewalk as they chant. If there are two or three hundred people, the pounding can make it sound like an army has arrived. At all times marshals should keep control of the demonstrators, making certain that there is no shouting to passersby.

Good natured waving to strangers is permitted. Often people standing along the sidelines will have favorable comments. No one should leave the demonstration to argue with the opposition.

The rally is much the same as a demonstration, but is used more for immediate action. It is less formalized, and can be more spontaneous. Pro-lifers rally before they go to the clinics to counsel or before they set out to campaign, leaflet, or lobby. The rally sets the mood for another action.

When the demonstration or rally ends, there should always be an announcement of some specific action to be taken. "Go from here to counsel at the clinics"; "Go from here to contact your senators to pass this bill." Demonstrators should always leave a demonstration or rally with the intention of doing some significant pro-life work foremost in their minds. The director should also compliment all those who participated, advise them of which TV or other media to monitor for the story of the event, and end with a prayer.

A march should always head somewhere with the intention of causing something to happen. When we march it is always to an abortion clinic or to a legislative office or to the Supreme Court. It is important for those just becoming involved in the pro-life movement to know that they are doing something real to stop abortion and that they are not just carrying out a symbolic act. Symbolism is fine, but it is not enough. It is certainly not enough for a genuine pro-life activist who intends to shut down the abortion industry.

6 THE COUNTER-DEMONSTRATION

The counter-demonstration is frequently impromptu. The message arrives that the pro-abortionists are gathering for a demonstration against some new pro-life bill or to protest some pro-life activity.

The alert pro-life activist will use this opportunity to gather together a small band of pro-lifers and go to this event to counter it. The pro-lifers will generally not call the press. This is the abortionists' activity and they will have worked to get media coverage. Pro-life does not want to bring the media to the abortionists' function, but only to engage the media that is there. Frequently the press is more favorably disposed to pro-life activists who appear at abortion functions than they are to pro-lifers at their own events.

A counter-demonstration can be carried out successfully with a small group, perhaps only three or four people, although larger numbers are better. It is useful to have a few signs protesting the abortion activity and to have a bullhorn to counter their noise. When the pro-life group arrives at the site of the abortion demonstration, it takes up a position as close to their march or rally as possible and begins countering their chants, slogans, and statements, using the bullhorn. If they are singing, activist pro-lifers will insert words that confuse their songs.

Abortionists don't like this and will probably call the police or alert the police who are already there. The police cannot tell the pro-lifers to leave, but can only make certain the two groups don't clash. Since the pro-lifers are outnumbered, it is good that the police are there to keep the peace. And the presence of police giving instructions will draw the press to the pro-life group and give them an opportunity to get equal press coverage. This will infuriate the abortionists who have sought media for their own cause and are now having to share it with the enemy. A balanced story can be gained at very little cost of resources or time.

The Pro-Life Action League has had victories over the abortionists through counter-demonstrations on a number of occasions. Once, more than one hundred fifty abortionists were marching in the Federal Courtyard in Chicago protesting passage of the Hyde Amendment. Two of us showed up with a sign and a bullhorn. We stood on the edge of the

44

line of march and began shouting, "Sore losers." We inserted our words into their chants. They called the police. The police surrounded us and told us not to start a fight. We pointed out that we were outnumbered seventy-five to one. The police attention attracted every television, radio, and newspaper reporter present. We appeared later on three TV newscasts, and our remarks went out to homeward-bound drivers on the radio news reports that night. Our comments also appeared in two newspapers.

On another occasion twelve of us showed up to counter-demonstrate at an abortion coalition rally in the Daley (Civic) Center. We had purchased a box of 144 whistles and handed these out to passersby and a number of young boys and girls on a tour. We told them they could keep the whistles but had to blow them when we signaled. During the keynote talk, we signaled, everyone blew his whistle, and the speaker was forced to cut short his comments. The whistles were also blown during the singing of a pro-abortion ballad. In addition, two of our women with guitars played when the abortionists sang. If the abortionists played a fast song, our guitarists played a slow one, in a different key. If they changed to a slow song, our guitarists played fast, the music amplified by the bullhorn.

These tactics disturbed the abortion crowd to the extent that they broke up early and began leaving just before the press arrived. When the reporters began arriving, we hurried to the far corner of the plaza where we unfurled a ten-foot pro-life banner that effectively hid the abortionists' stage. We did several interviews. By the time these were over, all the abortionists had left. The press took pictures of our banner, but had no pictures of the abortion rally.

The abortionists, though, can be equally adept at staging counter-demonstrations. It is wise to be prepared for any eventuality. We welcome counter-demonstrations by abortionists because they introduce into the event the element of conflict, something the media finds newsworthy. We once planned a large-scale picket of an abortion clinic only to find upon our arrival that the abortionists had arrived a half-hour earlier. They were already picketing their own clinic, which seemed odd but did deprive us of our location.

We formed our picket across the street from the clinic. After most of our pickets had arrived, we moved to the sidewalk next to the clinic and adjacent to the pro-abortion march. The police, fearing conflict between two groups so close together, moved our picket onto the street directly in front of the clinic. The abortionists were still marching on the sidewalk. The police stood between the two groups, but the pro-life pickets were closest to the TV cameras and we got the best coverage. In time, the abortion group went home and we took over the sidewalk. Early media coverage was balanced, but late-arriving reporters cited the pro-life number of protesters as much larger than that of the abortionists because our people stayed on the scene longer. The footage taken at this picket has been shown repeatedly on programs dealing with abortion, because it has both groups marching side by side and exemplifies the intense conflict in the abortion controversy.

A counter-demonstration is usually called quickly with only a few pro-lifers going to the site of an abortion march or rally to introduce the element of conflict and to steal the press from the abortionists. Generally, the pro-life leader does not notify the press. It is best if the abortion event goes unnoticed. If the press is there, however, the pro-lifers insist on an equal opportunity to present their side of the debate. The ideal situation exists when there is no press coverage at all. This means the abortionists are being ignored by the media. When this happens, the counter-demonstration merely disrupts and confuses the abortionists.

If, on the other hand, the abortionists counter-demonstrate at a pro-life event, the pro-lifers use the element of conflict to their advantage, and count on this element to make the event more newsworthy than it would have been if the opposition had not come. Since the pro-life message is reasonable and humane and the abortion message is not, it is to our advantage to have our activities reported. As Paul Brown of the American Life Lobby says, ''There is no such thing as bad press. The only bad press is no press.''

7 REMOVE ABORTION ADVERTISING

Abortion is the premeditated murder of an innocent, unborn human being, and abortion advertising is part of that murder. It directs people to the places where this destruction takes place. It is imperative that pro-lifers do everything they can to counter such advertising.

In the case of abortion advertisements in newspapers, for instance, pro-lifers may contact the newspaper's ad department and ask to place pro-life ads recommending agencies that help pregnant women carry their pregnancies to term. One major problem with this is that, while the abortionists make money through their business and can afford to advertise, pro-lifers make no money saving lives and economically cannot compete with the abortionists.

While some pregnancy help agencies advertise on a regular basis, their ads are usually much smaller than abortion ads. On occasion, pro-life groups have obtained free advertising in secular newspapers. This worked successfully for us with the *Chicago Sun-Times* in 1974.

The *Sun-Times* had been running nearly a full page of abortion ads every day. Pro-life groups strongly protested these ads and had tried various methods to get them removed. We had met with the advertising department and with the editors. We had picketed, written letters, and made phone calls. But it was clear that they were not going to remove the lucrative ads. They even claimed that they would be sued by the clinics if they refused the ads.

So, we designed a leaflet and went to the *Sun-Times* to blanket every department in the building. We were ordered from the building six times, but returned until our job was done. The leaflet asked *Sun Times* employees how they liked working for an abortion promoter. The single-page leaflet reproduced dozens of the abortion ads and in the middle of the page, in bold letters, asked the leading question of the *Sun-Times* employee.

At first we weren't aware of how successful the leaflet had been. But we learned that a contingent from the paper had gone to the directors of the advertising department and demanded that if the abortion ads could not be removed, the newspaper would give a free ad to pro-lifers. The employees said they did not like working for an abortion promoter.

This request was granted, and our office was notified that we would be given space in the *Chicago Sun-Times* and its sister publication, the *Chicago Daily News*. The ads would run every day that abortion ads ran. They would be placed in the center of the ad page, and the text could be changed on a weekly basis. They would not cost us a cent. We accepted the offer.

For the next four years our ad ran along with the abortion advertisements. There were some occasions when the abortion page was omitted and our ad ran by itself. If our ad missed appearing one day, we would call and demand that it be reintroduced. It was always as large as the largest abortion ad. At first it contained one telephone number for women with problem pregnancies to call, but in time we had to include four numbers because of the large volume of calls. On many days we received up to forty calls from women who had seen the pro-life ad while looking through the abortion listings.

The free ad remained in the newspaper for four years, until the *Chicago Sun-Times* ran its famous "Abortion Profiteers" series. The horrendous conditions in Chicago abortion clinics as reported in the series prompted the *Sun-Times* to drop all of its abortion advertising. Consequently, the pro-life ad was also dropped. We calculated that the ad had saved between five and ten thousand women from aborting their babies during its four-year run. It would plead: "Your baby's heart began to beat at three and a half weeks. Don't abort your baby." Or, "Your baby has detectable brain waves by six weeks. Don't abort your baby." And, "Your baby has fingerprints. Don't abort your baby." Rightly, many women took our ad seriously.

By a strange twist of fate, it was the success of our pro-life ad in the *Sun-Times* that eventually brought about its loss. Because so many women who saw our ad called our office with reports of botched abortions, abortions that were raced through, patients who were charged double, and doctors who operated without anesthesia, we suggested to the *Sun-Times* an investigation that later became the "Abortion Profiteers" series, which ended up getting our ad dropped.

Even more aggressive methods of removing abortion ads can be used. In 1973, an abortion clinic was placing its ads at train stations managed by the Chicago Transit Authority (CTA). Our pro-life organization asked permission from the CTA Board to put up pro-life ads alongside the abortion ones. We submitted an ad, but it was rejected. We said that if the CTA would not accept our ad, it should remove the abortion ads. They agreed. We asked them to put this decision in writing. They sent us a one-line statement of their intention. Our pro-life group went to the media and announced the CTA's decision to discontinue abortion advertising at train stations. This decision was confirmed during interviews on radio, television, and in the newspapers. The abortion ads ceased.

Several years later, when some abortion ads appeared again at train stops, our office called the CTA and ordered that they be removed. After we reminded the CTA officials of our agreement, the ads were immediately taken down. But then, a year after that, abortion ads again began appearing. This time, however, there was a new ad department management which refused to remove them. Our diplomatic efforts failed.

Then an interesting thing happened. The abortion ads began to disappear. The telephone number and address on the ads were mysteriously painted out. We had wanted to call a press conference to point out the CTA's betrayal, but had feared that if we brought the issue to the media, photographs would be taken of the signs, thus proliferating the abortion ads with the telephone number and address. Now, with the disappearance of this offensive information, we were free to go to the media, which we did.

Although the ads at train platforms remained out of commission, the CTA began placing them across the tracks in the underground stations. Anyone who wanted to remove the ads would have to cross the dangerous electrified third rail. Imagine our surprise, then, when we walked through the long tunnel under the Loop one Monday morning to find that all the abortion signs had been covered with contact paper. Every telephone number was obliterated under a sheet of sticky, gray paper. The CTA gave up. The abortion battle of the train stations was over. As of this writing, abortion ads have not been seen since at CTA stations, although in 1984 Planned Parenthood sued the CTA to place abortion ads on buses and trains. They won their suit in federal court. The CTA appealed the decision of Judge Milton I. Shadur and a temporary injunction on placing the ads was sought. Planned Parenthood eventually got permission to place its abortion ads, but these did not remain for very long either.

We have discovered abortion ads in programs for music festivals, in theater notes, in foreign-language newspapers. In every case we have used the system of graduated pressure to get them out. First we talk, then we get people to write or call. Finally, we go to the press, we picket, and we use pressure. We do not start with pressure, but rather with diplomacy. We end with pressure.

On one occasion, we went to the major advertisers of a musical event and persuaded them to help us get an offensive abortion ad out of the program. They threatened to remove their ads if the abortion ad remained. It was dropped. On another occasion, we got an abortion clinic ad out of a movie guide by pointing out that many of the theaters in the chain were family theaters and that the ad was highly offensive to many patrons. The ad did not mention the word abortion, but when we pointed out that the "facility" was actually a notorious abortion clinic, the ad manager dropped the ad.

Driving west on Devon Avenue in Chicago one morning, I noticed a large abortion ad painted on the side of a building. The letters were four feet high with a telephone number that could be seen half a mile away. I stopped in the building and asked the man in charge if the space would be up for rent soon. He said the ad had run out several months before but he would not remove it until he had another contract.

I signed up for the space right on the spot. It cost $300 for a year, and I would have to provide my own paint job. The following Saturday, another pro-lifer, Patrick Trueman, and I were on ladders putting up our ad. We nearly broke our necks. But for the next year our ad gave an abortion alternative to drivers heading west on Devon Avenue.

In Chicago, we have had the battle of the ad benches, the battle of the billboards, and even graffiti battles. Few companies managing ad benches at bus stops will take abortion clinics' ads in Chicago. It doesn't pay. Somebody always takes a paint roller to them and covers up the abortion ads. In some instances another "vandal" will come along with a stencil and place an anti-abortion message where, a few moments before, there had been an abortion ad. We pity pro-lifers who live in cities where abortion ad benches abound. Where are the pro-lifers with imaginations?

8 ADVERTISE PRO-LIFE

While it definitely pays to advertise, advertising can be very expensive. A full page ad in a paper like the *Chicago Tribune* or *Chicago Sun-Times* will cost around $10,000. It costs even more to advertise in the *New York Times* or the *Washington Post*. The price can be whittled down for non-profit organizations, and if the ad doesn't appear in the full circulation of the paper, but in one or more specific zones, it will cost even less. Position in the paper has something to do with costs. An ad in the business section is not going to cost as much as one in the main news. It is essential, before running any ad, to decide how much money there is to spend, how important the message is for this particular area, and what is to be achieved by the ad. Sometimes a good size ad can be had for two or three thousand dollars with some clever bargaining for a special rate.

A newspaper advertisement should always have a picture in it to get the readers' attention. The headline should be catchy and brief. Remember that the pro-life ad is competing with those of thousands of other advertisers, many with large budgets, who are able to take up full sections of the paper. The pro-life ad will need something special to make it stand out.

The ad will also have to be approved by the newspaper's legal staff. Since it is a pro-life ad, they will be very critical and make harsh demands. But it can still get in. It is even possible, with enough persistence, to place some hard-hitting photographs, though no big city newspaper we know of has yet agreed to showing a picture of an aborted baby in an ad for pro-life.

Advertising rates for magazines are prohibitive. Only the national pro-life groups can at this point afford them. Still, it is worthwhile to call on the magazine salesmen or go to their advertising departments to check their rates.

It is wise to compare advertising facts and figures, and to find out when special editions are scheduled. Advertisers frequently call pro-life offices soliciting ads for special sections. The pro-life organizations on a tight budget should be leery of these offers. Frequently the special edition will be so crammed with advertising that few will read it.

Small local newspapers will sometimes print a free pregnancy help ad, especially if the paper already runs ads for abortion clinics. Persistence in pressuring them to drop abortion advertising may gain free space for a pro-life ad by way of compromise and an appeal to their consciences. This does not happen often, but when it does it helps save lives.

Renting billboard space for pro-life ads is another option to consider. Many groups have done this and appropriate billboard ads are available from several pro-life companies. Refer to the end of Chapter 21 for their addresses. Ad space is also available on benches or on public transit.

There are many other less expensive ways to advertise the pro-life message effectively: bumper stickers, decals, stamps, labels on your mailings. Many groups employ these on a routine basis. It has been estimated that anything that goes through the mail will be seen by at least fourteen people before it reaches its destination. Nearly every method of telling the pro-life story is worth the effort: pins, buttons, bracelets, tie pins—anything that catches people's attention and can serve as a good conversation piece. The Precious Feet and Rose for Life are actually sophisticated forms of advertising. They are conversation starters and they draw people out. These methods should be used and should never be looked down on. Their use can result in some real pro-life gains. Nearly every pro-lifer has a story of an inspirational experience resulting from the wearing of a pro-life visual.

Once, when I was boarding a Western Airlines flight to Omaha, the captain greeted me with, "I see you are wearing the Precious Feet." I was taken by surprise since only pro-lifers refer to the button by its proper name. We had a long conversation about the pro-life movement and his efforts to talk about abortion with the crew and many of the passengers. My wearing of the Precious Feet has generated hundreds of interesting conversations on abortion. I now carry a pocket full of them to hand out to people who comment favorably on the ones I wear.

Advertising costs can be prohibitively high, so it is best to find ways to procure ads without spending much of your own money. One method used by a number of groups is to solicit names of those who would like to help cover the cost of running a newspaper ad, and print the names of the donors in the ad that results. Not only does this cut your costs in placing the ad, but it gives people a chance to broadcast their pro-life commitment. This method is used most frequently in ads run on Mother's Day and also on the anniversary of the Supreme Court abortion ruling. Everyone likes to see his name in the paper. For a dollar or two his name appears with others who espouse the pro-life cause.

Special ads representing the clergy, doctors, or other community leaders and their stand against abortion are often placed in local newspapers. While the main purpose of running these ads is to get the pro-life message to the public, the use of people's names has positive advantages besides helping to defray costs. It manifests the pro-life strength in the community and encourages others to join.

9 TELEVISION AND RADIO EDITORIAL REBUTTALS

An excellent way to get the pro-life message out without spending a cent is to apply for rebuttal time for editorials on radio or television. Rebuttals are a public service that all broadcast media are required by law to present in order to air both sides of an issue.

Whenever any editorial espousing any view counter to the pro-life position is aired, pro-lifers should call the station immediately and ask for the editorial department. They should tell the editorial director that they have just heard or seen the station's editorial, and they wish to present a rebuttal. It is wise to ask if anyone else has also applied.

Sometimes these editorials are broadcast in the middle of the night or on a weekend when few people are at the station. Obviously, calling them is useless. But to be certain of securing rebuttal time, it is best to send a mailgram, making certain that it is dated and that the time you originally phoned is also included. This can prove critical, as the person whose mailgram is dated the earliest gets to supply the rebuttal.

Another way to handle the weekend editorial is to wait until Monday morning and call as soon as the offices open, about 8:30 or 9:00 A.M. If the request for a rebuttal is accepted, the rebuttal should be written as soon as possible. Should you have missed all or part of the station's editorial, they will send you a printed copy on request. They will either rush a copy by messenger, arrange for a pick-up, mail it, or read it to you over the phone so that the reply can be written quickly.

Remember that the reply must deal specifically with their editorial. As a *rebuttal*, it must counter something they said.

This does not mean that the entire editorial has to be challenged. Perhaps the editor listed, among the things he opposed, restrictive abortion laws in upcoming legislation. It may only be a small part of the editorial. Sometimes the life issues may not even be specifically attacked. For instance, when radio or television stations promote the United Way fund drive in your area, you may apply for a rebuttal if some of the money raised by the drive will support Planned Parenthood or other abortion-referral agencies. Since pro-lifers cannot support the fund drive, you can use that element of their editorial as a basis for a rebuttal.

The rebuttal must conform to length requirements. But usually the writer can get a little extra time, and it is wise, in writing the rebuttal, to include extra copy that can be removed without damaging the force of the rebuttal. The station may approve the rebuttal itself but say that it is too long. They may suggest that an important element be cut for the sake of time. The writer can say he won't take *that* out, but will take out the less important element. In this way, the integrity of the rebuttal is preserved.

The station will generally allow a rebuttal to run the way it is written. The writer should not be afraid that the rebuttal will be rejected because it is strong and precise. We have gotten away with presenting graphic description of abortions through dismemberment, suction, D & E, and salting out. Sometimes we have been asked to tone down our descriptions, but not necessarily the descriptive elements. For instance, we were once asked to use "unborn baby" instead of "baby". One time we were asked to drop the word "baby" and use "fetus". We told them that we would not do that. They then asked us to describe the baby so that the public would know it was not yet born. We agreed to call it an unborn baby, and they accepted that.

The writer should use terms he is familiar with and that tell the story. He doesn't have to use their language. The editorial rebuttal should be a precise, educational piece so that the public knows exactly where the writer stands, what happens in an abortion, and why the original editorial was so objectionable.

The rebuttal is generally aired at the same time that regular editorials are aired. While it may be scheduled in some undesirable slots in the middle of the night, it will probably get some prime time day and evening spots as well.

It is surprising how many people listen to rebuttals. The more precise it is, the more words like "abortion", "baby", and "killing" are used, the more apt the message is to affect the public.

The editorial rebuttal need not be presented by its writer. Sometimes it is good to ask someone new to appear on behalf of the organization. Some rebuttals are best given by a woman. Others come off better when given by a man.

Pro-lifers should be alerted to the upcoming rebuttal, asked to watch it and to tell their neighbors to tune in so that the rebuttal gets as much exposure as possible. It is even smart to send out copies of the editorial in mailings to special interest groups and individuals, to let them know that an offensive editorial statement was challenged. Since the media to

some extent gauge the importance of issues by the number of requests
they receive from listeners or viewers for transcripts of rebuttals, have
pro-lifers contact the station for copies of the rebuttal.

10 LETTERS TO THE EDITOR

A letter to the editor in any publication is both a valuable source of information to the public and a free, effective way to correct media mistakes, of which there are many. You should never be surprised when a letter you have written shows up in a newspaper. Always have two or more letters under consideration at editorial offices. If you are ever surprised to see one of your letters published, that means you are not writing enough. You may have to write a dozen letters before one appears in print, but if it takes that many, then resign yourself to write that many.

Letters have a greater chance of being accepted if they are concise, courteous, to the point, brief, and *mailed*.

When possible, letters should be typed, using double spacing. Handwritten letters do get accepted, but it is easier on the editors if your letter is typewritten, as handwritten ones are more difficult to mark for typesetting, and may have to be typed by the editorial staff, forcing them to take extra time and effort to publish it.

Most publications are required to provide space for dissenting opinions. But even without such a fairness policy, most publishers want to hear from their readers and will publish their views. These letters tell them whether they are serving the needs of the community. If they don't hear from pro-lifers, they will never know what pro-lifers think about the newspaper's stand on abortion.

The most important thing you do whenever you write a letter to the editor is drop it in the mailbox. Letters should be mailed as soon as possible, while the subject is still timely. Some issues will not retain their interest very long, such as a particular bill before the legislature, or a minor candidate running for office. When the vote is over or the election decided, it is too late. Comment on the issue while it's hot.

It is helpful, in order to get your letter published, to refer to something that appeared in their newspaper, such as a story, column, editorial, or letter, and to reply to or correct any erroneous items. If your letter is not printed after a long wait, it may be wise to call the newspaper and ask for the editor in charge of editorial page letters. You might advise him to correct a sentence or change a word in the letter, and by that, turn his attention to your letter. Your call may cause it to go to the top of the pile. The call also gives you an opportunity to inquire whether they are going to use your letter, and if not, why not?

If they fail to publish an opposing view on abortion, they cannot say it is because no one sent one in. Your call may force them to print something they would prefer not to print. Of course, you cannot call the paper every time a letter doesn't get printed, but there are times, such as when the controversy is heated and the paper is not presenting balanced reporting, that a follow-up can make the difference between the pro-life view being represented or buried.

A particularly good letter should be sent to newspapers across the country, to the *New York Times*, the *Washington Post*, the *Los Angeles Times*. They may accept it. Editors like to receive letters from out of town. It indicates wide readership of their paper. It doesn't matter whether the writer reads or subscribes to the paper or magazine. The local librarian can supply the newspaper's correct address. Some of the major papers are listed at the end of this chapter.

Letters should also be written to the major news magazines—*Time*, *Newsweek*, *U.S. News and World Report*. These magazines are read around the world, and your letter may reach millions of people. Isn't that worth a little effort and a postage stamp?

Letters to major magazines must be brief and to the point. Since it is an achievement to get a mere one paragraph letter printed, every word must count.

Always remember to include your name, address, and telephone number. Some editors, for purposes of validation of authorship, will not publish letters without a daytime phone number where the writer can be reached.

Many publications have a policy of acknowledging receipt of letters from readers, even if they don't print them. Pro-lifers who don't have a file full of such cards are not writing enough.

Seldom does a day go by without some biased or incorrect editorial, story, syndicated column, cartoon or letter to the editor appearing in print. If we don't write letters to set the record straight, the confusion will remain. The unborn can only speak through our voices, pens, and typewriters. We are their voices, and we must keep speaking for them.

THE NEW YORK TIMES   CHICAGO TRIBUNE
  229 W. 43rd St.   435 N. Michigan Ave.
  New York, NY 10036   Chicago, IL 60611

TIME
  Time-Life Building
  Rockefeller Center
  New York, NY 10020

NEWSWEEK
  444 Madison Ave.
  New York, NY 10022

U.S. NEWS & WORLD REPORT
  2300 N Street, NW
  Washington, DC 20037

CHICAGO SUN-TIMES
  401 N. Wabash
  Chicago, IL 60611

LOS ANGELES TIMES
  Times-Mirror Square
  Los Angeles, CA 90053

THE WASHINGTON POST
  1150 15th St., NW
  Washington, DC 20071

11 GET YOUR STORY IN THE PRESS

Getting your story into the news requires that you have *news*. The media are generally not interested in your philosophy. They are interested in the news, and this is something many pro-lifers don't realize. They think the media's hostility toward them explains why they won't print their stories. It is true that the major media are prejudiced against the pro-life movement. But there is also the possibility that we are not giving the media news.

It is important to create news events. A picket is not necessarily news. Pickets are carried on routinely all across the country. It is true that if those picketing are respected by the media, such as gays or liberals, the press will probably cover the event. But if the subject is abortion, there is the added disadvantage that the media is generally opposed to the pro-life position. So we have to work extra hard to get our stories in print.

What makes a story newsworthy? People are news. Try to have a newsworthy person at your picket or event. Events that are different, such as giving an award to a judge who refuses to allow an abortion, are news. Who ever heard of a judge doing something like that? We gave a protector award to Judge Randall Hekman of Grand Rapids, Michigan. He had the courage to buck the abortion trend and to save a baby's life. That was news.

Add a little flavor to your news story by revealing something the people wouldn't ordinarily know. For instance, several years ago we tracked down a twelve-year-old girl who was going to have an abortion, so that we could talk her out of it. Talking a woman out of having an abortion is not news. But tracking her down by using a private detective is. That was the angle we played up to the media. They were critical of our action, but it worked. An editorial written against us appeared in the *New York Times*. We did more than thirty radio interviews from Dallas to Detroit, dealing with the event. The media were interested.

In our interviews we were able to clarify what some members of the press considered a violation of privacy. We pointed out that if we had tracked down a young girl to give her a large sum of money and that if we hadn't found her within a certain period of time, she would have lost the money, the media would *not* call our tactics a violation of privacy. They would say we were doing the person a favor. But since we were offering to help this young woman through her pregnancy, offering her a live child and a clean conscience, we were considered "violators of her privacy". What the media considered "good" apparently did not include unborn human life. Through this argument we were able to convince many listeners that we had a valid reason for using a private detective to find the girl. It was the use of a detective which made this a good news story.

Good visuals are also an asset. They give the camera something interesting to focus on. For instance, the introduction of thirty baby caskets into our marches and parades is a device the media has found fascinating on many occasions. The nature of your signs such as large banners instead of small ones, a printed statement of intention and purpose, few words instead of complicated sentences, can all attract the cameras. An effigy of the person being picketed also makes a good visual.

Conflict is always newsworthy. When you are going to go to a clinic, it helps get the press there if you tell them that you are going inside the clinic. If there is a chance of confrontation, the press are more likely to cover the event.

We announced in one press release that we were going to visit a number of clinics. A rumor began to circulate that there was going to be a confrontation and perhaps even violence. We did not deny it. The rumor brought out the press. We didn't plan any violence, of course, and we did not want any, but we didn't tell the press that. They showed up. On that march, during which we visited five Chicago clinics, *Newsweek* trailed along and took a photograph of part of our group in a Michigan Avenue clinic. We were holding flowers and a cross and reading a statement to the women in the clinic. The story that ran in *Newsweek* was not flattering, but it told of our concern and our dedication, and it made us look strong. It also got us a color photograph and a cover story in a national magazine with wide circulation.

You can have the best story in the world, but if you don't contact the media, they are not going to write it. You must have a regular mailing list of media outlets, including your local newspapers and weeklies, plus the news magazines in your area. Get to know the feature writers, and send them news releases. Have the addresses of your radio and television stations. Be aware of the community newspapers and radio stations. When you write a story about something your pro-life group has done, know which members of your group live in what neighborhoods, because neighborhood papers are always looking for stories about local people. In that way you will tell the whole story, but have it written around the people from a particular area.

Do not be afraid to use the phone to get your story out. The method we use is to send out a press release to the media two or three weeks in advance of the event. Then, a few days prior to the event, in time for the media to assign reporters, we send them another press release. The day before, we get on the phones and call all of the media. We remind them that we have sent them releases and ask if they received them. If they haven't we hand deliver new ones or read them aloud over the phone.

Be certain that you contact the wire services (United Press International, Associated Press) that will put your story out on the wires for newspapers, radio, and television stations to pick up across the country. One of the first organizations you should contact in your own city is the city news bureau. If you have a good news item, they will probably put it on the wire service in your city. It doesn't cost you anything if your story is accepted.

Then, on the day of the event, have someone on the scene call the local media who have not arrived, and give them a brief account of what is going on. If there are reporters already on hand, tell the media you are calling that other news people are there and encourage them also to cover the event.

Always put someone in charge of media and provide them with a list of media phone numbers. If your event is on Saturday, some radio and TV stations will not have anyone at the switchboard. Some will have a special news number that bypasses the switchboard. You should know that number. Call the studio and ask them how you can get through to a reporter when you have an event on a weekend.

Have lots of factual information at your fingertips. If you call in a story, be sure your facts are accurate as to the time, the place, the event, the number of people. If you give statistics, have proof for them. Pro-lifers have to be accurate in all of their reporting, checking out all of the facts, even checking the spelling carefully. The story must be as factual as possible. Pro-lifers must be more exacting than the media are. The press is going to make mistakes and we don't want to give them a head start by providing them with mistakes of our own.

Get to know news people. Visit newspaper offices. Meet the writers and editors. If you like someone's story, call him up and congratulate him. If you don't like it, call him up and tell him what was good about it, then point out what wasn't. Perhaps you will make a contact. Get to know people in the media by offering to take them to lunch. Get them to talk, to help you find out what is going on, and what may be coming up.

Try to get advance notice of what will be appearing on radio and television. Call the stations. They will put you on their mailing list and send you a calendar of events so that you will be aware of upcoming programs. If something is going to be aired that is against your pro-life philosophy, you will be prepared to watch it, listen to it, and refute it.

It is always better to send too many press releases than to send too few. When the media routinely receive your press releases, they will, even if they're opposed to your position, give you coverage because of the interest you have shown in their resource. Flood them with press releases, but send only one at a time. A package of press releases is like saying, "Take your choice. Which event do you want to cover?" This is not a good idea. It is easier for them to concentrate on one event at a time. Don't send them releases on things that aren't newsworthy. But any time you have an event coming up, take a chance. If you get only one reporter there, that's one story you wouldn't have had otherwise.

Don't hesitate to write your own stories. If you have an event that should have been covered by the press and wasn't, write it up yourself and send it in after the fact. If you have good pictures, send them along too. Many newspapers are willing to take a story that is already written. Sometimes they don't have the manpower or the interest to write it themselves, but will print it if you will write it for them after the event. Give yourself a by-line, but tell them that they can do the story without your by-line or even with that of one of their own reporters.

Sometimes it is better to omit the by-line so that you can quote yourself in the story. If you want to have your exact statements expressed, a direct quote is the easiest, most effective, most interesting way to do it. If you have a good story, but it is brief, get a good picture and send a caption along with it. A caption is simply a brief description of what is going on in the picture. Your chances of getting that in might be better. When we picketed President Reagan the day he made the announcement of his appointment of Sandra Day O'Connor to the Supreme Court, we went out to the airport a couple of hours before his arrival, while the light was still good. We held up large letters spelling out, LIFE YES, O'CONNOR NO. We had pictures taken of the pickets against the Air Force landing field sign in the background, so that people would know that this was where Air Force One came in. We used that picture, with cutlines, and sent it all over the country.

Eventually it got into newspapers in New Zealand and Australia. It got into twelve national publications. It was simply a picture with a cutline. We didn't have to send a long, involved story with it. The picture itself told the story. We think this story helped organize a strong drive to help educate Sandra O'Connor—and the President—on the importance of the abortion issue. Just look at how well she's been doing ever since.

It is advisable for any pro-lifer who has access to a press pass to get one. Join the press club in your city. Rub elbows with media people. There is nothing better than getting to know them. It was because of some contacts we had in Chicago that we were able to get the ''Abortion Profiteers'' series started in the *Chicago Sun-Times*. We knew some reporters on the paper and called to see if they were interested in a story on the rotten conditions in Chicago's abortion mills. They were.

Imagination and innovation are critical for getting media attention, and you have to have a certain flair for writing interesting stories. You can't be afraid to call a press conference. A press conference can be a devastating thing if nobody comes, especially if you've invited a celebrity. That happened to us. We staged a press conference with an ex-Playboy bunny who had become a pro-life speaker and we assumed that she would draw the press. Hardly anyone came. It was very embarrassing. I brought her in from Virginia to give a talk. Three reporters came, all from very small newspapers. Her only interview was with some high school students.

At other times you may call a press conference and get a good turnout, but have a very antagonistic press. Don't be afraid to call a conference if you have something worthwhile to announce. Some of the reporters may think, ''Well, we've got it on the wire.'' They won't call you. But others will call in, even if they don't send a reporter. They wouldn't do that unless you called a press conference, because they are afraid someone else might get the story that they didn't get.

Once, a local television station was doing a story on rape. A bill had been passed excluding rape as a reason for abortion. They wanted to do an interview. I knew they would be hostile and would try to make me look like an ogre for being against abortion for rape. So I called a young lady I knew who had been raped and had gone ahead and had the child. I asked her to bring her little boy with her. He was about four years old. When she arrived I asked her to go outside into the yard. She was out there playing with her little boy when the TV crew and reporter arrived. The interviewer wanted to sit down and talk to me. Instead, I suggested that he go out and talk to the young woman who had been raped but who had kept her baby. I told him to ask her what she thought about abortion for rape and to ask her little boy what he thought about it. They got a much better story out of this arrangement than they would have with just a straight interview with me.

Always remember that you're trying to reach people with your message, and you need to use the press to get that story out. Don't worry about their attitude, whether they are for you or against you. If they are good journalists, their reporting will be objective, and you will get your story to the people.

Remember Paul Brown's slogan, "There is no such thing as bad press. The only bad press is no press."

12 HOW TO GET ON TALK SHOWS

When you are considering making appearances on talk shows, be aware of which shows handle controversial subjects like abortion. Watch and listen to talk shows. Get to know the host and the sort of guests he has on the show. You can start on the local scene simply by calling the shows or sending them a biographical sketch of yourself or some other pro-life spokesman you want to get on the program. Tell them when you are available.

Once we printed up a piece telling about our organization and sent out more than ten thousand copies to talk show hosts across the country. While we did not get many takers, at least we let them know about us, and presumably they filed our brochure for future reference. From time to time we still get calls from radio stations asking if we are available to be on their show. Sending out the circular worked.

You can also call in to the talk shows in progress when you hear an adversary. Ask them to invite you to debate the issue or allow you to present the other side. That is one way to get an invitation. When they want you to debate a pro-abortionist, they may ask you to suggest someone to be your adversary. Never suggest your own adversary. It is their job to find someone. I once suggested three names for them to choose from. They invited *all three*. I have never suggested anyone since.

To appear on a talk show, call the host or producer and simply ask to be on the show. You have a good chance of being accepted if abortion is currently in the news, which it generally is. For instance, if a pro-life amendment is up for a vote in Washington, if a bill is before your local legislature, if there has just been a statement by the President, a bishop, or Mother Teresa, if there is a current story dealing with abortion or infanticide: that is the best time to call them.

Sometimes the station will call you when abortion is in the news if they have your name and number on file. Always be available. Never turn down an invitation to go on radio or television or do an interview. Whether you have to do the interview by phone or go to the studios, accept the offer. Whether it is a local college radio station or ABC, do it. You are going to be talking to *somebody* and possibly you will convert someone to the pro-life cause.

When you are on a talk show, do not get upset if the host favors the opposition. While that is a sure sign that he is not a good moderator, it won't hurt you. A good host, however, will not let his position on abortion be known. He will remain neutral. If he sides with you too much, he will scare off calls from the opposition. People won't call in if they know there will be two people against them. You may feel good with a friendly host, but it is better to have one who does not show his hand. A hostile host can gain sympathy for you. If you think he and the opposition are ganging up on you, mention it on the air. Say, "I didn't know I was going to have two opponents." Try to make light of it and perhaps the host will realize he is appearing to advocate abortion and may try to compensate for it by giving you more time to explain your position.

If you are on a show discussing a specific subject such as abortion, don't let anyone steer you off the subject and into other areas, no matter how persistent he might be. If the host, your opponent, or a caller starts asking your opinions on birth control, the nuclear freeze, capital punishment, or anything else not directly related to abortion, pull the conversation back to the subject. Say you came on the show to talk about abortion and that you refuse to get off that subject. You will come back on the program and talk about these other issues at another time. Usually that is all it takes to get back on the subject.

In a talk show, always try to keep a sense of humor. Graciously accept slurs against yourself. "Well, no one is perfect." Don't be afraid to use *their* terminology in a humorous way. Frequently the opposition insists that we can't impose our morality on others. So, if you get into a situation where they are insisting that you denounce violence, fire bombing, and kidnapping, you might say, "Well, I wouldn't firebomb a clinic or kidnap anyone myself, but I can't impose my morality on others." You can sometimes demolish a line of attack by using a little humor.

The talk show is a wonderful opportunity to reach thousands of people with the facts. Pour on the facts during the entire time you are on the program. Never answer a question with "yes" or "no". Always go into depth on *why* the answer is yes or no. Give examples and clear, graphic proof of why abortion is illogical and why the defense of human life is logical. It is a sign of a good talk show participant to launch into areas he is best qualified to discuss. If you are asked about the dangers abortion poses to women, talk about these, but also discuss the psychological effects of abortion. Talk about organizations such as Women Exploited by Abortion (WEBA) that aid victims of abortion. Emphasize the fact that women are so traumatized by abortion that they have had to band together.

Talk about your own experiences. People are interested less in philosophy than they are in events and experiences. You can keep an audience glued to the talk show by telling them things you and others have experienced. Real life events hold interest better than statistics and theory.

The talk show should target the issue. Pick up leads from what your opposition says. On one talk show a pro-abortion doctor slipped and used the word "mothers" instead of "pregnant women". It was close to Mother's Day. I picked up on it, and congratulated the doctor for using the proper term, since women who go into an abortion clinic *are* mothers about to destroy their motherhood.

Rarely use the opposition's terms in the way that they use them. When they talk about "pro-choice", avoid that term. Use "pro-abortion". Pro-choice means nothing. If they make an issue of it, ask them to define choice. It doesn't mean anything unless the thing chosen is indicated. What they choose is abortion and consequently, they are "pro-abortion". Insist on using the more accurate term.

Insist on accuracy throughout the discussion. If they talk about "eliminating", "removing", or "interrupting" the pregnancy, call it instead "killing a new human life". They don't interrupt life. You interrupt someone's conversation, but you don't interrupt someone's life. Don't let them get away with deceptive terminology.

Rarely use the word "fetus". Use "baby" or "unborn child", because we must give dignity to the child in the womb, the dignity that they deny it. Never use their terms, even if you want to get along with them. You don't have to surrender to their vocabulary. They won't use yours except by accident. The host is likely to slip up, too. He will say something about "the fetus" or "the embryo", and then start referring to it as "the baby". They often refer to the pregnant woman as "the mother", because that is the way we talk when we're not discussing abortion. They will start using your terms if you use them.

When you tell the talk show host or any member of the media where to reach you to do a show, always include your home telephone number. If you are going to be out of town, leave a number where you can be reached. You can interview by telephone from anywhere. I have done interviews from motel rooms, phone booths, hospitals, barber shops, and at home in bed at 2:00 A.M. And you don't need to have a file cabinet of resources with you to do interviews. Carry your resources in your head so that you are always able to speak articulately on abortion anywhere you are.

13 RECEIVE THE ABORTIONISTS' MAILINGS

It is crucial to stay aware of the abortionists' activities and plans. One way to stay informed is to get their mailings. You can be sure they are receiving ours.

If you are not known to the abortionists and are not on any pro-abortionists' mailing lists, send your name and address to all the pro-abortion organizations and ask to receive their mailings. You may have to send them a few dollars for their subscriptions. Some people balk at sending money to pro-abortion organizations, even for their publications, and this is understandable. But if you want to f nd out what the enemy is doing—and it is essential to know your enemies in order to counter them—you must get their literature. Justify the donation by being determined to cause them enough trouble to more than make up for the few dollars you send. You are going to be using their literature to their disadvantage. Besides, a number of pro-lifers do this routinely.

Have their mail sent to you at your own residence or office. In this way, your name will be placed on a number of similar lists.

Get on the National Abortion Rights Action League (NARAL) list and on Planned Parenthood's lists. Planned Parenthood has a number of publications. The National Organization for Women (NOW), the Religious Coalition for Abortion Rights (RCAR), Catholics for a Free Choice (CFFC), even the OB-GYN News should be sending their publications to you. (See the list of these organizations' addresses at the end of this chapter.) The advantages of getting their mailings are obvious: you will know when their meetings and rallies are being held, who their speakers are going to be, what they are planning to do legislatively. Frequently they will indicate when they are going to lobby and what bills they are most interested in working for and against.

You should keep files of all your pro-abortion literature after you have read the material carefully. Their literature will help you strengthen your arguments and reinforce your credibility. It will help you become aware of their greatest weaknesses. The best possible way to improve your arguments against the abortionists is to read the literature in which they present the fallacies that they use in defending abortion and their other crimes against humanity.

There is not a great deal to be said on the positive side about pro-abortionist publications except that they are generally professional-looking and slick. They have the money to pay for good layout and design. They frequently use two colors and often full color, which is very expensive. They use attractive type, good design, and high-quality paper. Their publications generally look good. It is what they say that is so bad.

If your name would be recognized by the abortionists as a pro-lifer, they won't accept your subscription; so, to receive the literature, have a friend subscribe for you. Select someone they won't suspect. It will take longer for you to get the information since it won't be delivered directly, but you can make arrangements to pick it up from your friend shortly after it arrives.

Pro-abortion organizations are constantly quoting from pro-life publications. We should return the favor. They sometimes comment on the effectiveness of our activities. Once, when we invaded an RCAR prayer service in the New York Avenue Presbyterian Church in Washington, D.C., we were too busy to take any pictures. The RCAR publication, *Options*, printed half a dozen pictures and a lengthy story on the event. It was a delight to read in their publication about their reaction to our "invasion".

Abortion-Promoting Organizations:

AD HOC COMMITTEE FOR
ABORTION RIGHTS
c/o Abortion Rights Association
  100 E. Ohio
  Chicago, IL 60611

CATHOLICS FOR A FREE CHOICE
  2008 17th St., NW
  Washington, DC 20009
  (202) 638–1706

THE ALAN GUTTMACHER
INSTITUTE
  360 Park Ave., South
  New York, NY 10010
  (212) 685–5858

PLANNED PARENTHOOD OF NEW
YORK CITY
  380 2nd Ave.
  New York, NY 10010
  (212) 777–2002

RELIGIOUS COALITION FOR
ABORTION RIGHTS
  100 Maryland Ave., NE
  Washington, DC 20002

REPRODUCTIVE RIGHTS
NATIONAL NETWORK
  17 Murray St.
  New York, NY 10007
  (212) 267–8891

ILLINOIS WOMEN'S AGENDA
Midwest Women's Center
  53 W. Jackson
  Chicago, IL 60604
  (312) 922—8530

NATIONAL ABORTION RIGHTS
ACTION LEAGUE
  825 15th St., NW
  Washington, DC 20005

NATIONAL ABORTION
FEDERATION
  201 Massachusetts Ave., NE
  Washington, DC 20002
  (202) 547—6599

NATIONAL ORGANIZATION FOR
WOMEN
  425 13th St., NW
  Washington, DC 20004
  (202) 347—2279

PLANNED PARENTHOOD
  810 7th Ave.
  New York, NY 10019

PLANNED PARENTHOOD
ASSOCIATION/CHICAGO AREA
  17 N. State St.
  Chicago, IL 60602
  (312) 781—9550

PLANNED PARENTHOOD WORLD
POPULATION
Planned Parenthood Federation of
America
  515 Madison Ave.
  New York, NY 10022

VOTERS FOR CHOICE
  1300 19th St., NW
  Washington, DC 20036
  (202) 296—7326

WOMEN ORGANIZED FOR
REPRODUCTIVE CHOICE
  P.O. Box A3423
  Chicago, IL 60690

WOMEN USA
  76 Beaver St.
  New York, NY 10005
      also:
  P.O. Box 8214
  Washington, DC 20024

WOMEN'S CAMPAIGN FUND, INC.
  1521 New Hampshire Ave., NW
  Washington, DC 20036
  (202) 332—1000

WOMEN'S EQUITY ACTION
LEAGUE
  805 15th St., NW
  Washington, DC 20001

14 ATTEND ABORTIONISTS' MEETINGS

One of the best ways to understand the abortionists' mentality and find out their plans is to attend their meetings and conventions. You can do this publicly, with them knowing who you are and that you represent pro-life, or while remaining incognito.

I attended the first National Association of Abortion Facilities (NAAF) convention in Chicago in the fall of 1976, as an "abortionist". Since they were unaware of who I was, I was able to spend three days at their meetings. I even managed to be invited to one meeting at which only six people were in attendance, discussing in depth how best to counteract pro-life pickets and sit-ins. It was so "closed" that it was held in a private room. I obtained a great deal of valuable information during my three-day stay, and wrote a number of stories on what I had found out. Since then, I have attended dozens of abortionists' meetings and conventions, some undercover, but most as a known pro-life activist.

At the National Abortion Federation (NAF) convention in New Orleans in 1983, Andy Scholberg and I registered under our own names but not under the real names of our organizations. We were identified before the opening meeting began. Since we had paid our registration they had to let us stay. At the 1984 meeting in Los Angeles, we both registered by name, and I sent a check from the Pro-Life Action League, complete with our decal saying, "Abortion Kills Babies. Choose Life." They accepted it.

Pro-lifers should make it a policy to attend as many pro-abortion meetings and conventions as they can get into, simply for the benefit they will derive from hearing the abortionists present their twisted philosophy, discuss their abortion techniques, reveal their political plans, talk about their problems, lament over their professional burnout, talk about their troubles with patients and staff, and discuss their fears.

Even if you are a known enemy, you can often find out how they plan to counter pro-life strategies. They often expose their plans, and they always make it clear, either directly or in a roundabout way, that they are concerned about pro-life activism and its new militancy.

The humanity of the unborn victim of their lethal trade also concerns them. While they attempt to suppress the medical facts about abortion killing a human being, they also talk a great deal about the qualities of the product of conception (P.O.C.). They worry about the information pro-life street counselors give women concerning the child's humanity and the dangers of abortion. These two subjects trouble them.

They are uneasy about the fact that the humanity of the unborn is becoming so well known to the public. At one meeting, an abortionist admitted that it could well be that pro-life is right, that human life is of value from the moment of conception. One abortionist told his audience that if they are true liberals, there may come a time when they will have to accept the pro-life philosophy and stop doing abortions. If unborn children are human beings, with meaningful life from the moment of conception, he argued, true liberals will be forced to side with pro-lifers. At the 1984 convention, one abortionist recommended that his listeners read Rev. James Burtchaell's thoughtful study of abortion, *Rachel Weeping*. It is amazing that at these workshops the audience does not seem to be disturbed by such statements or recommendations!

At a recent National Abortion Federation meeting, in fact, the first segment addressed such questions as "When does life begin?" and "What is a human being?" Some of the talks sounded as though they were being given by pro-life doctors. Many of the speakers believed that life begins at conception, although they qualified their statements by saying that it is not "meaningful" life, or has no "value", and that it is not as important as the woman's life. One speaker gave evidence of having reverence for the humanity of the unborn child. A "Catholic" theologian, Marjorie Maguire, however, later assured the group that the tissue in the womb doesn't become a human being until the pregnancy is accepted by the mother, and that the woman can withdraw her "covenant" with the child and send it hurtling back into "non-humanity" at any time.

It is important for pro-lifers to hear such things. It is necessary to see the moral struggle that some abortionists are having, and to find out how many of them do not like to be known as "abortionists". There is still a stigma attached to abortion. It hovers over doctors who perform them and the people who work in the clinics.

From these meetings you can also learn which pro-life activities bother the abortionists most. For instance, it is important for us to know that when pro-life pickets are outside a clinic, complications and confusion inside the clinic increase by as much as 400 percent. One woman announced that the average complication rate under normal circumstances was about two percent, but that when pro-lifers were outside, the complication rate rose to eight percent. This was common. From this report we can conclude that if they really cared about the health of the woman, they would refuse to perform abortions on the days that pro-life pickets are present. Obviously, they are so greedy that they will proceed with abortions no matter what the conditions.

We found out that their methods to counter pro-life activities are basically ineffective. Consequently, they are at the mercy of pro-life activist tactics. In the past, they have preferred to avoid court action against pro-lifers because their lawyers will not take their cases on a contingency basis and they lose most of the decisions. Recently, they have become bolder in taking legal action against pro-lifers, although they continue to lose the majority of cases and still have large legal bills to pay. They seem to be trying to "scare off" pro-life activists.

If you are on the abortionists' mailing lists you will find out about their meetings. Sign up to attend. If you can't get into a pro-abortion meeting yourself, send someone else. Many times when our people attend, they are unaware of our presence. If they do find out that pro-lifers are in attendance, they usually curtail their discussions, try to move to another location to exclude pro-lifers, or simply go on with their meeting, though reluctantly.

Be sure to tape their meetings, or at least take copious notes. Buy their tapes so that you can disseminate their information. It is encouraging to see how many problems they have managing the abortion industry.

One of the most valuable by-products of attending their meetings and conventions is your renewed conviction that they are absolutely wrong and you are absolutely right. There is no question about who is right after spending time listening to the abortion providers. Their arguments are so weak that they have a hard time convincing those already in their ranks.

Impromptu polls taken at these meetings are often useful in telling us how effective our pro-life activities are. From their own show of hands we learn what disturbs the abortionists most and what we do that is most effective. From these polls we may get ideas for future, previously untried activities, such as sending coverts in to ask if they can have the body of their baby following the abortion and if it will be baptized.

Attendance at their meetings also serves to reaffirm confidence in our own activities. It is inspiring to hear them tell how disturbed they are by pro-life pickets at their clinics. If we pro-lifers realized how much our presence bothers them, we would be at the clinics in such members that it would not be long before there wasn't an abortion clinic left operating.

Consider that if our presence at clinics causes four times more confusion and complications than there would be if we were not there, then it is obvious that we should be there every time they operate. The abortionists say we rejoice at the increase in complications when we picket a clinic. We aren't happy with the complications, but with the evidence this report provides that the abortionists are willing to go ahead with abortions even though they know there is a much greater chance of complications with pickets outside. This proves how little they care about their clients' health. They would not think of delaying the procedure until they have optimal conditions, as a reputable physician would do. The money means more to them than the women's health.

We will not accept blame for their complications because we believe it is more important to prevent murder that it is to worry about a woman's disposition while she is having her baby killed. We are not responsible for complications because we warn women about them and try to convince them not to have abortions. The only way to avoid complications is to avoid abortions. They cannot keep us away from the clinics. Pro-life activists intend to keep going back to the clinics even when the abortionists bring lawsuits and injunctions against us and even when we are routinely arrested.

Every pro-abortion meeting, convention, seminar, and workshop that you hear of should be attended by someone from your group. Spread the information you pick up at these meetings and expose the abortionists for what they are. If you hear about an upcoming abortion meeting but no one from your group can attend, call another pro-life organization and encourage them to send someone. No abortion gathering should be without its pro-life infiltrator.

15 GET PRO-LIFE BOOKS INTO THE PUBLIC LIBRARIES

It should not be difficult to get books that deal with abortion from the pro-life perspective into public libraries, but it is.

Libraries are well stocked with pro-abortion literature and have been for years. Go to any library and look in the catalogue files under "abortion". You will find that most of what is listed is pro-abortion.

The first thing to do to remedy this situation is to get pro-life books into the library. Purchase a number of hardback pro-life books yourself, then present them to the library. The books will be catalogued and put on the shelves. There are several sets of pro-life books that can be purchased in lots. These sets are assembled specially for this purpose. One good set is the "Library Pack", which costs about $50 and includes *Aborting America*, by Bernard Nathanson, M.D., *The First Nine Months of Life*, by G. L. Flanagan, *Handbook on Abortion*, by Dr. and Mrs. J. C. Wilke, *The Right to Live: The Right to Die*, by C. Everett Koop, M.D., *Unmarried and Pregnant: What Now?* by I. Critelli and T. Schick, and *Who Broke the Baby?* by Jean Garton. For this set write: Life Cycle Books, 15 Oakland Avenue, Harrison, NY 10528.

There are many other good pro-life books available. You can make a collection of them on your own and present them to your library.

You may also suggest books for the librarian to order. After all, it is your library too. But the recommendation will often be received cooly. Such suggestions may be referred to a library board, where they will get caught up in red tape, and will require a lot of follow-up on your part. It may take some persistence to get pro-life books into your own library where they are needed most, and it will take work to keep them there.

Remember that the books you donate must be hardback. Libraries are not as interested in paperbacks as they are in hardbacks because they fall apart more quickly.

Consider making a formal presentation of your books to the library. Tell the librarian that you are coming in to present a packet of books, then call your local newspaper staff and ask them to take a picture of you making the presentation. Indicate the books' content and explain why you want to make sure there is a balance of information available to students working on term papers or preparing for debates on abortion. On a controversial subject such as this, students should be exposed to both sides of the argument. Insufficient resources on either side of the issue is a violation of the students' right to be informed. Totalitarian states present only one side of an issue. This, however, is a democracy.

You will have to keep an eye on these pro-life books to make sure they get into the card catalogue or the computer. Check the listings from time to time until you see that they have entered the system. Frequently check on the books themselves. Try to check one out to see where it is and how long you must wait to get it. You may find it has been listed as "lost", in which case you should present the library with another copy. Don't be surprised to find that pro-life books disappear. Pro-abortionists have no qualms about throwing them out. Some librarians, if they are pro-abortion, might conveniently misplace them. We have seen these books mysteriously disappear from the shelves, so keep your eye on them. We checked our own local library several times and found that none of the pro-life books we had donated were still there. They all had to be replaced.

So be prepared to fight to get pro-life books into the public libraries, and be ready to fight to keep them there. Customarily, only one side of this issue has been aired. That is the side that says it is useful to kill unborn children. While most educators cater to children and want young people to come to them for advice, many seem not really to like children. Many are liberal and pro-abortion. That is the reality pro-lifers must deal with. Getting pro-life material into public libraries and keeping it there is a challenge. When this material becomes standard fare in all libraries, it can't help but bring many into the pro-life movement, if there is any truth to the adage, "Truth will out."

No single organization in the country, or for that matter the world, is a greater enemy of the pro-life, pro-family movement than Planned Parenthood. Planned Parenthood has been around for more than sixty years, and it still follows the philosophy of its founder, Margaret Sanger. It rejects a moral value system and aims at glorifying sex at the expense of the family and the unborn child.

Planned Parenthood's founder believed strongly in the program of eugenics. Her idea was that society should be made up of a breed of thoroughbreds and the inferior members should not reproduce. She believed sex was an end in itself. Sex could be used for reproduction by those who *should* reproduce, but for those who should not, the poor and minorities, it should serve strictly as a form of entertainment. The value system that underlies Planned Parenthood is an attack on morality, the family, even the human race.

Their slogan, "every child a wanted child", suggests that some children will be unwanted, namely those who were not "planned". And what do you do with unplanned children? If they are in the womb, you abort them. In the United States alone, Planned Parenthood operates more than sixty abortion clinics. It is constantly justifying abortion, recommending abortion, fighting legal battles to retain lax abortion laws, sending women and girls to abortion clinics. In areas where it does not perform abortions, it has referral services.

Fighting Planned Parenthood is of paramount importance to the pro-life movement, since their philosophy is antithetical to ours. Their programs should be exposed. Hard as it is to believe, many people are still ignorant of their real philosophy and aims, thinking of Planned Parenthood as a kind of philanthropic organization that arranges activities for teenagers and educates mothers on pre- and postnatal hygiene. Nothing could be further from the truth. Planned Parenthood presents a real and constant danger to youth, to the family, and to this country. It is important to work against local Planned Parenthood organizations and to try to get them out of the community by exposing the dangers they present.

Pro-life groups throughout the country have fought Planned Parenthood from the beginning. They have picketed their offices and exposed their materials, such as their film *All About Sex*. They have canvassed neighborhoods attempting to keep Planned Parenthood from opening new offices.

In Chicago, when we learned that Planned Parenthood was planning to set up fifty satellite clinics in the area, we began targeting specific communities where clinics might be set up. We talked with the mayors and village counselors. We talked with the heads of real estate agencies. We went to the churches and gave talks, telling the congregations why they should help keep Planned Parenthood out and that when Planned Parenthood gets into a community it can destroy the family structure.

When a clinic does become established in a community, despite our efforts, we try to alert the public to the dangers present and ask parents not to send their children there. We picket, protest, and run advertising that exposes the fact that Planned Parenthood will give sex information to children, which most likely is contrary to the information their parents want them to have.

Planned Parenthood gives this information without parental knowledge or consent. They will also give out contraceptive drugs and devices and make abortion referrals without parents' knowledge or consent. They even go so far as to advise young people not to tell their parents of a pregnancy if they think their parents will object to an abortion. All parents should resent Planned Parenthood's takeover of parental responsibility and their children's lives. The damage they can cause both physically, through contraceptive drugs and devices, and morally, through condoning and encouraging sexual activity outside marriage, can be irreparable. Planned Parenthood's "value free" sex education and free contraceptives give young people a false sense of security, encourage them to do things behind their parents' backs, and even encourage them to destroy new lives through abortion, which Planned Parenthood advocates as a back-up form of birth control.

Planned Parenthood has often, by its own admission, been unsuccessful in its programs. In its own reports it admits that the increase in the use of contraception has helped increase promiscuity, unplanned pregnancies, venereal disease, and abortions, rather than diminish them. It is clear that the only thing these programs accomplish is to create a need for contraceptives, which results in more unplanned pregnancies and, thus, more abortions. The full impact of Planned Parenthood's programs on society may not be known for generations.

Since Planned Parenthood poses a threat to our society, pro-life groups across the nation have declared an all-out war against its anti-family programs. They are trying to get Planned Parenthood clinics out of their communities, cut off its state, federal, and international funding and turn community sentiment against it. Utah has a parental notification law and only a few Planned Parenthood clinics. The Planned Parenthood office there must notify parents if their children are using their facility. This has discouraged many young people from visiting Planned Parenthood. In the first year the parental notification bill was in effect, there were eight percent fewer teen pregnancies and thirteen percent fewer abortions. Three out of five teenagers stopped going to Planned Parenthood and other "family planning" clinics. This one instance indicates that less Planned Parenthood means fewer teen sex problems, not more. Many believe the less Planned Parenthood the better.

A typical program to prevent Planned Parenthood from entering a community would consist of contacting pro-life leadership and holding a meeting with community leaders who recognize the dangers of Planned Parenthood. At this initial meeting, someone will be appointed to contact the mayor or village manager and pastors of community churches. Someone should run a check on possible sites for the proposed facility and contact real estate offices from whom Planned Parenthood may be seeking office space.

Someone in charge of publicity will contact the local news media with the story of their pro-life efforts and place a statement in the newspaper giving the names of community leaders who oppose the presence of Planned Parenthood. All concerned residents may subscribe to this ad and pay a few dollars for its placement, thus making up the cost of the advertisement. All of their names should appear with the ad.

At a second leadership meeting, the slide presentation "A Critical Look at Planned Parenthood" or a similar audiovisual presentation should be made, strengthening the community leadership's conviction that Planned Parenthood is a danger to community standards. This meeting should include educators, religious leaders, and as many representatives of municipal agencies as possible, including the mayor and police chief.

Plans should be made at this meeting to hold a larger, community-wide meeting at which a more formal presentation of the facts will be made. Planned Parenthood representatives may be invited to attend to debate the issue and present their arguments. Plans for implementing the program to keep Planned Parenthood out should not be discussed in detail at this meeting, the purpose of which is to get the community solidly behind the effort and to encourage those present to carry the message back to the rest of the community.

If the campaign to keep Planned Parenthood out is successful, a constant vigilance must be maintained. If, despite the best efforts on the part of the community, Planned Parenthood forces its way in, a campaign to get it out commences. This is similar to efforts used in trying to get any abortion facility out of the community—pickets, sidewalk counseling, leafleting, and a program of educating the community about the danger to family and youth.

Here are some useful resources for educating your community about the dangers of Planned Parenthood:

MARY SENANDER
  1205 Pennsylvania, North
  Golden Valley, MN 55427
"A Critical Look at Planned
Parenthood" (Slide Presentation)

AMERICAN LIFE LOBBY
  P.O. Box 490
  Stafford, VA 22554
"Planned Parenthood Must Be
Stopped" and "Planned Parenthood
and the Christian Family"
(brochures)

CATHOLICS UNITED FOR LIFE
  New Hope, KY 40052
"Margaret Sanger, Father of
Modern Society" (paperback book
by Elasah Drogin)

NATIONAL RIGHT TO LIFE
EDUCATIONAL TRUST FUND
  419 7th St., NW, Suite 402
  Washington, DC 20004
"The Victory is Won: Planned
Parenthood Abortion Crusade"
(booklet)

CATHOLIC LEAGUE FOR
RELIGIOUS AND CIVIL RIGHTS
  1100 W. Wells Street
  Milwaukee, WI 53233
"Family Planning Clinics:
Cure or Cause of Teenage
Pregnancy?" (brochure, by
Michael Schwartz and James H.
Ford, M.D.)

17 THE VALUE OF THE TAX PROTEST

The tax protest idea was bobbing around on right-to-life waters even before the 1973 *Roe v. Wade* Supreme Court abortion ruling. Taxpayers in California balked at paying for abortions in the late 1960s and New Yorkers discussed protesting payment of abortions under Governor Nelson Rockefeller in the early 1970s.

None of these efforts was organized on a large enough scale to be effective. When the U.S. Supreme Court dropped its abortion bomb in January 1973, no one thought seriously of launching a tax protest until the truth dawned on citizens that the abortion right invented by the court might be paid for with tax money. Few anticipated that a right so private that women could not be advised of its dangers or told of the humanity of the unborn child would be paid for with public funds.

As soon as it was clear that federal, state, and local taxes were supporting welfare abortions, tax protests on a small scale were instituted. There were sporadic calls for massive tax protests. Pleas, plans, and programs for tax protests fill the early pro-life literature. Nearly all of these were begun with enthusiasm, but failed to get off the ground or elicit sufficient public support to be effective.

This did not mean that the tax protest could not work or that it would not be a powerful tool for fighting abortion. It might have been. It might be in the future. But it was never given a chance. Some pro-lifers still believe the abortion ruling could have been reversed overnight through a national tax protest if it would have had the right leadership.

A Tax Protest Committee was formed in Lansing, Illinois, in 1975 to advise Cook County real estate taxpayers in protesting payment of a portion of their real estate tax that paid for abortions at Cook County Hospital. This was in anticipation of a class action suit against the county.

For seven years, beginning in 1970, three years before *Roe v. Wade*, Joseph Fahy of Sauquoit, New York, waged a quiet, successful battle with the Internal Revenue Service. Fahy fended off the federal bureaucracy singlehanded and won his case before the federal judiciary. He refused to cooperate with the killing of innocent unborn humans through the state's Medicaid program.

Former Minnesota attorney William E. Drexler paid no taxes at all for ten years, arguing that the Internal Revenue Service has no right to collect taxes, much less to spend it to murder the unborn. He pointed out that each year twenty million Americans either fail to file, refuse to file, or file a protest return. Only a few go to prison. He said that a thorough knowledge of the law can prevent prosecution.

Consider what the effect might have been on the abortion issue if on January 23, 1973, the day after *Roe v. Wade*, all pro-life church leaders, from the National Council of Catholic Bishops to the anti-abortion heads of pro-life Protestant denominations, speaking in unison, had called for a national tax protest until the abortion ruling was rescinded.

Imagine what a statement by the American Catholic bishops to fifty million Catholics commanding them not to pay their federal, state, or local taxes for as long as the government permitted abortion might have done for the cause of life.

If the evangelical leadership, the heads of the Mormon church, and the leaders of other religious groups that believe abortion is murder would have announced that no God-fearing Christian could financially support a government that allows such a grave evil, they would have nipped the "abortion right" in the bud.

Citizens outraged at a ruling that defied history, science, law, and morality would have joined church leaders in a national tax boycott, and such a bold, forthright appeal in response to the abortion ruling would have had a profound effect on the future of the country.

Many non-churchgoing people would have responded too. There would have been allegiance to any leadership that opposed a ruling that shocked so many decent people. Ninety percent of Americans opposed liberalized abortion laws in the early 1970s and nearly *all* polls taken at that time indicate that a change in the abortion law would not come through the people or their representatives, but only through the courts. State referenda showed that the people did not want liberalized abortion, and some states that had liberalized abortion reversed their laws. And even though some states had liberal abortion laws, none had laws as liberal as those imposed by the Supreme Court's 7−2 decision.

If millions of people had withheld their taxes under moral conviction, there probably would have been few investigations or arrests by the IRS. The government would have been in a quandary. When all efforts to "reason" with church leaders had failed, rapid steps would have been taken to remedy the situation.

Even if such a strategy had not worked, the effort would have been a permanent tribute to religious leadership and its belief in the value of human life.

But instead of action, Americans received volumes of strong, stirring, impressive words against abortion. They heard the abortion ruling condemned. They did not see it challenged.

Consider the plight of the unborn on January 22, 1973. All laws protecting their very existence were suddenly removed. Permission was given to exterminate them at will. For 365 days a year it was open season on the unborn child. This would soon translate into one painful, brutal killing every twenty seconds. Yet, their avowed protectors, committed by their belief in God and their promise to Christ to defend the helpless and defenseless, came forth with only words denouncing the new ruling. No significant action was taken or even suggested.

It has been said during the current abortion holocaust that the unborn child has fewer friends to defend him than have dogs, cats, and raccoons. At least these animals have humane societies to rescue them. But the unborn child has weak, poorly organized, frightened negotiators, often ready to compromise their case rather than lose their respectability. The only defense unborn children receive are words calling abortion an unspeakable crime. If it is so unspeakable, why didn't church leaders *do* something to stop it?

But a few valiant souls did more than talk. They put the tax protest to use as best they could, hoping to start a trend but invariably going out alone on a limb.

One hero of the tax protest was Dr. John Kelly of Oak Park, Illinois, a wiry, red-haired father of fourteen, whose own father had been chairman of the Cook County Hospital Committee and had helped procure federal, state, and county funding for the hospital. After January 22, 1973, Dr. Kelly wanted to be sure none of his tax money was used for funding abortions. While the Bartlett Amendment was in force, no federal funding of abortions was possible. But when Dr. Kelly found that his *county* taxes were being used for abortion, he withheld the percentage of his real estate tax that he estimated was being used to kill unborn babies. The amount was less than two dollars, but he refused to pay it. He withheld this amount for three years and was finally charged with non-payment.

The county threatened to auction off his home to collect the $5.75 he owed in back taxes. At that point in his fight the Bartlett Amendment failed to pass, and Dr. Kelly, knowing he could not fight both federal and county tax agencies and unwilling for reasons of conscience to help finance abortion, sold his home and moved to Ireland, taking most of his family with him.

His departure on St. Patrick's Day, 1975, was a colorful media event that educated a whole new generation of pro-lifers who needed to know that abortion is an important enough issue that some people will risk home and profession to fight it. He said good-bye to relatives and friends at O'Hare Airport and left for Ireland, where he remained for three-and-a-half years. Making his stand against the unjust use of taxpayers' money to pay for abortion meant leaving behind a well-established medical practice and his family home, but he was willing to do it.

In 1980, Cook County board president George Dunne ordered the abortion ward at Cook County Hospital closed. Dr. Kelly, who had returned to reestablish his medical practice in Oak Park, testified at the hearings that ended abortion funding at the hospital that had played such a vital role in his life.

A more current tax protestor is Edmund Starrett of Livonia, Michigan, who refused to pay his state tax. His story is not unique, but has followed the pattern of courage and dedication, threats and intimidation, hope for pro-life support, and a lonely battle.

We spoke with Starrett during a visit to Livonia and were struck by his determination to fight the case through with a conviction that the protest is a viable method of fighting abortion.

It is. But pro-lifers will never realize the tax protest's real potential until they can convince a large number of people to unite in their efforts. It would undoubtedly prove to be one of our powerful tools.

Protesting the use of tax money to finance abortions is perfectly legitimate and is something every pro-lifer should do without hesitation. There is a proper legal method of protesting that must be followed to avoid prosecution. In Cook County, Illinois, the law requires the use of a properly worded formal protest at the time of payment of your tax. The next step is the filing of a legal objection to the use of tax money for abortions. This can be done individually, at each taxpayer's personal expense, or by forming or joining a class action suit against an agency (such as the Hospital and Medical Services Governing Commission) performing abortions with tax money. You cannot get a judicial hearing until your real estate taxes are paid under formal written protest. Then you can demand a refund of the portion of your taxes used for abortions. If you wish to engage in a tax protest in your area, be sure to obtain legal advice.

Here is a copy of one tax protest form used in Cook County, Illinois.

PAYMENT OF REAL ESTATE TAX UNDER PROTEST
(this form is to remain attached to my tax bill)

TO: COUNTY COLLECTOR OF COOK COUNTY

I, _____, a citizen of Cook County, as an owner of certain real estate in Cook County, have received a real estate tax bill for real estate taxes assessed and levied against said property as set forth in said tax bill and as set out in the Cook County Collector's Warrant Books Vol. No. _____, Permanent Index No. _____. Total amount of tax for the year _____ is $ _____. Total amount paid is $ _____. Total amount of this installment is $ _____. This payment shall be applied to the taxes of all taxing bodies pro rata, subject to a refund of .1 percent [1]of the total _____ tax which is paid under protest and is objected to on the ground that:

1. The Cook County Hospital Governing Commission, an appointed governing body, has the legal responsibility for setting policy at Cook County Hospital. The said Commission has allowed the Cook County Hospital to perform abortions at the hospital, without regard to whether or not said abortions are therapeutic. Non-therapeutic abortions are, in fact, performed at County Hospital.

2. Abortions are performed at County Hospital even though life has begun in the unborn child and without regard to that life.

3. No consent to abortion has been obtained from a guardian of such unborn child in which life has begun, nor notice and an opportunity to be heard afforded to a duly appointed guardian of the unborn and the father of the unborn.

4. Certain therapeutic medical needs of residents of Cook County have remained unfulfilled at the same time County Hospital engages in non-therapeutic abortions.

5. I, the undersigned, a citizen and real estate taxpayer of Cook County, in violation of my rights, have not been given the opportunity to choose by a vote at an election those goverment officials who have assumed the power to choose which unborn children live and which shall be exterminated, nor was I given the opportunity by referendum to vote on the Hospital Governing Commission.

6. The levy of real estate taxes for the purpose of performing non-therapeutic abortions and/or abortions which result in terminating the life of the unborn child violates the undersigned's constitutional rights as guaranteed by the First, Fifth, Ninth, and Fourteenth Amendments to the United States Constitution, and Article I, Sections 1, 2, 3, 5, 12, 23, and 24 of the Illinois Constitution. [2]

Name, Address, and Phone Number:

_____

_____

_____

Signed: _____

Cook County Real Estate Taxpayer

_____

1 This percentage will vary. Check your own county.
2 Find the appropriate article, if any, in your state.

18 HOW TO INFLUENCE YOUR ORGANIZATIONS

Most people belong to some kind of fraternal or social organization such as a church group, the American Legion, Knights of Columbus, or Rotary. Whatever group you belong to, make it a point to bring up the issue of abortion. Perhaps you can get your organization interested in supporting pro-life efforts or making contributions of time or money to pro-life projects. Your encouragement should be in the form of an all-out effort to get them to be active, to attend pro-life meetings or, better still, to take part in abortion clinic pickets and sidewalk counseling.

Don't hesitate to bring up the issue of abortion to your group. You may do it by getting up in front of the group and announcing that there is a crisis in our country that many don't understand. Be diplomatic. Perhaps it will be best for your group if you first bring up the issue with a small number of people within the group, such as a committee you are on, to try to discover who is with you and who against. You will have to be the one to decide which approach is best.

But be sure to make it a priority to influence your organization for the good of the unborn. Maybe there is something timely in the news such as a bill before the legislature. Maybe the President made a statement on abortion. The issue that stimulates the conversation can be negative such as a clinic fire-bombing or the discovery of the bodies of aborted babies. Use whatever device it takes to bring up the issue and get a discussion going. You will soon learn who the pro-lifers in your group are. You will also know who supports abortion and who is trying to remain neutral. And you will become the pro-life spokesman. People will come to you with their questions. Sooner or later someone will ask you about a problem pregnancy and whether or not to have an abortion. Other questions on infanticide, letting babies starve, *in vitro* fertilization, and other life issues will be brought to you. You will be the person your friends and enemies alike will turn to for authoritative answers. Let it be known where you stand on the abortion issue.

Even if you are in an organization whose members are mostly pro-abortion, it is probably wiser to be outspoken in defending your position than to remain silent, unless you believe you can work better without declaring your stand on abortion. In some instances, that is the best way to be effective. But however you approach it, you should keep bringing up the subject of abortion. Even if you decide not to be openly pro-life, you can cause people to think about the issue. Most people have not carefully considered whether they really want to support abortion. They simply believe that almost everyone else does. If the opportunity arises, speak to them about their feelings about abortion.

Also, relate your own experiences. Introduce new ideas to the group. Encourage them to invite speakers who have had experience with abortion, such as a member of WEBA (Women Exploited by Abortion), who has suffered an abortion or someone who has worked as a counselor in an abortion clinic. Schedule a physician specializing in prenatal life. Bring in a lawyer to talk about the legal problems with the Supreme Court's 1973 abortion ruling.

Use your imagination and you will find there are many ways to influence your organization. Hand out pro-life literature, discuss books on abortion, discuss the current news on abortion. In short, use anything that will educate and inform your group on the issue.

All of this will help to keep the issue alive. Don't worry about losing friends over abortion. Do you really have a ''friend'' who is pro-abortion? You will be surprised to discover how many people are pro-abortion simply because they haven't had time to research the issue. Once they get a little information on the subject, they realize they really are not pro-abortion after all. They may have fallen for the slogans and empty philosophy of the abortionists without ever really thinking deeply about it. Facts can turn people around. Every pro-lifer has seen it happen.

Documented information on what abortion is, what it does to the unborn child, how it damages the mother, and what it does to society are weapons that can at least neutralize a person on the issue. Rather than eliciting a firm, pro-abortion stand, these tools will sow the seeds of doubt in their minds. These seeds will grow, and will eventually prompt a thorough investigation of the subject. When people have looked into the abortion issue objectively, they will invariably come over to our side.

19 INFILTRATE ABORTION GROUPS

It takes courage to join a pro-abortion organization, pretending to be on their side, but it can be very educational. Infiltration can be done by going to individual abortion meetings as you learn about them or by actually joining an abortion group and paying your dues. Pro-lifers have managed both successfully, and much of the information used in countering the abortionist's efforts comes from infiltrators.

If you are infiltrating an abortion group on a long-term basis, your pro-life activities will necessarily be somewhat curtailed. You will have to go underground and not be seen with the pro-life group you are working for. Your contacts with pro-life will have to be few and carefully guarded until you are ready to go public.

You have to reconcile this arrangement with your conscience. You will have to pay the abortionists some dues. You cannot do anything to encourage abortion, counsel for abortion, or do anything else contrary to your beliefs. But you can still justify a financial contribution by determining to make up for it by using the information you acquire to diminish the harm they do.

Infiltration is a difficult thing to do. Most shy away from it, and not everyone is cut out to do it. But it is important for us to have pro-life people in various abortion organizations. We need the information. Once you have made a decision to infiltrate, you should go about it with enthusiasm and a determination to do the best job you can even if you plan your stay to be short-lived. You may be found out, or you may find it is not necessary to stay with the group long. You may get the information you need quickly. If you leave without being detected, try to stay in touch with the group. Keep their trust as long as you can, and remain on their mailing list so that you will be able to keep track of their activities.

A young woman who worked for a Chicago abortion clinic visited our office to tell us all she knew about the abortion clinic where she was employed. Her information was helpful. She brought us copies of their reports and their forms, and she helped us learn a great deal about the management and routine of the abortion clinic where she worked. She said she had problems working for them and accepting their money. I met with her after work at a restaurant and talked about the situation in the clinic. She wanted to quit her job because it depressed her and she could not get along with many of the people who worked there. She was not directly involved in doing abortions but knew all about the clinic's malpractice suits and their other legal and financial dilemmas. Some of the clients at the clinic, she reported, would come from the waiting room to her office to talk with her about their doubts and difficulties with their abortion decision. We learned from her how concerned the clinic was over the problems of the women who had had abortions there, and she reported the effect our activities had on clinic personnel.

One other method of gaining information is a quick "blitz" type infiltration of a pro-abortion event. This can be effective whether you are known or not, since you don't intend to gain their confidence, but merely gather some instant information and perhaps upset their meeting, challenge their security, and even capture some media attention. If you are not known, you will have an opportunity to learn from those abortionists who are willing to talk over their plans with a stranger. You should press this opportunity. If you are a well-known pro-lifer, you may not gather as much information as if you were unknown, but they cannot scuttle the meeting on your behalf and you will end up learning something useful.

If you are known to them, try to have some unknown or genuine infiltrator at the same meeting with you, so that they can let you know later what effect your presence had on the abortionists. These reports can be helpful to you in future confrontations with the abortionists at their meetings and seminars.

20 GET DENUNCIATION OF ABORTION BACK INTO THE MEDICAL OATHS

All medical oaths prior to 1973 had a clause that condemned abortion. The Hippocratic Oath read, "I will give no deadly medicine to anyone if asked, nor suggest such counsel, and in like manner, I will not give to a woman a pessary to produce abortion." The Oath of Geneva contains this pledge: "I will maintain the utmost respect for human life, from the time of conception; even under threat, I will not use my medical knowledge contrary to the laws of humanity." These and other oaths taken by doctors and by medical students, when they entered medical school and when they graduated, always contained a condemnation of abortion or inflicting any harm to the unborn patient. Since 1973, however, medical schools have gradually dropped the section of the oath dealing with abortion and respect for the unborn, obviously to accommodate their medical practice to the Supreme Court's ruling permitting abortion, and to prepare themselves for dealing with infanticide and euthanasia.

What some of us have done to call attention to this sad state of the medical oath is to go to the ceremonies when new students are introduced to medicine or when the graduating class is taking its oath and pass out flyers that put the denunciation of abortion back into the oath. We ask those present to insert these phrases at the time the oath is read. Even if a great number do not, some will still read it into the oath. And we have always managed to have confederates in the audience to read the portion that has been left out. In some cases, we have used a bullhorn to stimulate participation. When the class comes to the section where the part is missing, we insert the missing lines—loudly—so that they can be heard over the rest of the audience. The audience then has to stop its recitation and listen to our statement before it can proceed. The desired effect is to make a major issue out of abortion during a ceremony that is attempting to ignore it. The program is marked by confusion from then on! If word of the planned interruption leaks out, the authorities will inevitably denounce the insertion before the recitation of the oath. This simply serves to give it more attention.

At Northwestern Medical School's graduation in 1982, leaflets were passed out telling the audience to insert into the oath the section against

93

abortion. The master of ceremonies announced from the stage that some people had made this request and he urged that the whole gathering pause long enough to allow the graduates and their guests wishing to recite this part to do so.

There are other ways to try to get this traditional denunciation of abortions back in the medical oaths. We could start a movement on the campuses of medical schools to reinsert this portion. The odds are presently against us. It is possible to have the proposal brought up for reconsideration at each medical school. It would be helpful if medical schools with religious affiliations would simply put it back in and insist that their graduates adhere to the oath, even though abortion is legal.

While some will call such a proposal impractical, it is an important undertaking, the type of thing we as pro-lifers must do. We have to remind the public constantly that there are dissenting groups which will not accept abortion as the law of the land. We must establish the fact that there are many doctors who will not be involved in abortion because they consider abortion a medical and moral blasphemy. We need to remind society constantly of the barbarism of abortion, because some people don't even want the Supreme Court ruling to be questioned. We have to be the voices that remind the public that if members of the medical profession did not so readily pervert their profession as healers, abortion would not have taken root in this country. If doctors had taken a firm stand in support of their professional oath to be healers, they would not be murdering their patients through abortion.

If doctors honored their oath, liberal abortion laws would have no effect. It is important for a condemnation of abortion to be in the medical oaths. We must work for this by keeping the issue alive. Putting it back in temporarily may work toward getting it back permanently. We predict that some day the condemnation of abortion will again be an important part of the oath taken in medical schools across America. We are not predicting when that will be, but we are optimistic, and will continue to use direct action to hasten that day.

21 USE PRO-LIFE STICKERS, LITERATURE, DECALS, STENCILS

It is important for us to use every means at our disposal to bring the issue of abortion to public attention. Fortunately, this is not hard to do. There are literally thousands of pro-life promotional materials—bumper stickers for your car, badges to wear, decals to put on the windows of your home, car, or office. These all serve as reminders of the controversial nature of abortion. Some stickers suggest alternatives to abortion: "Adoption, Not Abortion". Others make a straightforward statement or ask a simple question: "Abortion Kills Babies" and "Does Your Doctor Kill Babies?" These are powerful statements and searching questions, and there are literally hundreds of them to choose from.

A pro-lifer should have a pro-life bumper sticker on his car. Sometimes a stranger will park next to your car and your pro-life sticker will encourage him to strike up a conversation. On the highway, people will sometimes honk as they pass you and point to your sticker. They're pro-life, too. While sometimes you will get an adverse reaction, at least you get a reaction, and that shows your message got across to someone.

One pro-lifer who has carried the bumper sticker to its limit is the Reverend Olga Fairfax, a Methodist minister from Maryland, who has at least thirty bumper stickers and signs on the back of her car. Once, I arrived for a television show in Pittsburgh and spotted a station wagon in the parking lot covered with pro-life bumper stickers. I knew right away that Olga was also a guest on the show. She is known far and wide for her traveling-billboard car—in addition to the large oilcloth poster she carries around and unfurls, displaying a picture of an aborted baby and an anti-abortion statement.

The use of buttons, pins, and the Precious Feet can be excellent devices for creating interest. People sometimes wonder what the feet represent. You explain that this is the size "your feet" were when you were ten weeks old in the womb. This graphically dramatic device has reached many people with the story of prenatal life.

There is an enormous selection of pro-life literature, colorful and interesting pamphlets that can be left in doctors' offices, at the dentist's, with the hair dresser, or the barber. Walk in and drop off a few pieces of literature or take it with you when you have an appointment.

Bumper stickers can be applied to many places besides on a car. Pro-lifers have even been known to stick them on windows or doors of abortion clinics. Bumper stickers encourage pro-lifers and inform the public from telephone poles, lamp poles, construction fences, even the sidewalk. It is inspiring to walk down the street and see these pro-life messages. We have all noticed pro-life billboards and posters in towns we have visited. They give us a real boost. They also upset the abortionists who are reminded all the time that we are out there, buying space or finding space to put up these labels, posters, decals, and billboards. Even homemade or commercially made stencils can be used to place pro-life slogans at construction sites. On a large wooden fence erected at a building site on Michigan Avenue someone stenciled "Abortion Kills Babies" twelve times in two-foot tall letters for the length of the block. Thousands saw it. People still talk about it as "the pro-life billboard on Michigan Avenue". It attracted the attention of a reporter who took pictures which appeared on the front page with a story on the "graffiti war".

Some people customarily use pro-life stickers on their envelopes when they pay their bills and mail letters, so that others are reminded that abortion is still a hot issue. Since every letter is seen by at least fourteen people before it reaches its destination, this is cheap publicity.

Sometimes people even have pro-life statements printed on their checks. They may, for instance, have a picture of a slogan such as, "Abortion is Murder, Pass the Human Life Bill." This is just another reminder that the abortion controversy is raging and will not go away. (See also Chapter 30.)

Besides offering a wide variety of pro-life books and pamphlets, the following companies also sell decals, posters, and bumper stickers:

LIFE CYCLE BOOKS
   15 Oakland Ave.
   Harrison, NY 10528
pro-life buttons, balloons, fetal development models

HERITAGE HOUSE '76
   P.O. Box 730
   Taylor, AZ 85930
Precious Feet pins, necklaces, earrings, T-shirts, pendants, decals, bumper stickers, envelope stickers, tote bags, postcards, billboards

RIGHT TO LIFE LEAGUE OF SOUTHERN CALIFORNIA
   1616 West 9th St., Suite 220
   Los Angeles, CA 90015
license plate frames, balloons, decals, buttons, stickers, billboards

DELUXE CHECK PRINTERS
Any bank, or write:
   Ron Campagna
   6225 N. Harlem Ave.
   Chicago, IL 60631
pro-life checks

HAYES PUBLISHING CO., INC.
6304 Hamilton Ave.
Cincinnati, OH 45224
slides, cassettes, leaflets, books

IDEA
(Information from the Dominican
Educational Assoc.)
P.O. Box 119
Elmwood Park, IL 60635
Rose for Life, self-sticking,
embroidered appliqués

INFOMAT-RIGHT TO LIFE
P.O. Box 5033
Torrance, CA 90510
envelope stickers (Aborted Babies),
(Abortion is Murder)

RIGHT TO LIFE OF LOUISVILLE
132 Breckenridge Ln.
Louisville, KY 40207
license plates (Love Life)

CATHOLICS UNITED FOR LIFE
New Hope, KY 40052
envelope stickers

RIGHT TO LIFE CALENDAR
133 Ridgewood Dr.
Metairie, LA 70005
appointment calendar

CINCINNATI RIGHT TO LIFE
EDUCATIONAL FOUNDATION, INC.
INC.
P.O. Box 24073
Cincinnati, OH 45224
billboards, posters, and other items

VOICES FOR LIFE
409 S. Grandview
Dubuque, IA 52001
billboards, posters, and other items

22 CONVERT THE PROFESSIONALS

Everybody should use his God-given special talents to fight abortion. If you are a writer, write about abortion. If you are an artist, use your artistic skills to make posters and construct visuals for the pro-life effort. If you happen to be a printer, print pro-life literature and help pro-life people with their printing jobs. If carpentry is your profession, make a set of baby caskets for abortion clinic pickets and build the platform needed for a pro-life rally. If you are a doctor, offer to help pregnant women and become a pro-life speaker. There is prestige in your title that garners respect for the pro-life message. If you are a lawyer, you are a potential expert on the Supreme Court abortion ruling. Use your professional specialty for the unborn.

Converts continually come into the movement. Once they have seen the evil of abortion, they feel an obligation to fight it. Some professionals come into the movement late and make up for lost time by working especially hard for the pro-life cause. We know an attorney who will not come out on the street to fight abortion with us, but he offers us his services free. Once, when we offered to pay for his services, he refused, saying that we were sacrificing our time and energy so that there would be a better society for his children to grow up in, and this was payment enough for him.

Professionals should be prepared to give pro-lifers the benefit of their experience and training. Doctors, attorneys, professional counselors, and the clergy can address abortion from a unique perspective, using their expertise to train pro-life laymen and enabling them to present the arguments themselves in a professional manner.

It is important not only to convert professionals, but to put their skills to use in the cause. Professional artists help us with our posters, signs, brochures, and programs. People in the print media, in television, in all walks of life, want to share in the inevitable pro-life victory. We have doctors in hospitals keeping us informed as to the number of abortions being performed and alerting us to cases where babies are aborted alive or instances where a young woman is being coerced into having an abortion.

Sometimes professionals will work together in helping save a life, as in one instance when a pastor informed us of a teen being forced to abort, a pro-life lawyer filed for an injunction, while a friendly doctor kept us informed of the situation at the hospital. A pro-life judge granted the injunction to prevent the abortion, and a friendly media contact gave us a good story. Pro-life professionals all along the line were called in to help in this effort to save a baby's life and to help save a young woman's dignity.

While this particular case ended with the father prevailing on the young girl to have the abortion, the spirit of cooperation among these professionals remains to this day.

23 PRODUCE A PRO-LIFE RADIO OR TELEVISION SHOW

It may sound ambitious to produce your own radio or television show, but it is not that difficult. A group of us in Chicago presented a live radio show every Sunday afternoon for two years. We pre-recorded the program for about six weeks and then decided it would be simpler and more interesting to do it as a live call-in. We also had some excellent guests on the show, either live or on long-distance telephone hook-ups.

Producing the show was not very expensive. It cost about $150 per week to rent the studio. The station we broadcast from was in Evanston, Illinois, and it reached only the north and northwest sides of Chicago, but we had a good following and got some positive response.

Among the guests we had on our short-lived program were Mother Teresa of Calcutta, Congressman Henry Hyde, and Attorney John Mackey. We invited any pro-life dignitary visiting the city to be on the program. We had telephone interviews, a news wrap-up, and discussion of current events. Regular hosts, besides the author, were Thomas F. Roeser and Fr. Charles Fiore, O.P. It was an exciting two years.

It doesn't have to cost a fortune to produce a radio show. We solicited contributions on the program and usually received the $150 it cost us each week to stay on the air. Our half-hour program was only $75 a week, not something that was going to bankrupt us.

Almost any established pro-life group could set up a radio program, especially if it is in a community where there are numerous stations. Call the station management to see if there is a half-hour slot available. Even fifteen minutes would be enough time for the pro-life news of the week, some appeals, and a brief guest commentary. But a half-hour is better to work with.

If you get a fairly decent broadcast time, people will start tuning in and you will soon have a following. Nearly any time slot is useful, though, since someone is listening to the radio at any hour of the day or night. Once you begin this project, exciting as it is, it will take a lot of preparation and require a regular commitment each week. But there is satisfaction in knowing that *somewhere* the pro-life message is being broadcast honestly and fairly over our airwaves.

It is more expensive to conduct a regular television show, although, in some areas, the cost might not be prohibitive if you can find a sponsor. Otherwise, you will probably have to sell advertising. A pro-life television program every week would be a boon to the movement, but at this time we don't know of any regular television programming sponsored by a pro-life organization.

We were able, however, to do a ninety-minute television documentary. We found someone who wanted to pay for the production, so we rented a studio for a day, got all of our guests and props lined up beforehand, and ran a very tight schedule. In the course of the day we filmed the entire ninety-minute documentary. We then presented it to a Christian station in Chicago, WCFC-TV, Channel 38, and, after some negotiating and prayers, they gave us a ninety-minute segment of free time on a Saturday night.

We set up a bank of nine telephones which were manned throughout the airing of the show and for several hours afterwards. We had a simulated phone bank in the program picturing nine women answering phones, which was worked into the film three times. The night of the program, these women came to our office to answer calls for pledges. Like clockwork, when the first appeal was made on the program, the phones began to ring at our office. Over $5,000 in pledges came in during that program and we added two hundred new members to our mailing list. The calls were still coming in several hours after the program ended. It was a profitable and useful venture, educating many area residents on the facts about abortion. We called it "Abortion: Exploding the Myths".

The program presented the entire pro-life issue. We showed pictures of fetal development and of abortions. We interviewed two young women who had had abortions. We talked to two ministers and a doctor. Through these volunteers we showed what abortion has done to society—not just to the unborn victims, but to their mothers, the doctors, and all those who come in touch with the abortion industry.

We had to publicize the program in newspapers, and the ads cost us two thousand dollars. The ads were effective, however (see picture at end of this chapter), and we recommend a project like this to all pro-life groups. It will give your group a little prestige if done professionally. Later we turned the film over to a cable outlet for further showings.

Don't hesitate to look into this medium for reaching the public. You may be surprised to find out how feasible it is.

If you cannot have a radio show every week, have one once a month.

If you cannot buy time for a regular television show, do a documentary. You can donate your documentary to a cable TV station and it will air all over the country. Venture into these areas of communication. You may find it to be a profitable and effective way to spread the word and help bring about the collapse of the abortion industry.

PRODUCE A DOCUMENTARY ON ABORTION FOR TELEVISION

"ABORTION: Exploding the Myths" was shown twice in the Chicago area and reached half-a-million viewers through advertisements like this in the metropolitan dailies. This ad was also handed out in leaflet form at churches and in shopping centers.

THE YEAR'S MOST CANDID TV DOCUMENTARY

ABORTION: Exploding the myths...

"If the birth of a child is a miracle, the killing of a child by abortion is a great tragedy..."
— Larry T. O'Neill

"Right to life is accused of calling abortion murder...but the abortion providers now call it that...just listen to them..."—Joseph M. Scheidler

"During the years I have counseled young women, I've met many who would give anything to undo their abortions and have their baby back." — Kathy Carter

"The Bible clearly states that God directs life in the womb...even non-Christians know life in the womb is a miracle." — Dr. Joel Nederhood

"I wonder if America isn't already being punished for its abortion culture...what kind of moral capability do we possess?" — Rev. Harold O. J. Brown

"America, like other countries, is experiencing an epidemic of short- and long-range physical complications from abortion." — Dr. Eugene Diamond

ABORTION...No topic has so divided the nation since slavery... what is the abortion issue really about... who really suffers most from abortion?... Watch this factual, honest documentary and find out... listen to a doctor who knows the damage abortion can cause not only to a woman but to her future children...hear a learned discussion of abortion and the Bible by two prominent Protestant theologians... and listen as two young women who had abortions tell of the deep regret they feel over the loss of their children... "ABORTION: EXPLODING THE MYTHS" is a true story you won't soon forget.

HOST: BILL BERG

SATURDAY, OCT. 6 • 8:30-9:30 PM • WCFC-TV, CH 38

103

24 SET UP A PRO-LIFE FILE

One of the most important tools any pro-lifer can have is a comprehensive file of pro-life subjects. We began setting up our file in 1973, shortly after the Supreme Court ruling, and we have found it invaluable for keeping at our fingertips documents, dates, newsclips, magazine articles, and anything related to abortion. Our file includes a much earlier collection dating from the early 1960s given to us by a friend who saw legal abortion coming, and it is useful for going back and discovering how we got into the abortion culture. Other pro-lifers who keep extensive files also send us copies of their material, and this exchange program helps build a first rate pro-life file. Included in the file should be correspondence, speeches, and essays, as well as news stories.

There are several ways to organize a file, the most convenient of which is by the obvious heading—the person, the event, the organization. After a while, as the file grows, these develop sub-headings. An appropriate sub-heading is the year of the event.

Keeping a card index of the contents of the file saves you from rummaging through the files every time you want an item. You can flip through your card index instead to see where the item can be found or whether you have it in your file at all.

Cross-indexing is a good idea. If you have an article by columnist Nick Thimmesch, you file it with Thimmesch's columns under his name. But if he has written something on Planned Parenthood, a copy of that should be in your Planned Parenthood file. We often photocopy three or four copies of each article and put these in several files for cross reference. It might be filed under the author, the subject, the publication, and perhaps the year of publication. That way we are less likely to overlook it.

You should become familiar with your files and go through them frequently, cleaning them out occasionally so that they don't get cluttered with useless items. You may, for a while, be interested in a particular candidate while he is running for office, but if he loses and drops out of politics, it is useless to keep a large file on him. Go through your files periodically and sort out outdated items. Keep only the bare bones of dead issues.

You will find that the file is invaluable in preparing a story, writing letters to the editor, trying to convince someone of facts, statistics, and dates. The file, in conjunction with your up-to-date library, gives you many of the tools you need to carry on a pro-life educational program.

You should publicize your file. Let other pro-lifers know that you have it. We have received phone calls from the Moral Majority, from the Ad Hoc Committee in Defense of Life, from the American Life Lobby, from people all across the country who needed information on infanticide, fetal experimentation, the complications of abortion. We have put together packets of photocopied material on these subjects and have sent them out by express mail. One time we needed to rush some materials to a pro-life organization for a court case. We sent twelve pounds of copy, and those files turned out to be valuable in winning the case. People across the country know about our files and often contact us, sometimes coming in to spend the day at our office putting together materials they find there. We let them take any duplicates from the file and make copies of the originals. We provide a photocopy machine and do not charge for copies, as we don't want people to skimp on what they take with them. Getting the right information out to the public is one of our most important functions as a pro-life organization, and we are glad to bear the expense. Sometimes after using our file, people leave behind a donation.

Your file should constantly be expanding. Our organization now has eight large file cabinets full of material and is always growing. You will never regret having too much material, especially when you need it.

25 GET ABORTION OUT OF YOUR INSURANCE POLICY

Trying to get abortion coverage out of your insurance policy may sound like a very ambitious undertaking. It may be. Check your policy carefully. Make sure that abortion is in fact paid for by your policy before you start trying to get it out. Many insurance companies are becoming sensitive to the abortion issue and are offering abortion only as an option, or rider, for which a person needs to pay extra.

Strictly speaking, if you have a policy that does not automatically cover abortion under gynecological services, then perhaps you are about as well off as you can be with your policy. If a special arrangement is necessary to get abortion coverage, most people are not going to pay it. Some of those who might want it will not want to admit it, so they will forgo having the operation covered. Consequently, you may consider that situation very close to non-involvement, since the money you pay for your policy is not going to pay for someone else's abortion.

However, if your policy does have abortion in it, perhaps you can join with other policyholders to protest this coverage. You might consider buying shares in the company and attending their shareholder's meeting to try to get abortion out. Another way to get abortion coverage out of your policy is to lobby for state laws that prohibit insurance policies from including abortion. There have been efforts on the federal level to cut abortion out of policies.

There are several other things you can do to try to get abortion out of your policy. Meet with the directors of the company, with other shareholders, or with other policyholders. Make an issue out of the abortion coverage. Let them know that you resent paying for abortion in any way, that this is an elective and lethal surgery that you want no part of.

If you cannot get abortion out of your policy, discontinue it, if you can, and investigate special policies that do not include such coverage. There is now a pro-life insurance company that offers competitive policies that will not pay for abortions, and there are also Catholic insurance companies that do not cover abortion. The coverage is not always as comprehensive as the better known insurance policies, and rates may be a little higher, but the peace of mind and of conscience you will have is worth the added expense. And, as more people switch to pro-life policies, the rates and coverage will become comparable to those of other policies.

These are some companies that will not cover abortion:

PRO-LIFE INSURANCE
AGENCY, INC.
  P.O. Box 1232
  Northbrook, IL 60062

PRO-LIFE ASSURANCE SOCIETY
  1612 S. Prospect Ave.
  Park Ridge, IL 60068

HOLY FAMILY SOCIETY OF U.S.A.
  1 Fairlane Dr.
  Joliet, IL 60435

26 GET YOUR ORGANIZATION KNOWN

There is something sad about pro-life organizations that are never heard from. They may be doing good or even excellent work. But if no one knows about them, they cannot be very effective in spreading their message. No one who needs them can tap their resources or share information and ideas with them or receive training from them. A pro-life organization, if it is doing its job, should be known to other pro-lifers and to the public. Its directors should know how to reach out and become known and make their organization available.

One of the worst things anyone involved in a social issue can do is be "unavailable for comment". If you are a public figure, the press must know your phone number. They have a right to know you by name, to know your address, and your organization's phone number. While it is true that by being available a person exposes himself to some inconvenience, being known and available to the press is very important.

Pro-lifers should have walk-in offices, where people do not need appointments to talk to someone, where they can come off the street into the pro-life office to talk, debate, or just pick up literature and have a cup of coffee. While an arrangement like that can upset your schedule, it also allows those looking for help to walk right in and get it.

Let people know your telephone number. Publish it. You will invariably get a lot of crank calls, even death threats, but at the same time you are going to get some very valuable calls that you might otherwise miss. Let people know your home phone number. When you put out a press release, include on it both your office *and* home numbers so that people can be sure to get hold of you. Many contacts will be made while you are at home, even at two or three o'clock in the morning. You may get calls from the City News Bureau or reporters with a story just off the wire. Be willing to do talk shows and news interviews from your bed at strange hours of the night or on weekends. Being available is extremely important in our line of work.

But it is not enough just to be available. You have to *publicize* your availability and let people know that you are not in hiding. You have to let the press know that you are not afraid of the public. At the same time, you have to let the public know that they won't be imposing on you, because you are in this business to be available, night and day, to everyone.

It can be difficult to remain available if you can do pro-life work only part time because you have a business or job to maintain. You have to be careful about how much business time you can use for pro-life activity. But whatever the circumstances, the dedicated pro-lifer should try to be available whenever other duties do not prevent him.

Try to make your group's name evident in all of your activities. Along with our signs that say "Abortion Is Murder", "Choose Life", "Abortion Kills Babies", we also have a few that proclaim "Pro-Life Action League". We space them throughout our pickets and carry them at demonstrations. We have a ten-foot sign which we place on a platform at our demonstration that says simply, "Pro-Life Action League". That lets people know who we are. We are not afraid to be identified with our activities. We are glad to be known as pro-life activists and are proud to announce that we are leaders in the fight against abortion.

When we tape editorial rebuttals or participate on talk shows, we make certain that the League name is used and that our phone number is given out. Publicize your organization's activities at every opportunity. Brag about the work your organization does.

As you become well known, you will be contacted by the media for information. This is as it should be. Don't be humble and self-effacing. That may be virtuous in private life, but you are a public figure in the most important social and moral issue of our time. It is criminal to hide your talent under a bushel when the unborn children need your leadership shining out from a candlestick. No more false humility. When people think of pro-life, they should think of you and your organization. If not, you are missing out on many opportunities to get the pro-life issue before the public.

27 HOLD A SPEAKERS' WORKSHOP

Pro-life organizations need to train people to carry the pro-life message to the nation. A speakers' training session can be a source of invaluable information and inspiration to pro-lifers. It can either be a small-scale event—nothing but an informal meeting featuring one speaker at an activist's home—or a large-scale workshop in a rented conference room at a hotel with several speakers and film and slide presentations. The point of each is to train people to present the pro-life story.

Whether you are holding a large or small training session, it is essential to publicize the workshop and make arrangements ahead of time to have good speakers and some kind of visual presentation. You must also supply learning materials for people to take home, such as books, pamphlets, slides, fetal models, decals. The workshop should be planned and organized so carefully that by the end of the day, attendants will be able to go out and give a convincing pro-life talk themselves.

Some time during the workshop you should arrange a list of all those in attendance who want to be speakers, noting their special talents and their areas of expertise. You should tell them to be prepared to be called upon and sent out to speak at high schools, college campuses, clubs, church groups, women's groups, fraternal organizations, and any other gathering that invites them in to present the pro-life message.

The speakers' workshop should be set up to begin and end at a precise time, and it is important to start and end promptly. This will help establish for those present the necessity of staying on schedule when they eventually go out to speak. Talks on public speaking should be given by an expert in the field, ideally someone with a great deal of experience in public speaking. He should be a compelling speaker himself, one who makes his listeners want to become equally proficient. He should inspire them to want to go out and give talks.

It is helpful to conduct a series of on-the-spot talks with members of the audience. Get people up before the group and give them a chance to express themselves, to tell about themselves and their jobs, or anything that will help to break down their fear of facing an audience.

Immediately following the "how to" segment of the workshop, the lecture should move quickly into a pro-life education program. It will take two, maybe three hours to present all the basic facts. In explaining fetal development, the methods of abortion, and the dangers to women, the visual and printed materials that the instructor uses should be carefully explained, as these are probably exactly the same materials that the novice speakers will be using.

This program is double-barreled. It deals with how to speak, while at the same time it is a comprehensive education on what to speak about. A detailed outline of the "How to Tell the Pro-Life Story" presentation should be prepared and handed to each person attending so that on leaving all have with them a step-by-step lecture presentation, as well as a complete slide presentation of fetal development and the methods of abortion. All the slides will be explained in this speech outline.

If there is time, special lectures can be arranged to train people in their own specialties. For instance, there could be a lecture on the legal aspects of abortion conducted by a lawyer, a physician's lecture for physicians, and a lecture for nurses. In some pro-life educational organizations it is customary to send out two or three specialists to speak together, instead of a solitary speaker. For instance, a layman might appear on a program with a doctor and a lawyer. The layman could give the general talk while the doctor would handle the medical aspects of abortion and the lawyer the legal aspects. In time, each speaker should be capable of presenting the entire program by himself, including the medical and legal aspects.

Do not underestimate the value of having speakers available to go out into the community to tell the pro-life story. Equally important, though, is making sure you assign speaking engagements to all those who attended the workshop. They need the experience and want to be called on.

They can start out by addressing small, friendly groups. They may start out with younger audiences, such as classes of sixth, seventh, and eighth graders. If they do well and enjoy speaking, they should be moved up as they chalk up more experience. Your speakers want you to make use of them and their talents, or else they wouldn't bother attending your training session. There is nothing more frustrating to an enthusiastic speaker, prepared to go out and talk, than never to get an assignment. One of the most frequent complaints in pro-life circles is from those who took the speakers' workshop, but never gave a speech. People want to use what they have learned.

As requests for speakers come in, new people should at first be sent out with experienced speakers so that they will feel more confident and see how it is done. After a few talks, they may find that they enjoy speaking; they will grow in confidence, and will do a good job of educating the public.

A good pro-life speaker can help the organization by bringing in volunteers and new members. Speakers should always let their audience know about the pro-life organization that is sponsoring them. They should take envelopes, cards, and printed information about the organization with them, so that immediately after the talk they can get people involved on the spot, while they are still enthusiastic. The speaker should take along a tablet to get names and addresses of those interested in joining the pro-life movement. The speaker should make it easy for them to join his organization. Many of them will want to become active if they have been inspired by a good pro-life talk. They will want to become members of a good pro-life organization, and it may as well be yours.

The speakers' workshop can be an effective tool for spreading the pro-life message. The pro-life movement has all the information, pictures, and appeal that any movement could ask for. The pictures alone tend to draw people in. The pro-life story, if presented enthusiastically and with confidence by a well-informed, well-organized speaker, is practically irresistible. The pro-life story is *truth*, and presented honestly it is a faultless formula for conversion.

Imagine how the abortionists, with their appeal to selfish convenience, denial of biological fact, pandering to the lowest animal instincts and specious statistics, defense of illicit sex and human degradation, must envy their pro-life opponents.

It is a great privilege to train pro-life speakers. Here is a typical example of a pro-life speaker's outline:

RIGHT TO LIFE AS A SOCIAL MOVEMENT

Introduction

Relatively few people behind great social movements:
American Revolution
Communism
Will you join this, the most important social movement?

Part I. Nature of past social movements

Underlying philosophy based on a discovered truth

1. Slavery: the Negro a man
   — Theology, Scripture
   — Science, anthropology
2. Pro-life: unborn child a person
   — Religion
   — Science: fetology, biology

Part II. Truth important enough that it must be promulgated

Need for education

Part III. Truth important enough that it must become law

Need for political and legislative action

Part IV. Truth important enough that it must be fought for

Need for *activism*: non-violent direct action
   1. Non-violent
   2. Direct
Lobby, attract press effectively
Fight demands suffering, sacrifice

Part V. Truth important enough that we need to know how truth was lost

Thirty year breakdown of morals:
   1. Secular humanist education
   2. Playboy philosophy
   3. Feminist movement
   4. Weakening of churches
   5. Planned Parenthood, abortionists knew their job and did it!
      — 85—95 percent of people opposed abortion
      — No state had abortion-on-demand
      — Against all scientific evidence
      — PP's own admission that abortion kills
How they did it:
   1. Determined minority
   2. Sold semantics (fetus, problem pregnancy, contraceptive failure)
   3. Concentration switched from child to "victim" (woman)
   4. January 22, 1973: constitutional right to abortion
   5. Pro-abortion media spread lie:
      — Misrepresented *Roe v. Wade*
      — "Legal" is "safe"
      — "Catholic" issue

Part VI. Truth beginning to be recognized:

In every social movement, there is a time when inherent truth of one side and inherent evil and falsehood of the other side is recognized
1. Media is beginning to crack:
   — George F. Will, Joseph Sobran, Pat Buchanan, Nick Thimmesch, Stephen Chapman, William Buckley
   — Several newspapers turning around (*Sun-Times*)
2. Semantics being questioned:
   — ''Choice'' is whether to kill early or late, by salt poison, suction, dismemberment, strangulation
   — The killing is murder
   — No ''necessity'' for 18 million murders
   — Nathanson, California Medical Society ('70), First International Symposium
   — Every major religious body has condemned it as murder
   — Can't be Christian and pro-abortion or vice versa

Part VIII. What we can and are doing *now*

Replace pro-abortion congressmen with pro-lifers
Cut off funds (state, federal)
Pass city ordinances
Educate, picket
Go into clinics, stop killing, close clinics

28 AIDS TO EFFECTIVE LOBBYING

Effective lobbying is critical to the success of any social movement. Lobbying simply means persistent work with the legislature to get it to push the adoption of your bills, ordinances, laws, and amendments. You personally go to your legislature and convince lawmakers not only of the rightness of your cause, but of the necessity for change and the reasonableness of your bill or ordinance, as well as of its constitutionality. In short, you try to convince them of the correctness of what you want. You may not get everything, but you must work for as much of the bill as it is possible to get passed.

Lobbying consists not only of going directly to your legislators, but also writing, telephoning, and meeting them outside the legislative atmosphere. It means working for the election of politicians who support your bills. It means, first and foremost, generating enthusiasm for your bill.

Lobbying takes planning. It is usually effective to take a large group of people to lobby. It looks better to have large numbers and is also practical because you can contact every person in the branch of legislature that you are lobbying. You can contact some legislators more than once. You can talk about your bill with confidence that they will listen, because they see good support for your cause.

When you lobby at the state house or in Washington, D.C., try to schedule your appearance close to the date the bill is going to come up for a vote so that the bill and your lobbying are fresh in the minds of legislators. Before you begin, schedule a meeting with your people to plan a lobbying strategy. Provide a sheet with the names of legislators you intend to talk to, together with their photographs so that you will recognize them on sight. Almost every state house or city council has a booklet that gives the names, the party affiliation, and photos of the legislators. If you have time, prepare a list of the particular legislators each person in your group should contact. If you have a large group of lobbyists, each one may contact a single legislator, though it is best for several people to go together to talk with their own legislators.

As a general rule, lobby everyone in the legislative branch that is about to consider your bill. Even when you know that a certain legislator supports your bill, still go to see him. If he isn't in, leave your name, talk with his aides, and tell them to let the legislator know that you appreciate his support, that you will be glad to help him with other bills he is seeking support for, and that you will work for his reelection. Stay friendly with your pro-life legislators.

Usually it is unprofitable to speak with any legislator who is adamantly opposed to your bill, especially if he has a long history of pro-abortion voting. But it cannot hurt to pay him a visit, especially if he is your own legislator. Stop by and pay your respects. Many pro-lifers have established good relationships with the enemies of pro-life, partly in the hope that a bill will come along that is neutral enough for them to vote for. If you have befriended them, they may want to give you a vote some day. Or they may vote for a pro-life bill simply because they are not being pressured to vote otherwise.

The legislators to concentrate your efforts on most are those who are undecided. Those are the votes you need to go after. When you talk to these legislators, be extremely friendly. As a rule, never show anger or resentment. Never call legislators names. They are generally sensitive to public opinion and can be vindictive if you upset or insult them. They can turn against you forever. Granted, we can all make mistakes and can sometimes say the wrong things, but no purpose is served by threatening a legislator or saying that you are going to work for his defeat. He may make your issue a special project and work for the defeat of a bill you want. Control yourself for the sake of the unborn child.

Our opposition has frequently worked for us unintentionally. Legislators have been alienated and pushed over to our side. Many legislators report that feminist or abortionist lobbying is actually advantageous to pro-life because so many of those lobbyists are vindictive and hateful, thus giving their cause a bad image. This may no longer be as true now as it once was since the left has learned to be more polite, and has acquired some political savvy in recent years, but we still hear negative characterizations of them.

When you enter a legislator's office, approach the secretary and politely ask if the legislator is in. If he is, ask if you can see him for a few minutes. If he is not, leave your name and ask when he will return. When you do go in to see him, introduce yourself and those with you. Tell him where you are from. If you have someone there from his district, be sure and mention this. This is important since that person represents a reelection vote. Have him first talk about the folks back home and the people he is speaking on behalf of, then present your case.

Know the bill number, its provisions, and its purpose thoroughly. If you want to talk about a number of bills, know specifics on each of them. Give the legislator some pertinent literature and briefly summarize each bill for him. Tell him you and your constituents hope you can have his support on this bill, and tell him why it is so important. Then ask him if he will support you. If he gives you nothing but double talk, try to pin him down, and ask him what it will take to convince him. Don't presume that he is evading the issue. It may be that he has a genuine misconception of the bill. Be prepared to supply him with any information he needs, and if you don't have everything with you, tell him that you will send him whatever he needs. Mention the names of other legislators who are supporting your bill, especially ones he may respect. There may be a legislator who is close to him. If you can prove that this legislator supports your bill, it may encourage him to support it.

After you have presented your case and you have a good idea where the legislator stands, politely dismiss yourselves. Tell him that you will be in touch and will be watching the vote on this bill. Politely remind him that he will be graded on his vote.

After leaving his office, record whatever position he seems to have taken, because you want to keep track of the votes you have for your bill. If he seemed nebulous or uncertain, schedule another meeting with him later, and make a note to have his constituents call or write him. Your representative for his district is the one you want to send home to generate mail. Some people think mail is not important, but it is, *extremely* so. Sometimes, when you visit a legislator, he will indicate that he has received a lot of mail about your bill or that he has received little mail or that most of his mail is from the opposition. It is important for you to have drummed up support for your bill back home, prior to your visit, so that by the time you arrive at the legislator's office, he will have a stack of letters in favor of your bill.

Here are some helpful hints on lobbying: If you are going to take a busload of people with you, you can get a lot of work done on the trip. Have a speaker in the front of the bus, and have experts presenting a training course on pro-life issues as you travel toward the Capitol. Give the passengers printed material about the bill. Prepare them for a pep rally when they arrive at the statehouse. Plan to have a central meeting place at the Capitol, and after everyone has finished a couple of hours of lobbying, gather them together for a brunch or luncheon to break up the day.

Lobbying can be tedious. It can be hard work. Perhaps the legislature is in session when you arrive and you cannot visit legislators in their offices. Gather your group at the entrance to the House or the Senate and contact your legislator by messenger or in whatever way is customary in your state. In Illinois, there are guards at the door of each chamber, from whom you get paper to write a note to your legislator. The guard delivers it. If the legislators are not in the middle of a vote, they will come out to look for you. Stay by the door. If a legislator comes out and you are not there, he will return immediately and you may have a hard time getting him to come back out. When he comes out, he will ask for you by name. You should be able to recognize him by sight, so that if you are cordoned off into a restricted area, you can call him by name and direct him to where you are standing. Initiate the conversation. Make it brief. You may ask simply if he is planning to vote for your bill. If he says yes, thank him. If he says he is not familiar with it, be prepared to explain it to him. If he says no, ask him why not and be prepared to answer his objections. Try to get him to say at least that he will give it more thought.

As we pointed out, it is important for people to contact their own legislators, and it is good policy to have with you people from each district. But even if you don't, contact every legislator anyway. It is also important to have people phone their legislator from their hometown. If the vote is going to be close and you need to pressure a legislator, you might call his hometown and get his pastor, business partner, a relative, an old schoolteacher, or his neighbors to call him up and help you get his vote.

It is important, in lobbying, for any friends you may have in the legislature to use their influence. Once, an elder senator was dying of cancer, and many of his fellow senators were willing to do him a favor by voting for a pro-life bill before the Senate. Several were indifferent toward the bill and one even opposed it, but out of deference to his years in the Senate and his condition, they voted for it. As it turned out, we won the vote by exactly the number needed. Whenever you are running a tight contest and need an override vote, use every form of persuasion you can to turn out the vote.

When you have finished lobbying for the day, hold a rally. If it has been a long, hard trip to the Capitol and you need to head right back, choose a place to stop and relax on the way home. As I said, lobbying is hard work; it is not always rewarding. Many people don't like it and some are even afraid of it, so you have a responsibility to make lobbying appealing.

We developed a custom in Springfield that if our bill came up, was voted on, and we won, we all went out to an old-fashioned ice cream parlor near the statehouse and celebrated. Consequently, a kind of esprit de corps developed among our lobbying group. When you have lobbied many times, you get to know the people and the routine and it can become an experience with many pleasant moments. But even if you lose the bill, be sure on the way home to stop and celebrate the day. You have all worked hard, making contacts you can use for future bills, so whether you won or lost, you have actually won.

The American Life Lobby has a vast library on lobbying. Write them:

AMERICAN LIFE LOBBY
  P.O. Box 490
  Stafford, VA 22554
  (703) 659−4171

29 USE BILLBOARDS, AD BENCHES, AND OTHER DEVICES TO GET YOUR MESSAGE ACROSS

In every city there are companies that rent ad space at such places as on billboards, on ad benches, at bus and train stops. There is no reason why you can't try to get pro-life advertising anywhere you see something else advertised.

You can rent billboards from a number of companies. A large billboard in a good location in a big city rents for thousands of dollars, but for much less you can get smaller billboards a little farther back from the main road but still readable from the road. If you have a well-designed billboard ad with contrast, a picture that attracts attention, and strong, simple wording, you will engender interest and give information.

You should keep your message short: only eight or ten words. Remember that if people are driving by or riding the train, they are not going to have time to read a long statement. The message should say who you are and what you do. The ad should be clear, specific, and brief. If possible, include a picture in your ad. You should also display a phone number so people can get in touch with you.

To raise money for ads and billboards, use regular fund-raising techniques, and let people know that you are collecting money for an ad campaign. While some people see something undesirably aggressive in an organization that intends to advertise, usually people are happy to support your ad campaign because they see something forthright in advertising your cause. A pro-life ad campaign is encouraging to many.

Frequently you will find that you cannot rent ad space because the abortion issue is too controversial. Also, there may be strong reaction to advertising the pro-life position. Sometimes the ads will be vandalized. You may get crank calls and hate letters as a result of posting your telephone number.

Sometimes you can get an ad placed for a period of time by buying space on the side of a building. We did this. We rented a building site for a year and painted the ad on it ourselves, thus saving several hundred dollars. When it came time to renew the ad we declined, but since no one else bought the space, the ad remained for another six months at no charge.

Ad benches at bus stops and along thoroughfares are less appealing than billboards because they are not read as widely. They are smaller, and they are also relatively expensive. Generally you have to rent a group of benches to assure that your ad will be widely seen.

There are other advertising devices that get your message across such as bumper stickers, posters that you post yourself, stencils, banners, even balloons. In Chicago, some pro-lifers pasted up 1,200 posters one night, two on every lamp post in the downtown Loop. They posted them high so that they were difficult to tear down. When people went to work the next morning, they saw pro-life posters on every lamp post. Each post had two, facing in opposite directions. The posters pictured the basket-babies and the caption, "Abortion Kills Babies".

Wooden panels with words cut into them, such as "FIGHT", "STOP", "MURDER", "BABIES", "KILLS", "ABORTION" can be arranged into a variety of sentences, such as: "ABORTION IS MURDER", and "ABORTION KILLS BABIES", "STOP ABORTION", "FIGHT ABORTION". These can be placed on temporary construction site fences and other temporary structures, but you must not deface private property. *Do not* stencil on a permanent wall or building. Construction board walls are temporary and are going to come down eventually. Stickers can be removed and don't cause permanent damage. They may be used in many places. Never spray paint a message on a building or scratch glass or cause damage. We must keep in mind that, even if it is an abortion clinic or a building that houses an abortion clinic, it still is private property. Pro-lifers are not vandals. We do not damage property. Billboards, ad benches, posters, stickers, and other forms of advertising are better than stenciling, and should be used whenever possible.

What all these graphic devices are attempting to do is keep the abortion issue before the public and let them know that the issue is not going to go away. They also send a message to the abortion crowd that there is some daring in the pro-life ranks, and encourage other pro-lifers to keep up the fight.

TELLING THE ABORTION STORY WITH BILLBOARDS

One way to get public attention focused on the abortion debate is to rent billboard space on a public highway and place a graphic photograph and your caption for all the world to see. This billboard was placed by Voices for Life and the Pro-Life Action League on a main thoroughfare in Dubuque, Iowa. It engendered letters to the editor, invitations to talk shows, condemnation by pro-abortion groups and requests to buy the display from all across the country (Photo by Richard O'Connor).

30 GIVE A SLIDE PRESENTATION

The most important thing a pro-life activist does is educate. Talking a woman out of an abortion is imparting education. Pickets, demonstrations, rallies, and sit-ins all educate the public to the injustice of abortion. As soon as we learn the facts about abortion, our impulse is to spread this knowledge. When we start out in the pro-life movement, we believe that educating the public will stop abortion and make people believe the way we do. This is a good concept, but it is only partially true. Many people don't want to know the facts. Others remain indifferent to the information given them. But many people will be drawn to pro-life when they learn the facts about abortion. There is great value in informing the public. One of the best ways to do this is to show them pictures of fetal development and abortion.

You should watch a number of slide presentations before you decide which pictures you want to use. Dr. Jack Wilke has an excellent slide presentation, and most pro-life groups either adopt it or develop some variation of it. You can change your presentation to fit different situations. I have one presentation with only twelve slides—six on fetal development and six on abortion—and another with one hundred slides. The larger set includes pictures of pickets and demonstrations and other pro-life projects. Keep in mind that people quickly become tired of still pictures and that you should not leave a slide on the screen for more than fifteen seconds. If you are going to present a long talk with only a few pictures, present the slide program first. Don't leave a picture on the screen while you go on with your talk. This distracts people. Finish your slides quickly and continue with your talk.

Do not be afraid to shock your audience. Abortion *is* shocking. Prepare your audience for it, telling them that some of the pictures they are about to see may be upsetting. But tell them that this is what abortion is all about and that these are the pictures the media won't show. So we have to show them. These pictures frequently motivate people to become active in the pro-life movement.

Reproduce sets of these slides so that if someone in the audience who likes your presentation wants to repeat it, you can give him a slide set plus a step-by-step explanation of each picture. We have reproduced dozens of our sets.

Let people know that you are available to give slide presentations. Call the principals of high schools, directors of youth groups, and pastors. Encourage students to use abortion as a subject for debate. Students can drop into our office to take slides with them to present as a class project.

Groups that meet on a regular basis are always looking for speakers on controversial subjects, so get into the Kiwanis, Lions, or Knights of Columbus. Organizations that are learning the art of public speaking may invite you to speak as an example of a speaker attempting to persuade. Accept these invitations. While they are observing, you will be educating. One talk will generate others as word spreads about your presentation.

Never turn down a speaking invitation, no matter what the group. Once I gave a presentation at a Unitarian Universalist Church. When I arrived, I asked my contact if I would be talking before, during, or after the service. He said, "You are the service." I showed them the slides. The audience was so hostile that I left in a hurry and forgot my projector. I had to return to retrieve it. I was able, though, to convert one or two people, and that made it worthwhile.

Use your slides often. Have them ready to use at a moment's notice. Store them in the carousel, and wherever you go, use your own equipment—projector, screen, extension cord—so that you can avoid confusion when you arrive. Get a lightweight projector that can be carried easily. And, of course, be ready to travel.

There will be times when groups will ask you to speak but tell you not to bring your slides. In cases like that, I usually say, "That will be easy. If you don't want my slides, I won't be there either." Sometimes that is enough for them to agree to let you bring the slides. Sometimes you will not be allowed to use them. If you are debating the abortionists, you will frequently be told that, since the abortionists do not have slides, you shouldn't have any either. You can say that you have *their* slides, and that half of your presentation consists of *your* slides on fetal development, while the other half is *their slides* on death by abortion.

But whenever I am told I can't bring slides, I bring them anyway. If it is a matter of leaving the slides behind or not going, go. Use the fact that you were denied the right to show pictures as part of your talk. Abortion is so horrible, you can explain, so unspeakably ugly that you have been denied the right to show it. Describe in detail the pictures you are prohibited from showing. You can be almost as graphic in your verbal description as if you had shown the slides, so that the result will be the same. You can even do this on TV talk shows: "What I'm talking about, abortion, is such an inhuman activity that the studio will not let me show pictures of the dismembered, burned, pitiful remains of aborted children." Describe the methods of abortion, painting a picture to work on the imaginations and emotions of your listeners.

You can order Dr. Jack Wilke's slides from:

HAYES PUBLISHING CO., INC.
  6304 Hamilton Ave.
  Cincinnati, OH 45224
  You can obtain other slide presentations from the following sources:

ILLINOIS RIGHT TO LIFE   LIFE CYCLE BOOKS
COMMITTEE   15 Oakland Ave.
  53 West Jackson Blvd., Rm. 1264   Harrison, NY 10528
  Chicago, IL 60604
  (312) 922−1918

31 HOW TO RAISE FUNDS

Fund-raising to support your pro-life organization is a challenge. There are as many ways to raise money as there are of spending it. One of the biggest challenges of any pro-life group is to stay out of the red. In the movement today, with so many pro-life organizations clamoring for money, it is a victory to make enough money to pay the rent, the printing, the telephone bill, and a few salaries.

To learn how best to go about fund-raising, contact successful fund-raisers who are interested in your cause and who will discuss their fund-raising techniques with you. Set up a finance committee. Appoint a chairman who wants the challenge of keeping your group financially sound.

One reason for appointing a special finance director is that it leaves others free to do pro-life work. Some pro-lifers spend as much as ninety percent of their time trying to raise money. That leaves ten percent of their time for doing pro-life work.

You can, however, promote your cause at the same time you raise money. Sell pro-life books and materials. A book such as this can be used as a fund-raiser. Every red-blooded pro-lifer wants to know how to shut down the abortion industry. Granted, it takes time to advertise and sell a book, and it requires ordering and mailing, but selling educational materials could make money for your organization.

Direct mail is always effective. Design a flyer that tells about your work in such a way that people will want to support you. Give them the opportunity to do so by including in your mailing a card that they can return with their name, address, phone number, and amount of their donation in an addressed, postage paid envelope. This can be either a one-time donation or a pledge to donate regularly. In either case, add the donor name to your list and continue to send fund-raising letters on a regular basis.

There is a lot of literature on how to implement a direct mail campaign, and at the end of this chapter there are some books on fund-raising that you can read. For a successful direct mail project, rent mailing lists. These are expensive, and though you rarely pay the cost of a mailing using these lists, you will pick up new members, and that is what you are aiming for.

Send out a regular mailing to your members and benefactors. It can be a monthly newsletter or other publication. With every mailing you should include a self-addressed return envelope, so that your members will have a ready means of sending in their contributions. Keep very careful records of all contributions. If your group is a 501(c)(3) tax exempt organization, include in your mailing the fact that contributions are tax deductible. But if you are not such an organization, let people know that too. They may be even more supportive knowing that you are unable to entice contributions on the basis of offering a tax write-off.

A mass mailing will customarily garner one new member for every 100 pieces sent. At twenty-five cents per piece, that means that for every twenty-five dollars you spend, you may get one five dollar donation, a net loss of twenty dollars per hundred pieces, But that new member may, in a year's time, send in several larger donations. So if you send out a mailing that costs a thousand dollars and get less than half of the cost back, still if the piece brings in twenty new members, in time those members should donate far in excess of the initial investment.

Do not be shy about asking for money. Many people feel so strongly about abortion and the horror of killing a child every twenty seconds that they *want* to write a check to an active pro-life group. When I first read about the Supreme Court ruling in 1973, I wanted to find someone who was fighting abortion so that I could write him a check, even if I couldn't afford it. I wanted to write a check for a thousand dollars. That would have been a great sacrifice for me, but when I realized what abortion was, I wanted desperately to support someone who was fighting it.

The Pro-Life Action League frequently gets letters from people saying, "Thank God you are there", "We appreciate all that you are doing", "I want to support your efforts". One of the ways they support us is financially. Because they are caught up in the business of making a living they are not able to get involved in active pro-life work. But they feel they can be part of this effort if they give money to those who are doing the work they wish they could do.

There are many ways to raise funds besides sending letters. We have had yard sales which we advertised extensively. We asked people to go through their attics and bring items to our office, or else give us a call so that we could go pick them up. Some of our yard sales brought in as much as $3,000.

You can also make money from bake sales, the backbone of many small organizations' fund-raising efforts. Ask churches to sponsor a bake sale for you. Other organizations will work for you if they like what you do. A church group may sponsor a car wash or rummage sale or sell roses on Mother's Day and turn over all or a portion of the money to your organization. If you get enough organizations to do this, your gains will be substantial.

If you are frequently invited to speak to clubs and organizations, ask them what they customarily give as a stipend. Many have a set amount. If they don't, you should suggest a stipend to cover at least your travel expenses. Remember that the laborer is worthy of his hire.

Another way of raising funds is by advertising in newspapers and magazines. While we have found that placing ads in local papers is next to useless, some organizations have had good luck with this method. We once ran a $1,200 ad and got only $700 back in contributions, but the ad gave us new membership, a long-term investment. Getting new members may cost initially, but it pays off in the long run.

Hold a raffle. We have found that raffling gold is profitable. We buy one or two twenty dollar gold pieces and sell tickets for only a dollar. People seem to like the idea that for only a dollar they can win a twenty dollar gold piece, which is generally worth between $500 and $1000, depending on the current price of gold and the numismatic value of the coin. Also, people like to win something that they can store away and anticipate an increase in its value.

Of course, not everyone is aware of the value of gold coins, so be sure to advertise the approximate value of the coin(s) being raffled. One of our gold raffles netted almost $7,000. The gold piece was worth $800. Subsequent gold raffles, with little effort, netted us between $2,000 and $4,000.

Before you send raffle chances through the mail, using your fourth-class, non-profit mailing permit, however, check with the post office officials for current postal regulations. You may want to mail them first class, although that is expensive and would cut into your profits.

Another successful fund-raising technique is the use of collection cans. These are cans with a slot in the top and a slogan on the label, such as "Save the Babies, Pro-Life Action League", along with an appealing picture of a baby. Volunteers take these cans out on the streets and ask people to make a small donation. A series of these collections totalling $4,000 paid our office rent for six months. This method is best used in congested areas, during parades, at shopping centers, at sporting events, wherever crowds of people are walking or driving. If you solicit contributions while standing in the street, walking from car to car as motorists wait for the lights to change, notify the police that you will be there. You may need their permission.

You may also leave these cans on counters in restaurants, drug stores, beauty shops, and barber shops, with the owner's permission. If you get flack from the proprietor or if he gets complaints from customers, it is generally better not to fight back. Replace the cans about every two weeks.

Some pro-life groups have been successful making money selling candy, Christmas cards, or Christmas wreaths, especially after they have established a buying market and a reliable clientele.

Most pro-life groups, sooner or later, set up prayer breakfasts, banquets, brunches, and dinners as fund-raisers. The formula is simple: rent a place, buy the meals, and sell them for more than they cost. Invite a well-known guest speaker. Figure out how much people will be willing to pay and what you can afford to spend, remembering that you are going to have to advertise, send invitations, decorate, and pay a speaker. Often, a low-budget organization can survive for a year on a good banquet turnout.

A modern twist to the banquet fund-raiser is to invite people free of charge, and then take up a collection at the end of the banquet. This has worked well for many, but is risky.

Theaters can be good money makers. One Christmas we bought out the entire theater for one night's performance of Charles Dickens' *A Christmas Carol* at the Goodman Theater in Chicago. We owned all the seats in the theater that night and raised the price of the ticket enough to make a profit. It was a risk, and we had to have tickets and posters printed. We also advertised. We feared that we would not be able to sell all the seats. But we ended up making a profit on the play and had a gala evening, with a welcoming talk before the play. It was an enjoyable way of turning a profit.

Other fund-raising ideas include cocktail parties, excursions, cruises, dances. Possibilities are limitless. Decide if the expense of the event and the work it involves will bring in enough money to make it worthwhile. Any fund-raising event takes planning, time, and effort.

Remember that even fund-raising events should be educational and should promote the pro-life cause. A banquet should include a speaker who has done something outstanding for the pro-life cause. Give out awards to your best workers during the affair. We give Activist Awards to the twelve most active pro-lifers of the year. This helps build organizational spirit and creates a clientele of supporters who like what you are doing and want you to keep doing it.

A final word of caution: Never be too optimistic going into any fund-raising venture. Always keep a healthy pessimism about your anticipated profit. That way, you may be pleasantly surprised.

Emergency letters should be used sparingly, and should telegraph a real and present crisis. The Pro-Life Action League had prided itself on never using this measure of desperation, but when two major financial set-backs hit us in late 1984, we had to send out a letter asking for immediate contributions. It was successful and the response sent us a clear message that many of our supporters wanted us to continue our work. Many were willing to make financial sacrifices to assure that we would remain in the fight. We had asked for an immediate $21,000. Within one week we had reached that goal.

Some suggested reading on fund-raising:

Special Resources:

AMERICAN ASSOCIATION
OF FUND-RAISING COUNSEL, INC.
  500 Fifth Ave.
  New York, NY 10017
  (212) 354—5799

FUND-RAISING INSTITUTE
  Box 365
  Ambler, PA 19002
  (215) 628—8729

INSTITUTE FOR FUND-RAISING
  333 Hayes St.
  San Francisco, CA 94102
  (415) 896—1900

Books:

NATIONAL INSTITUTE
FOR CAMPUS MINISTRIES, INC.
  885 Centre St.
  Newton Centre, MA 02159
  Fund-Raising, Leo A. Piguet, Ed.

SAMARITAN ASSOCIATION, INC.
  Elkhart, IN 45614
  Fund Raising for New Agencies, by
  R. J. Ross

32 SIT-INS

The abortion clinic sit-in has been misunderstood and maligned even by some who are deeply concerned about saving the unborn. Still, the fact remains that it is a powerful tool for saving lives. However, it should be understood by those who are contemplating a sit-in that it is an activity that may result in arrests, jail sentences, and fines. Nevertheless, some pro-life activists have weighed the consequences and decided to go ahead and conduct sit-ins.

The decision to conduct a sit-in must not be made lightly, especially if arrests are anticipated. It must be carefully planned and choreographed.

The sit-in has three major objectives. First, it is undertaken to save lives. During the sit-in, abortions are generally not performed. While the sit-in is in progress, protestors may come in contact with clients and clinic personnel. Counselors taking part in the sit-in have a better opportunity to talk with clients than they have outside the clinic where lack of time and the presence of hired guards or clinic escorts, also known as "goon squads", often prevent fruitful conversation.

The second objective is to give public testimony to the seriousness of abortion. Even those who may react negatively to the sit-in, will recognize the "witness" given by the protestors. Many who have taken part in sit-ins have learned that they receive a kind of grudging respect even from those who are pro-abortion. This witness will often be presented by the media. A sit-in is usually more of a media event than picketing or a demonstration because there is something convincing about people who are willing to be arrested, handcuffed, and taken away in a paddy wagon, that is dramatic enough to demand public attention even by the traditionally cynical press.

I recall the first major sit-in that we held in Chicago at Concord Medical Center on Grand Avenue. Twelve people had been arrested and were being taken from the clinic in handcuffs. Every time a pair, handcuffed together, came out of the clinic and were led to the paddy wagon, a cheer went up from the picketers gathered outside. Meanwhile, I was being interviewed by a reporter from one of the television stations.

This reporter had interviewed me before, and she had always been condescending. But on the day of the sit-in, the reporter was extremely serious and respectful. I noticed as she took notes that her hand was trembling. It was obvious that even this reporter, who was by no means pro-life, felt respect, and even fear, when she saw this well-organized, carefully orchestrated sit-in at an abortion clinic. During the news that evening I saw for the first time in my experience, an objective report of a pro-life activity. The media treats pro-lifers deferentially when they see their strength and purpose. A sit-in manifests this.

The third purpose of the sit-in is present only if arrests are anticipated. Not every sit-in has to result in arrests. Much of the good inherent in a sit-in may be accomplished prior to when the police give warning that arrests will be made. Counseling, educating the public, and capturing the attention of the press can be accomplished without arrests. But a full-scale sit-in absolutely demands arrests, because of this third purpose: the introduction of the "Defense of Necessity", a defense which can be invoked when those arrested are eventually brought to trial, usually on charges of disorderly conduct or trespassing.

The Defense of Necessity, an element of common law, defends an illegal action on the grounds that it must by necessity be taken in order to prevent a greater evil from taking place. By that, it requires the court to set aside the lesser law. For instance, anyone may enter a private building to save life or property. A fireman may break into a locked home to put out a fire or police may enter a home to apprehend a burglar without being arrested for trespassing. It is not even necessary, in invoking the Defense of Necessity, for the individual actually to have saved life or property. All he needs to prove is that he had sufficient reason to believe that he was protecting life or property from grave harm.

This defense has been used with success in several instances involving political protests. In general, however, it has not been effective in pointing out the nature of abortion as the unjust taking of a human life. Many judges are under political pressure not to grant this plea or else they have a false notion of what the Supreme Court has said about abortion. Nevertheless, efforts to use the Defense of Necessity must continue.

It is important that defendants appear at the trial following their sit-in arrests in order that they may present evidence that they entered the clinic or barred the doors to save human lives. The trial could produce testimony by experts and present educational materials that have been mostly suppressed but may be picked up by the media and presented to the public.

Planning the sit-in is like planning a military operation. Those who take part in the sit-in must be carefully chosen: no hotheads, no one who is not able to grasp all of its implications. The consequences of arrest in the particular locale must be discussed: fine and possible imprisonment, the amount of bond money necessary to have on hand, which lawyers will be called in after the arrests.

The clinic to be targeted must also be carefully selected. Does it have easy access? Does it have security guards? What is its floor plan? Someone must case the layout beforehand. Its schedule must be known, as well as the number of personnel working there, and the time of abortions. Considerable, careful planning is required: rehearsals of the sit-in; signals that will be given; preparation of the coverts or "truth teams" to be inside the clinic before the sit-in begins; pickets organized outside during the sit-in; counselors to talk to the clients; a press team to contact the media; a spokesman for the sit-in team inside and a media spokesman outside; legal contacts at police headquarters; and the meeting place for the picketers.

The Defense of Necessity may someday set the stage for a court ruling that will begin the erosion of the abortion decision. It would require the court to investigate the evidence for the humanity of the unborn child, something the U.S. Supreme Court failed to do.

SIT-IN CHECKLIST
Advance Preparation:

1. Write and print press release and handouts.
2. Get phone numbers and addresses of all local media—TV, radio, newspapers.
3. Discuss all legal matters with counsel.
4. Assemble all literature to be left at clinic, used by counselors, or read aloud during sit-in.
5. Acquire camera, correct film, tape recorder, and bullhorn—also American flag and crucifix.
6. Print words to songs and chants to be used.
7. Scout clinic. Send in spy to see how they operate and what information they give, note floor plan, location of operating rooms, and waiting room.
8. Note best parking areas, best place to assemble prior to sit-in.
9. Invite all pro-life activists to planning meeting.

Planning and Training Meeting:

1. Emphasize purpose of sit-in: to save lives.
2. Answer all questions honestly.
3. Assign all leaders, spokesman for press, counselors, photographer, media callers, contacts at jail.
4. Announce exact location, address, room number.
5. Practice songs, chants.
6. Decide who will be arrested, who will leave.
7. Announce where all will assemble before entering.
8. Select couple who will pose as clients immediately before the sit-in to make certain clinic is open. They should ask for a pregnancy test.
9. Explain layout of clinic to all.
10. Discuss all contingency plans.
11. Collect or arrange for bond money.

Before Leaving for Sit-In:

1. Make sure you have everything. Women with children must have diapers and bottles.
2. Dress comfortably.
3. Carry as little as possible, but have identification.

When Sit-In Begins:

1. Park and assemble where instructed. Those who picket outside should assemble elsewhere if number of group might tip off clinic.
2. All sitters should enter waiting room and sit down. Remain calm if clinic staff gets abusive.
3. Begin counseling immediately if any clients are present.
4. Distribute literature and add inserts in magazines.
5. At signal from leader, begin singing songs or reading pro-life material aloud. No shouting.
6. Those designated should try to convince clinic staff members of the evil they are cooperating in.
7. If agreed on, and if the operating rooms are empty, block operating room doors by sitting down in front of them.

135 SIT-INS

When Police Arrive:

1. They will read you your rights and ask you to leave.
2. Try to stall them by explaining why you are there. Show them pictures of aborted babies and tell them they will be responsible for killing more if they make you leave.
3. Do not argue with or antagonize the police. They can be converted too. They may give you more than one warning.
4. Those to be arrested should remain seated so police must carry them out (optional).
5. Liaison person should keep those outside informed of what is happening inside, and vice versa. You want the press to arrive before the arrests are over.
6. Take pictures of arrests, but not of clients.

When Press Arrives:

1. Contact outside should direct press to clinic room and floor, so that no time is wasted.
2. Do not encourage TV cameras inside.
3. See that reporters receive press releases.

Outside Clinic:

1. Press callers should alert the press as soon as clinic is entered.
2. Distribute press releases or leaflets to all neighboring stores and offices.
3. Only those designated to do so should talk to the press.
4. Do not argue or debate with those who object. Keep the picket orderly.
5. Pickets should remain long after the arrest, in case other media come late.

After Arrests:

1. Photograph and tape record all activity by police, pickets, clinic staff.
2. Post bond at police station. Insist on rights of those arrested to prompt hearing for release.
3. Try to get a judge to ask for release of the whole group on their own recognizance, thus saving the posting of bond.
4. Have the picketers meet with the whole group arrested and have them relate their experiences as soon as possible.

Many pro-lifers believe that the sit-in will become an even more useful tool in the future for closing abortion clinics and have written extensively on its use and method. For copies of some of this literature, write to:

PRO-LIFE NONVIOLENT ACTION
PROJECT
  P.O. Box 2193
  Gaithersburg, MD 20879
"Shared Responsibility",
"No Cheap Solution",
"Human and Vulnerable",
by John Cavanaugh-O'Keefe

P.E.A.C.E. OF MINNESOTA, INC.
  1154 Ashland Ave.
  St. Paul, MN 55104
"Sit-Ins: Saving Babies from Death",
(May/June 1984 Newsletter)

  P.O. Box 6325
  Silver Spring, MD 20906
"Why Abortion Sit-Ins?",
by David Gaetano and Jeanne Miller

PRO-LIFE ACTION LEAGUE
  6160 N. Cicero Ave.
  Chicago, IL 60646
"A Case for the Sit-in" (*National Catholic Register*, March 1979),
by Bishop Leo A. Pursley

FELLOWSHIP OF
RECONCILIATION
  Box 271
  Nyack, NY 10960
"Non-Violent Direct Action"

For an example of how the Defense of Necessity can be argued in court, send to Americans United for Life Legal Defense Fund, Suite 1804, 343 S. Dearborn St., Chicago, IL 60604. Ask for *People v. Krizka*, No. 79—365 (Ill. App. 1980), *Leave to Appeal Denied*, No. 54663 (Ill. 1981). The case was written by Carmen V. Speranza. Esq.

Defense of Necessity Cases That Have Resulted in Acquittals:

COMMONWEALTH V. BERRIGAN
  472 Atlantic 2nd #1099
  Superior Court, PA 1984

COUNTY OF FAIRFAX V. BALCH
  General District Court of Fairfax County
  February 11, 1978
  Judge J. Mason Grove

STATE V. BLASCH
  #78 CRD 3701
  Ohio Municipal Court
  Hamilton County
  May 1, 1978

ST. LOUIS COUNTY V. KLOCKER
  Circuit Court County of St. Louis
  Division 13
  #419096
  June 15, 1979

CITY OF CLEVELAND V. O'MALLEY
  #76—CRB 22781
  Municipal Court
  December 15, 1976

COMMONWEALTH V. CAPITOLO
  471 Atlantic 2nd #462
  Superior Court, PA 1984

33 GET A WOMAN PROFESSIONAL PREGNANCY HELP

The pro-life movement has four thousand organizations throughout the country dedicated to helping pregnant women carry their pregnancies to term. Pro-life is sometimes accused of simply trying to stop abortions without concerning itself with the future of the mother and child. That is not true.

Ever since the legalization of abortion there have been pro-life organizations dedicated to helping women through their pregnancies. Birthright and similar pregnancy counseling services are made up of pro-lifers who specialize in providing pre- and postnatal care.

When our sidewalk counselors talk a woman out of an abortion, the woman will frequently need help adjusting her life to her new decision. She is probably unmarried, with no adequate income to cover her additional expenses. Perhaps she has been thrown out of her home or has been rejected by her boyfriend. When a woman becomes pregnant, many problems may arise and pro-lifers try to help her solve these problems. Sometimes she simply needs someone to talk to who will help her put things in perspective.

Not all pro-life activists are qualified or prepared or in a situation to help a pregnant woman. So we call on professional agencies that specialize in helping such women. Pregnancy help organizations can be found in every large city in the country. We must be certain that the organization to which we refer women is in tune with the pro-life philosophy. Some secular pregnancy help organizations, for instance, will, on occasion, counsel abortion or abortifacients. We must make certain that the organizations to which we send women believe in preserving the life of the unborn. Reliable organizations such as Birthright will help a woman through her pregnancy, get her medical care, find her a place to stay, find an adoption agency if need be, and see to most of her other needs. This includes giving her maternity and baby clothes.

There are other organizations such as Preservation of Human Dignity, Lifeline, Aid for Women, Alternatives to Abortion, and the Pearson Foundation which assist pregnant women. Whatever organization you send the woman to, several conditions are necessary. Be certain that this organization will help her and will not give her bad advice. To be useful to her it must be attuned to her disposition and needs. The people there must keep in touch with her throughout her pregnancy to make sure her needs are met. To stop a woman from an abortion but to offer her no help is cruel. It is irresponsible to tell her that her decision was wrong, but then offer no assistance in carrying out a better alternative. We must help change what seems like a hopeless situation into one that is optimistic and full of life.

Usually when a woman decides against an abortion, the gloom, depression, fear, and anguish disappear. Once she is oriented to giving life she becomes enthusiastic. We find that the women who go ahead and have their babies are grateful that they were talked out of an abortion. We find the exact opposite, however, among women who go ahead and have the abortion. We have met hundreds of women who feel remorse over their abortions, and they ask us why we were not at the clinic door to stop them.

Actually, no woman is enthusiastic about having an abortion. Most women who have the baby instead do not regret it. Whether they keep their baby or give it up for adoption, they have the satisfaction of knowing that they gave life. That attitude is certainly far superior to the attitude of a woman who realizes she has killed the innocent human life within her, that her body is a haunted house where the tragic death of a child took place—a child whose memory may haunt her forever.

Pregnancy Help Agencies:

AID FOR WOMEN
  8 S. Michigan Ave.
  Chicago, IL 60603
  (312) 621−1100

ALTERNATIVES INTERNATIONAL
  (800) 344−7211 (toll free)

BIRTHRIGHT OF CHICAGO
  11235 S. Western Ave.
  Chicago, IL 60643
  (312) 233−0305

CATHOLIC CHARITIES
  645 N. Randolph St.
  Chicago, IL 60606
  (312) 454−1717 (Maternity Dept.)

PREGNANCY PROBLEM CENTER
  5097 N. Elston
  Chicago, IL 60630
  (312) 454−1400

PROJECT SAVE OUR BABIES
  P.O. Box 2521
  Appleton, WI 54913
  (414) 713−3366

PRO-LIFE ACTION LEAGUE
  6160 N. Cicero Ave.
  Chicago, IL 60646
  (312) 77−2900

WOMEN EXPLOITED (WE)
  2100 W. Ainsley
  Chicago, IL 60640

In your own area, check the Yellow Pages of the local phone directory under "Birthright", "Salvation Army", "Catholic Charities", "Pregnancy Problem Center" or "Crisis Pregnancy Center", and similar listings.

34 OPEN YOUR HOME TO A PREGNANT WOMAN

Many pro-lifers have offered shelter to a young woman who decides not to go through with her abortion. We know one family that has had more than twenty girls live with them since the *Roe v. Wade* abortion decision. Sometimes they have had two or three at a time.

In order to provide shelter for a woman, you need adequate space for her, a room where she can be alone and have privacy. If your home is already too crowded or if conditions are too hectic, perhaps it would be unwise to bring a pregnant woman into your home. If you want her simply for a companion or to do the work or the babysitting, you are probably not being altruistic, but merely seeking free help. You have to be prepared to give her time to herself, time to think through her problems and work through her pregnancy.

Before placing a pregnant woman in a private home, the agency placing her usually checks into the type of home she is going into. Generally, if you have an orderly place for her and are understanding, it won't matter if you have children and a little confusion. The presence of children might even be good for her.

When a pregnant woman stayed in our home several years ago, we had only two little boys, but it was a good experience for her to have children around to keep her occupied and entertained. She had a private room, and from time to time her parents came to visit her from out of town. She helped around the house, but was not overburdened. She often asked to help. She was a delightful person to have around, and we had some wonderful visits together.

My wife, Ann, took her to her doctor's appointments, and as the birth drew near, we became as excited as if our own daughter was having a child. She got to see her baby, a healthy girl, but had decided from the beginning to put the baby up for adoption. There were some difficult times and some sad moments, but she was, overall, optimistic, positive, and outgoing. Even after she left, we heard from her from time to time. For a while she sent Christmas presents to our children. As our family grew, she got to know the other children through correspondence, and every year she would send a Christmas present to the new child. She is now married, has a family, and is very happy.

Her story was a positive experience for all of us. She was better off being away from her own family and friends, and she was able to return home a happier person after she gave birth. Only two or three people in her hometown ever knew that she had been pregnant.

There was one crisis. The father of the baby said he would marry her, but she assumed it was only to give the baby a name. Then, before the child was born, the young man was killed. His own parents, after the loss of their son, wanted to adopt the baby and give it their name. They were wealthy and offered to take care of both the baby and its mother. The young woman had difficulty deciding what was best for her and the baby. Finally she decided to turn the baby over to an adoption agency. It took a great deal of courage to make that decision. It was an ennobling experience, and she became a strong person in making the decision.

We never thought of her as someone who had sinned and deserved punishment. She had made a wrong decision, but out of it came a beautiful child and a stronger woman. If you open your home to a pregnant woman, you may have a wonderful experience or you may very well have a difficult time. But if your intention is to help her, you will.

35 GLOSSARY OF PRO-LIFE SONGS, CHANTS, AND SLOGANS

Sometimes it is helpful, before a rally or march, to print up a sheet of songs, slogans, and chants. These sheets can be distributed and used to help keep the rally or march from becoming drab and uninteresting. They may prevent participants from being distracted and disorganized.

Some of these chants are very simple, such as "Life Yes, Abortion No!" A variation of this is made by alternating the name of the target of the picket with the word "Abortion". For instance, if we are picketing pro-abortion Senator Ted Kennedy, we will chant "Life Yes, Abortion No! Life Yes, Kennedy No!" Another simple chant is the college yell, such as "Give me an 'L' ", with the crowd responding loudly, "L!". Then the leader continues, "Give me an 'I' " and so on to spell "LIFE". "What do we want?" "LIFE!" "What do we want for the baby?" "LIFE!" "Louder!" "LIFE!" This is effective and exhilarating, especially during a march with a large group. You can get an effective cadence, and walking between tall buildings will give a canyon effect that is startling!

"All we are saying is give life a chance!" is a chant based on the John Lennon song "All We Are Saying Is Give Peace a Chance". It is a simple, rhythmic melody, rather low-key, a pleading, plaintive kind of song that will calm a crowd and even touch the hearts of passersby.

It is important to have a chant or song leader, using a bullhorn or battery-operated megaphone, announcing and leading all chants and songs.

"Stop the killing now!" said in a loud determined monotone, gives the feeling of immediacy. Strong words like "killing" and "now" are direct and forceful. People like to use them. An alternate is "Save the babies now", a more positive, low-key statement. When a young couple is going into a clinic it is particularly effective to have a large group chanting "Save the babies now", or even, "Don't kill your baby; don't kill your baby."

The advantages of all of these chants, especially when the group is in the vicinity of an abortion clinic, is that they will penetrate into the clinic whenever the door opens. In most instances, they can be heard clearly inside. Once, while watching television coverage of one of our demonstrations, when the reporter was interviewing those inside the clinic, everything we were chanting outside could be heard clearly in the background, even though our group was quite a distance from the clinic. This is the advantage of the unified chant. If everyone is yelling something different, there is little chance that anyone's message will get through. But if everyone is chanting the same words in unison with a good cadence, the message will penetrate into the clinic and keep clinic employees busy trying to distract their clients. It will keep the women and men in the clinic aware of the fact that somebody outside cares about them and their baby.

You may wonder what good all this does. It does in fact do a great deal of good. The human voice is a very powerful instrument. The magnified word is a strong weapon. The things we say have specific meanings to us, but touch people in many different ways. Women inside the clinic may be having thoughts of turning back from their decision and the words in our chants may be just the thing that reaches them.

It is important to remember that some people are impressed by care and concern shown to them. We have known people who have left the abortion clinic because of the concern we have shown for them and their baby. One young couple told us that *our* concern made them see their unborn child in a completely new light. We cared more for the child than they did, and that impressed them. These chants and songs can help communicate that concern.

There are many songs almost everyone knows, and it is not difficult to get the group singing if you have a bullhorn to lead the melody. You can announce the words as the song is being sung. "The Battle Hymn of the Republic" ("Mine Eyes Have Seen the Glory of the Coming of the Lord") is one such song that is both strong and effective. Also, people equate this song with the victory of righteousness over evil. There are a number of other inspiring songs like that, such as Pat Boone's popular ballad, "Let Me Live".

If you have a religious group, you can sing traditional religious songs that most know and enjoy. Some groups make up their own. The words of a song that was popular in the Sixties, "Where have all the flowers gone?" can be changed to "Where have all the children gone? Killed in chambers every one. When will they ever learn?" It is good to have a number of these ready because you don't want your people to have to keep repeating one or two chants. They will get tired of singing the same thing over and over. Don't let the chants or songs get so complicated that people will garble them because they can't remember the words. Keep them simple.

For variety and interest it is recommended that you have the women call out one section of a chant and the men respond with the alternate section. For instance, the women would say "Life, Yes", and the men would respond "Abortion, No". Verses of the songs can also be done in this way. Sometimes you might want to have the children alternating with the adults. But be sure you have a leader with a clear, strong voice.

You cannot keep people chanting the whole time. You have to give them a chance to talk and develop a camaraderie while picketing. As a rule, discourage people from getting too loud or having too much fun on the picket line. You want the picket to remain orderly and serious. But talking and visiting are natural and good, and they make the picketing more enjoyable.

The importance of songs, chants, and slogans cannot be overestimated. They are the voice of the movement. That is why you should always have at least one bullhorn on hand at any function, so that the people at the far ends of the demonstration or picket can keep singing or chanting with the whole group. A loud voice is a sign of authority and with a megaphone your voice will be heard above the crowd. There is better unity in the group when you have this amplified voice. The abortionists respond to it too.

Learn how to use an amplifier and keep it in good condition. Keep it the proper distance from your mouth to get the best tone and volume. Some bullhorns, such as the one from Radio Shack, must be in contact with the mouth to get full volume.

Some picket directors don't like to use a voice amplifier because they think it overpowers the group and they will stop chanting when the leader stops. They have a point, and if you are more comfortable without a bullhorn, don't feel required to use one. Where the bullhorn is outlawed, it is best to comply, provided you have checked out the local ordinance. You should always do what works best for your group.

But with or without a bullhorn, keep chanting.

Here are the words to Pat Boone's popular pro-life song:

> Let me live.
>   Let me walk into the sunshine
> Let me live.
>   Feel my mother's arms around me
>   Feel my father's love surround me
>   Be a part of God's creation
> Let me live.

TO BE ALIVE

Chorus:

To be alive and feeling free
and to have everyone in our family,
to be alive in every way:
Oh, how great it is to be alive.

1. Everyday there's a newness,
   something else to do.
   The dawn of life is upon us
   so let the gladness ring through.

2. Wake up to a new sunshine,
   darkness no longer stings
   for the new generation
   will light the world today.

3. Tell the whole population
   the time has now arrived.
   We must learn the sensation
   that comes with being alive.

4. Ring the bell of new freedom;
   teach your brother to live,
   for the real joy of living
   is something we can now give.

BATTLE HYMN OF THE REPUBLIC

1. Mine eyes have seen the glory of the coming of the Lord:
   He is trampling out the vintage where the grapes of wrath are
     stored;
   He hath loosed the fateful lightning of His terrible swift sword;
   His truth is marching on!

   Chorus:
   Glory, Glory, Hallelujah,
   Glory, Glory, Hallelujah,
   Glory, Glory, Hallelujah,
   His truth is marching on.

2. I have seen Him in the watchfires of a hundred circling camps.
   They have builded Him an altar in the evening dews and damps.
   I have read His righteous sentence by the dim of flaring lamps.
   His Truth is marching on!

LITTLE ONES (Phil Keaggy)

Chorus:
Who will speak up for the little ones?
Helpless and half abandoned,
They've got a right to choose
Life they don't want to lose.
I've got to speak up, won't you.

1. Equal rights, equal time,
   For the unborn children.
   Their precious lives are on the line.
   How can we be rid of them.
   Passing laws, passing out
   Bills and new amendments.
   Pay the cost and turn about
   And face the young defendants.

2. Many come and many go,
   Conceived but not delivered.
   The toll is astronomical.
   Oh, how can we be indifferent?
   Little hands, little feet,
   Tears for Him who made you.
   Should all on Earth forsake you now,
   Yet He'll never forsake you.

3. Forming hearts, forming minds
   Quenched before awakened
   For so many deliberate crimes
   The Earth will soon be shaken
   Little hands, little feet,
   Tears for Him who made you
   Should all on Earth forsake you now,
   Yet He'll never forsake you.

JESUS LOVES THE LITTLE CHILDREN

Jesus loves the little children,
All the children of the world.
Red and yellow, black and white,
They are precious in His sight.
Jesus loves the little children of the world.

36 KEEP UP TO DATE

A pro-life activist must keep up to date on the entire movement. He must know the names of people, the bills up for vote, and the activities going on in other parts of the country and even in other parts of the world. The pro-life activist should know the names of the enemy: the names of federal judges, editors of the larger newspapers and magazines, columnists—pro and con, those politicians with us and those against us. He can never know too much.

We have to be reading all the time, and constantly updating the knowledge we have. We need to know far more than the basic facts of fetal development and the methods of abortion. We need to know everything going on in the pro-life movement, and to do this, we must read, listen, watch, and investigate all the time.

One pro-lifer who gives talks about the media and how to work with them, buys ten or fifteen newspapers every day, from all over the country. He carefully reads through all of these. On the weekends, he scrutinizes a dozen national news magazines and publications from the opposition.

It is important to know what the enemy is writing. It is important to read your own daily newspapers and subscribe to one or two big city dailies such as the *New York Times* and the *Washington Post*. Nearly all the big city dailies and national news magazines are pro-abortion. Read the *Wall Street Journal* too. Their editorial content is not restricted to business issues but frequently has editorials and features on pro-life. You should subscribe also to the three top news magazines, *Newsweek*, *Time*, and *U.S. News & World Report*.

Watch television and listen to the radio, especially the national and local newscasts and special programs such as talk shows, documentaries, interviews, and news specials. Try to get previews of upcoming programs from the television and radio public information offices. Skim through TV listings every week to keep abreast of upcoming shows that may be pertinent to the pro-life cause. Alert other pro-lifers to programs they should watch.

Stay in touch with other pro-life newslines and the opposition's hotlines such as *Women USA*. Keep at least half a dozen activists on

147

surveillance duty. These should be people who have the time to read the newspapers, listen to the radio, and watch TV and who can discern what is important.

Contract a clipping service. These services are expensive but worthwhile. Tell them to send you everything in the news about your organization, about abortion, euthanasia, and infanticide—the issues we are involved in. You can never be too well informed.

You could also start a telephone news hotline. When we first became active in pro-life we wanted to know in a hurry what was going on relative to abortion, but we had to wade through newspapers and circulars and even then didn't get all the news. On a trip to San Diego in 1974 we called a pro-life group and asked if we could receive their newsletter. They said they didn't publish a newsletter but contacted their members through a recorded telephone message.

That idea sounded so good that when we returned to Chicago we set up a news hotline that presented a recorded message containing all the latest pro-life happenings, upcoming talk shows, meetings, and news from around the country. It caught on, and our original newsline is still in operation.

The procedure is simple. You purchase one or two (or more, if you anticipate a lot of calls), recording machines with microphones, get a telephone line with a search system so that when one line is busy the caller will get the message on the second or third line. Since you will be receiving only incoming calls, your monthly charge is minimal and your initial expense is your major cost. The advantages of a call-in newsline cannot be overestimated. We use it to muster the troops for rallies, pickets, and meetings, to alert them to upcoming media events, to encourage letters to the editors and letters or calls to friends and foes of the pro-life movement, and to comment on blatant anti-life editorials, columns, cartoons and news stories. As of May 1985 our hotline recorded 3,000 separate messages and received nearly a million calls in its eleven years of operation.

Action newslines have caught on across the country. Some of the better ones are Art O'Brien's in Garden City, New York, and Marjorie Montgomery's in Louisville, Kentucky. Richard Freeman recently inaugurated one in Forest Park, Illinois, and Jack Ames has one in Baltimore, Maryland, Jim Condit is planning one for Cincinnati, Ohio. Why don't you try it?

Become familiar with the history of the press and its attitude toward abortion. Check back issues of news magazines and periodicals in the

public library, and discover how the secular press helped to encourage
the legalization of abortion.

I wouldn't advise anyone to subscribe to *Playboy*, *Penthouse*, *Hustler*,
or other such magazines that are full of pornography, but a pro-life
activist should be aware of the vicious contempt these magazines have
toward the unborn, the pro-life movement, religion, and the family, and
recognize their rabid defense of abortion as a woman's "right".

Study the material in Planned Parenthood's publications. Read the
Religious Coalition for Abortion Rights' *Options*, Catholics for a Free
Choice's *Conscience*, and other pro-abortion publications to see just
what kind of perverted thinking they employ. They are unpleasant to
read, with their attacks on reason, morality, Scripture, tradition, and
orthodoxy. They are depressing. But all of this study is necessary. A
pro-life activist cannot be caught off-guard by not knowing what the
enemy is doing. Pro-life confidence grows in the face of arguments by
the opposition. We see how shallow and full of fallacies they are, in
contrast with our reasonable arguments. It takes a great deal of work to
stay abreast of the movement. You should also know the latest news on
our issue from the Department of Health and Human Services and the
Center for Disease Control.

When you appear on a radio or TV talk show, know and discuss the
latest news item on abortion. Often, when you go on a talk show with a
fresh news story, you throw the opposition for a loss. They usually
know only the old material.

Know the tricks the abortionists use. Study their ploys and their
methods of argumentation. Know your own facts and statistics. Quote
recent polls and surveys. Have information at your fingertips so that it
trips off your tongue easily and with confidence. In this way, you will
prove to friend and enemy alike that you know the issue thoroughly.

After a while, the opposition will become cautious of going on
programs with you, and that will be to your advantage. When you arrive
for a talk show on which you are scheduled to debate the opposition and
they do not show up, this may irritate the host so much that he will call
them cowards and suggest that you are too strong for them. Consequently, you will have the entire program to yourself.

Keep up to date! This is a movement, and since a movement keeps
moving, the pro-life activist must move with it!

For a list of sources for pro-abortion publications, see Chapter 13.

Pro-Life Hotlines:

PRO-LIFE ACTION LEAGUE
Joseph Scheidler
(312) 777—2525

VOICE FOR LIFE
Art O'Brien
(516) 746—0198

ILLINOIS RIGHT TO LIFE
Gertrude Naumes
(312) 922—1920

KENTUCKY RIGHT TO LIFE
Marjorie Montgomery
(502) 897—LIFE (5433)

ILLINOIS PRO-LIFE COALITION
Ann Belanger
(312) 545—1200

BALTIMORE PRO-LIFE NEWS
Jack Ames
(301) 661—BORN (2676)

PRO-LIFE BROTHERHOOD
Richard Freeman
(312) 747—4725

37 PICKET THE ABORTIONISTS' HOMES

Whenever we propose picketing the homes of the doctors who perform abortions or those who work at the abortion clinics, some pro-lifers always get upset. They say that we are getting too personal or being too mean. After all, a man's home is his castle, they say, and you shouldn't disturb him at home.

While we understand their concern, we don't agree with their reasoning. We go to the homes of abortionists and to places they work other than the clinics precisely because they don't like it. They usually are not proud of being abortionists, and often they even guard the fact that they are involved in abortion from their community.

If it *were* widely known that they are abortionists, they might be very uncomfortable in their communities, and their communities might be uncomfortable with them. There is even the possibility that they may be forced to stop doing abortions. In some smaller communities, this has happened. Workers at abortion clinics are especially vulnerable. If it is going to be too much of an embarrassment to them to continue working at the abortion clinic, they may look for employment elsewhere. A person's reputation is always important to him. Since many people do not feel comfortable about their abortion involvement, it is important that we take advantage of this uneasiness and make their involvement public. This is done not because we hate them, but because we hate what they are doing, and we want them to stop.

The best way to call public attention to a doctor's abortion involvement is to picket his home. Find out where he lives, and pick a time when his neighbors will be home. A Sunday afternoon is generally a good time. Hold a public picket in front of his home. Carry signs that mention the name of the abortionist in conjunction with the word abortion. Leaflet the entire neighborhood around his home just prior to the picket.

In some communities it is illegal to picket private homes, even though the sidewalk is public property. If this is the case in your community, you have to be prepared. One effective strategem is to put a point on the bottom of the stick that holds your picket sign. When the police arrive, stick the picket sign in the lawn or hang it in a tree or in a bush—somewhere on the property of the abortionist. Then walk away. When you are no longer carrying a picket sign, you are a pedestrian out for a walk. Go to your cars and drive away. You accomplished your mission.

It is best to park your cars in different areas of the neighborhood so that the crowd can disperse as they head to their cars. When the police arrive, neighbors will come out to see what is happening. When they do, word will pass quickly that Doctor So-and-So is in the abortion business. The purpose of the demonstration was to bring attention to that fact. News of the picket will spread rapidly through the neighborhood.

Don't stay and talk to the police. Since you are no longer picketing when they arrive, they will go to the doctor's home to get the complaint. They may try to order anyone who lingers to remove the signs or explain what is happening. They may try to arrest someone. For that reason, do not designate anyone as leader of the picket. It is an event that you need not continue after your point has been made. It is merely an effort to deliver a message to the abortionist and his community. When you have done this, leave. Plan to meet afterward far from the picket site to discuss the success of the picket in a relaxed atmosphere.

Besides picketing abortionists' homes, it is also useful to picket their offices or even clubs that they belong to. Some abortionists have told us that being involved in abortion disturbs them, and that other doctors look down on them. Their patients never thank them for an abortion, whereas other obstetricians are always thanked for delivering a baby. Abortionists have no reason to take pride in their work. They are constantly fighting malpractice suits. And one of the things they like least of all is coming under the attention of pro-lifers. They especially dislike having the conflict brought to their homes.

It follows that if this is what bothers them most, then this is what we must do. In time, these pickets may make them think seriously about getting out of the abortion business.

The home picket must be carefully planned. It is often difficult to find out where abortionists live, but there are ways of getting this information. One way is to arrive at the abortion clinic early in the morning to see what car the physician drives. Take down the license number and check it out with the auto-license department.

Check to see if you have mutual acquaintances who know where the abortionist lives. Sometimes you can simply call the abortionist's office and ask his secretary for his home address.

If you get uneasy about such a project, try to remember what this man or woman is doing to the medical profession, to the community, to women, and to unborn children. Then think again on the methods he routinely uses to destroy innocent human life, and ask yourself if it is so terrible to provide him with an opportunity to rethink his commitment to killing instead of healing.

As we mentioned, it is advisable, just before the picket, to leaflet the neighborhood for several blocks around the abortionist's home with an educational piece on abortion. Link up the doctor with the "procedure" and ask the members of his community if they are happy to have an abortionist in their midst. This leafleting is perfectly legal and if you are told otherwise, challenge whoever tries to stop you. As with handing out any material, do not place it in the mailbox, but put it in the door latch, screen, or under the door.

While the immediate effect of picketing the abortionist's home is to dissuade him from engaging in abortion, the long-range effect is to alert other abortionists to what is in store for them if they remain in the business. It is also intended to dissuade other medical professionals from going into the lucrative abortion business. After all, who wants to get into a business that will bring with it embarrassing demonstrations at their homes on a Sunday afternoon?

On one occasion when we picketed the home of two abortion doctors, a husband and wife team, we left about fifty picket signs on their lawn. The next sign that appeared there said "For Sale".

38 ADOPT AN ABORTIONIST

Despite their violation of the ethics of their own profession, which is dedicated to healing and not to harming their patients, physicians who practice abortion are still open to redemption. They must live with their consciences and the reality that they destroy human life every time they perform an abortion. While abortion doctors who have converted to pro-life are few and far between, they do exist. Perhaps one of the best known is Dr. Bernard Nathanson, who was not only a pioneer in the effort to get abortion legalized, but had founded a chain of abortion mills in New York City which, by his own admission, had destroyed some seventy thousand lives.

In his book *Aborting America*, Dr. Nathanson gives us another good reason to turn away from abortion: the fact that many doctors in his own clinics were suffering serious personal conflicts due to their abortion involvement—nightmares, drinking, drugs, and divorce. Many pro-lifers have known doctors engaged in the abortion practice who have shown signs of distress. After all, nearly every doctor at some time in his training made a commitment to heal and to do good to his fellowman, and abortion is certainly a perversion of that pledge. It must be hard to live a constant lie.

One method that has been used successfully to get an abortionist to cut down on his practice and even to swear off doing abortions is for a pro-lifer to make him a target for conversion. The abortionist is addressed politely through letters, telephone calls, and in person. He is sent information, kept up-to-date on legislation, supplied with articles supporting life and statements by medical personnel defending the right-to-life position. Efforts are made to get to know this abortionist's family, his church affiliation, his memberships in professional organizations and clubs, and other facts about his lifestyle. Manifestation of this interest is always genuine, and persistent.

Pro-lifers who want to befriend an abortionist should not hesitate to discuss the medical, moral, legal, ethical, and religious ramifications of abortion with him. They should try to meet with him to discuss the issue.

"Take an abortionist to dinner" should be more than a humorous suggestion. It should be a genuine invitation. Pro-lifers may be surprised to discover that the abortionist may actually welcome the opportunity to try to justify his position on abortion and will take the invitation seriously.

In the early days of legal abortion, one of our pro-lifers decided he would "adopt" one of the leading female abortion advocates in Chicago. He accompanied her on lobbying missions to Springfield, following her from one legislator's office to another, all the time praying for her conversion. He attended her seminars and encouraged his friends to fill up the front rows at every lecture she gave. He challenged her to public debates, organized people to question her at her talks, sent her pro-life literature, and took every opportunity to try to get her to stop promoting abortion. He succeeded. She eventually got a job with a public relations firm. Several years later, in a chance meeting on Michigan Avenue, she assured us that she was still uninvolved in the abortion controversy and intended to keep out of it.

Examples abound of pro-lifers either encouraging abortionists to curtail their support for abortion or, in some cases, to change their position. On many occasions we have met with abortionists—the doctors, clinic owners, newspaper editors, advertisers, and reporters—to discuss in depth all facets of the controversy. At one meeting, an abortionist admitted frankly that in every abortion he performed he realized that he was destroying the life of a fellow human being. At another meeting, a hospital administrator told us that he knew of cases of live births resulting from abortions and the mothers sometimes requested the bodies of their babies for burial. He predicted that any form of lifetaking would be acceptable at his hospital so long as it were legal. Asked if this would include infanticide, suicide, and euthanasia, he replied, "If it's legal, we would provide the service."

Appealing to moral codes and ethical standards that may be lying dormant, or even appealing to values that the abortionist may apply to his own family and children, could provide the basis for a conversion. Dr. Naim Kasar said in a public address before the National Abortion Federation (NAF), that he found it difficult to perform abortions on women who were at the same term of pregnancy as his own wife. He found it distressing to remove arms and legs and heads of babies who were precisely the age of his own unborn but wanted child. So disturbing was the effect of mid-trimester abortions on Dr. Kasar that he urged the federation to seek ways of restricting or banning mid- and late trimester abortions.

Not long after Dr. Kasar had given this talk, I was picketing his abortion clinic in Kansas City. In the group of two hundred demonstrators was a young woman who told me she had had an abortion by Kasar and that she deeply regretted it but also felt compassion for him. I asked if she would consider "adopting" Kasar, pray for him, send him literature and even try to have a meeting with him. She agreed. Some other people in the group also wanted to adopt Kasar. A year later Dr. Kasar had stopped doing abortions and had moved to another region of the country.

Consider the effect it would have on abortion in America if every abortionist were "adopted" by an informed, pro-life activist who made every effort to engage him in conversation, and even befriend him, at his club, his clinic, his church. Think of the potential for good if every pro-lifer reading this chapter were to decide to "adopt" an abortionist— be it a doctor, counselor, clinic owner, pro-abortion columnist, legislator, or judge. We recommend that you adopt an abortionist right now.

39 LET THE ABORTIONISTS FURTHER OUR CAUSE

"Nobody knows when life begins."
"It's only a blob of tissue."
"Life begins at birth."
"Abortion prevents child abuse."
"Every child a wanted child."
"Abortion for population control."
"Interruption of pregnancy."
"Potential life."

These and other nonsensical slogans represent the stock phrases of a subculture bereft of logic, morality, or common decency. The abortionists employ every known logical fallacy in their arguments defending abortion.

They beg the question: "Wouldn't it be better to be aborted than to be abused?"

They exaggerate: "Before abortion was legal, 10,000 women died of illegal abortion each year."

They exclude the middle: "Nature aborts thousands of fertilized eggs."

They use non-sequiturs: "Better to destroy a fetus than the woman who is already living."

The use of such false arguments and illogical conclusions makes the abortionists their own worst enemies. The clever pro-lifer will let them bury themselves in their own devices. He will take every opportunity to debate the abortion spokesman and create opportunities that would not arise otherwise. There are no arguments for abortion, except those based on man's fallen nature, his propensity to sin, his baser animal instincts, and his desire for selfish gain. Pro-lifers, on the other hand, are supported in their defense of life by the highest forms of idealism and altruism, as well as logic and fact. Even a neophyte in the pro-life movement can outwit and out-argue the most pretentious abortion defender, since it is nearly impossible to sell the killing of children as a rational, moral, sane practice. The defense of human life is always reasonable. It appeals to man's nature and his highest aspirations.

Listen to an abortionist arguing in favor of the extermination of the

"P.O.C." (products of conception)—what abortion advocates call unborn children—and you will hear him deny that there is life in an obviously living organism growing inside the woman's body. He will deny humanity to a living organism who is the offspring of human parents. He must deny any value to an heir who can sue for millions of dollars if injured in the womb. He must deny a soul to a human being with a very active life principle. He must even deny reality to the greatest reality in creation, a living human being. To make these denials seem reasonable he must confuse, distort, and pervert the truth.

The pro-life advocate, on the other hand, need only appeal to nature, reason, and morality for his arguments.

For this reason, right-to-lifers should use the abortionists at every opportunity to promote the pro-life cause. It may take a little practice and research, and some observation, but nearly any pro-lifer can, with a good stock of facts, become proficient at arguing abortion, and in arguing, use the abortionists to confirm the reasonableness of the pro-life position.

On a television program several years ago, the pro-abortionist insisted that the pro-life spokesman use no photographs of intrauterine life or children killed by abortion, even though the studio had assured the pro-lifer that color slides could be used. Six color slides had been prepared for the show. The abortionist argued that he did not have any pictures. The pro-lifer argued that he had brought the abortionist's pictures, the ones of babies torn apart, burned by salt, and suffocated by abortion. But the request to use them was denied. During the program, the abortionist announced that she had aborted some "fetal tissue" nine weeks into her pregnancy.

"It was an indistinguishable mass", she assured the host.

"How old?" quizzed the pro-lifer.

"Only nine weeks", came the smug, confident answer.

"An indistinguishable mass?" asked the pro-lifer as he drew from his coat pocket a photograph of the hand of a nine-week old unborn child.

"This is what your baby's hand looked like", he said. "Complete with fingerprints and a lifeline. If this perfect hand is any indication of the rest of your baby's anatomy, you were carrying a lot more than a mass of tissue."

The abortionist stared at the photograph as the camera focused in to fill the screen with the tiny, perfect hand.

"That picture's exaggerated", she sputtered, and then fell silent.

The pro-lifer read the scientific definition that accompanied the picture, which had been taken by an abortionist. Once again, cold, factual evidence had crushed pro-abortion fantasy and lies.

The abortionists, with their hard line that abortion is a remedy for child abuse, seem unimpressed by the studies that show that there is no connection between unplanned pregnancies and unwanted children. Child abuse has burgeoned since abortion became legal. A segment of our society has apparently concluded that if life has no value before birth, it doesn't have much value afterward either. Yet, careful studies indicate that the vast majority of abused children were planned pregnancies. There is no evidence that unplanned pregnancies result in abused children. Our experience is that women we have talked out of having abortions come to love the children they once thought of aborting. Often they show a special love and devotion to these "salvaged" children.

The abortionists chafe at the suggestion that abortion is primarily used as a mop-up for sexual promiscuity. Yet, statistics show that three out of four abortions are performed on unmarried women and that the abortionists themselves often hold their patients in contempt, especially when they are repeaters, having their fifth or sixth abortion. They fear the venereal diseases infecting some of their clients. Abortionists try to deny the frequency of late term abortions, and yet the discovery of 17,000 aborted babies in a dumpster in Los Angeles, many of them fully formed, and frequent stories of abortion live births belie their denials.

It is easy to make abortionists appear both foolish and confused, simply because they are. Their position flies in the face of morality, natural law, and reason. Despite their use of doublespeak and psycho-babble, their facade of intellectualism is thin when pitted against the dagger-sharp arguments of trained pro-life spokesmen.

"But it's legal", they will say about abortion when every other argument fails.

"So was selling slaves, but that didn't make it right", is the obvious reply to such nonsense.

It is easy to make the abortionists look foolish, and to make them resort to name-calling and invective. It is easy to call their bluff. We should never hesitate to use every opportunity that is afforded us to engage them in public debate. It can only advance the pro-life cause.

40 HOW TO STAY OPTIMISTIC

People new to the pro-life movement frequently ask more seasoned activists whether they don't get frustrated and discouraged fighting for a cause that presents such overwhelming odds. Frustrated, yes. A person gets frustrated when he sees that his work is not achieving the ends that are sought and, also, when he finds so many pro-lifers not giving their all to the cause, or using ineffective methods. Consequently, a pro-life activist may become frustrated from time to time. But he never becomes discouraged.

You cannot become discouraged if you are confident that your cause is right. When your cause is the protection of innocent human life, you know that you are right in what you believe. Everything you do that conforms with your beliefs has an effect, even though you may not realize it at the time. Also, you know that ultimately victory is yours because what you are doing is good, and good always prevails over evil. Discouragement in the pro-life movement would imply a lack of faith in the movement, in the reality of the value of each human life, and in God, who is on the side of the righteous.

But it is not enough simply to remain free from discouragement. A good pro-lifer is always optimistic. Sometimes it is necessary to set up temporary goals, "little victories", that are relatively easy to achieve, in order to keep a positive attitude. We temporarily set aside the goal of stopping *all* abortions and settle for stopping one by talking someone out of an abortion *today*. There is cause for optimism when we can go to an abortion clinic and meet a young couple going in and, by talking to them and sometimes praying with them, dissuade them from killing their child. We know that what we are doing really works, that our method is useful, and that what we are doing is good in the sight of God.

In Chicago, for instance, the fact that our sidewalk counselors were able, under the leadership of Rich Freeman, to stop seventeen abortions in one morning at a single clinic gave us all cause for optimism. We were so optimistic that we announced our achievement in national publications in order to encourage others to share our victory. In that way, pro-life sidewalk counselors everywhere acquire an optimism that says, "We can all stop abortions, even large numbers of abortions, and we can stop them now."

We felt great optimism in Chicago when we closed down Cook County Hospital's abortion facility, when we put Associated Concern out of business, when we helped close down the Water Tower Clinic and Chicago's Women's Center, both on Michigan Avenue. Whenever we close a clinic or stop an abortion we want to share our excitement and tell pro-lifers everywhere that we have won a victory for our cause.

The resource within the movement that should give all of us the greatest optimism and keep us buoyed up is other pro-lifers. I find that visiting pro-life groups in Kansas, Nebraska, Indiana, Minnesota, Texas, California, New York, Florida, Alabama, Pennsylvania, and Virginia and indeed, all over the country, is good for the spirit. Everywhere I travel, in every organization I visit, I find the same dedicated, hopeful, cheerful, and ingenious pro-life people. I am always discovering new techniques for stopping abortion (which make it possible to put a book like this together). I return from every trip keyed up, enthusiastic, brimming with new ideas that we can implement in Chicago and introduce to other groups. I become optimistic when I see other pro-life groups adopt our suggestions and get results that we ourselves had never dreamed possible.

Another way to stay optimistic is to note the increased interest in the abortion issue. Sometimes even the secular press, with its lopsided, limited view of the issue, will come up with some gems. The *Philadelphia Inquirer*'s investigation into live aborted babies, entitled "Abortion, the Dreaded Complications", of August 21, 1981, was a godsend. The June 5, 1978, *Newsweek* article, "Abortion Under Attack", and its in-depth cover story, "Abortion", of January 14, 1985, the April 1983 *Life* magazine article on intrauterine surgery. *Time*'s special cover story, "Making Babies", September 10, 1984, were all causes for optimism because they showed us that public concern over abortion is growing. We know that people who will not be exposed to our pro-life literature are reached by these secular journals. That, too, is a cause for optimism. Articles on the aftermath of abortion, the anguish and the psychological reaction of women, the fact that a book has been written on the effect of abortion on the father, all of these are causes for optimism because they force the public to study this issue more intensely, and even reconsider their stand on abortion.

Another reason for increased optimism is the tremendous strides being made in the field of fetology. Even without intending to, the medical profession may once again become the protector of the unborn, by the sheer force of advancing technology. We now have fetal surgeons and fetal diagnosticians, as Dr. Bernard Nathanson points out in his book *The Abortion Papers*. Soon we will have fetal neurologists, fetal hematologists, fetal cardiologists, fetal endocrinologists, and even fetal psychologists. Advances in technology not only create new specialties, new techniques, and new ethical questions, but also new constituencies. Nathanson argues that when fetal medicine becomes a full-fledged field of medical endeavor, physicians will become the most aggressive advocates for the unborn.

Someday doctors will vie for federal funds, for positions within universities, and for their place in the medical pecking order, all in the name of their client, the human unborn. "This will be a bitter vindication indeed for those of us who are pleading this lonely cause in 1983 in the name of decency and simple humanity", Nathanson wrote.

But the day will come, and that is grounds for real optimism.

There was a program on abortion in Chicago one Sunday morning. It was a typical stacked deck. All four panelists were pro-abortion. Yet, in their half-hour discussion, the grief, anguish, fear, doubt, and despair caused by abortion came out in this one-sided discussion. Despite the host's best efforts to keep the negative aspects of abortion submerged, these realities came out. The program was, in fact, very anti-abortion, even though everyone on the program wanted it to be a pro-abortion presentation. Such things give a person cause for hope and optimism.

The most satisfying reality and the one thing above all that keeps us optimistic is the certain knowledge that we are on the right side of the battle between good and evil. Even when the situation looks dark and even if abortions continue at the rate of three a minute for years to come, we have to keep a spiritual view of life and of the evil that affects us. We are battling evil and we are winning the battle. Some of us will not see that victory in our lifetime, but we are confident of finding a place of peace and victory in the life to come. Everyone dies, whether *in utero* through an abortion, by getting cancer, being struck by a car, being blown out of the sky, or whatever. We all die, but death is not our end. It is our beginning. Death someday will be the beginning of our new life. That life will depend on how we lived our lives here, and what we did with our lives.

Congressman Henry Hyde gave one of the movement's most optimistic pro-life talks in Chicago at a fund-raising banquet. In what is now a popular soliloquy about the last moment in the life of a pro-lifer and the first moment in eternity, this eloquent defender of unborn babies said,

> When the time comes, as it surely will, when we face that terrible moment, the final judgment, I've often thought, as Fulton Sheen wrote, that it is a terrible moment of loneliness. You have no advocates there; you are there alone standing before God, and a terror will rip your soul like nothing you can imagine. I really think that those in the pro-life movement will not be alone. I think there will be a chorus of voices that have never been heard in this world but are heard very beautifully and very loudly in the next world, and I think they will plead for everyone who has been in the movement. They will say to God, "Spare them, because they loved us", and God will look at us and say not, "Did you succeed?" but "Did you try?"

If the belief that there is an eternal reward awaiting us for our small efforts in this world does not give us cause for optimism, then there is no meaning for that word. Optimum means "the greatest". That is what is in store for us. We need to believe in this so firmly that in the face of any frustration, anguish, or failure our optimism remains steady, constant, and persistent to the end.

41 MAKE YOURSELF AVAILABLE

I believe that one of the strangest things a pro-life activist can do is have an unlisted telephone number. I know activists who have gone this route. I have listened to their reasons and excuses but am seldom convinced. Except in rare circumstances, having an unlisted telephone number seems incompatible with being a pro-life activist, always ready to act. An activist has to be available. I have had friends come to Chicago and not bother to look up my number in the phone book because they assumed it would not be listed. I would not think of *not* being listed. We have to be available to everyone who wants to talk to us, even cranks.

When we put out a press release, we always give both the office phone number and the director's home phone number. As mentioned, I have given some of my best interviews from home at four or five o'clock in the morning. I might receive a call from a reporter who says a story on a Supreme Court ruling came in on the late wire and he just received it. Would I like to comment? In these cases I tell the reporter I haven't seen the text of the decision, so will he read it to me over the phone? With this brief summary we do an interview that may run on the morning traffic newscast and reach thousands of people.

The pro-life activist must use every opportunity to tell the public about abortion, even if he is not fully briefed on a particular ruling or current event. There is nothing wrong in admitting that you need to look further into a news item, while doing an interview with the information you have. Request that they call you back later for further comment.

The second most baffling thing a pro-life activist can do is answer "no comment" to a legitimate question by the press. Even if your lawyer has told you not to comment "on the advice of your attorney", don't let it appear that you are hiding something or that you are fearful. It is not difficult to swing a discussion around to another aspect of abortion since you have been sought out for your expertise on the issue.

How many times have we listened to a politician answer a question he doesn't know a great deal about or doesn't want to answer? He moves off the issue and switches the subject to something he knows about and wants to talk about. He never says, "I don't know much about that. Ask me something else." He uses the occasion to discuss his favorite program. He knows that most of his listeners don't know the answer either and probably don't remember the question. He will consider whatever aspect of the question he wishes to talk about. The audience wants knowledge and is agreeable to a variety of new information.

If you are asked about a court decision unfavorable to pro-life, talk about the anti-life bias that seems to be a prerequisite for being a judge today. Talk in general terms if you do not know the particulars. But whatever you do, say something to advance the pro-life cause. Don't let any opportunity to make a statement for the unborn pass you by.

There is nothing more damning than for a news commentator to say, "So and so could not be reached for comment." What does that mean? To the public it means you are scared, wrong, ignorant of the facts, or didn't leave a forwarding number. None of these is flattering. It is more than unflattering to a pro-life activist who is defending the unborn child. We are not advocates for ourselves but for the unborn. And the unborn are always in trouble. That is why we must always be available.

Many others are in similar situations, such as the doctor on call, the priest, the mother who has to get up in the middle of the night. These are hard things to do, but if it's your vocation, you must be available. You must be available to talk to high school students, grade school pupils, coffee klatches, or anyone who wants you. Do not turn away *any* opportunity to talk about abortion. Do not provide a substitute to speak for you unless absolutely necessary.

Don't be embarrassed to charge for your talk if the group can afford to pay you something. They will appreciate you more and work harder to get a large audience if you charge for your talk. Doing things free takes away some of the value of what you are doing. If they know they have to pay you, they will encourage more people to attend your talk.

Availability also helps your image. People who stand out in the pro-life movement are those you can call on any time and who are always reachable. They call you back when you leave a message. They follow through with their promises to send material or deliver a message. They are the types we need in the pro-life movement. Many names come to mind—Nellie Gray, Judie and Paul Brown, Curtis Young, Bob Tobin, Jim McFadden, Art O'Brien, John Jakubczyk, Franky Schaeffer, Jerry Horn, Norm Stone, Dr. John Kelly, Diane Rinn, Olga Fairfax, and many more—all people who consider the battle to stop the murder of babies to be their most important concern and not just a part-time job. These people are ready and available any time they are needed.

Who is available to us? Who can we call on at any time? God is always there waiting for us to call on Him. We take Him for granted, but that is the kind of availability we should use for our model.

42 HOW TO SET UP A TAX EXEMPT ORGANIZATION

Whenever sincere, interested, dedicated pro-lifers come to you and ask you to help them start an organization, don't tell them to launch right into raising money or even planning their program.

The first thing to tell them is to get incorporated. If they are serious about starting a pro-life organization, they should incorporate. They should be prepared to go through the red tape, fill out some troublesome forms for incorporation, get a tax status that exempts them from paying sales tax, get a mail permit to save on bulk mailings. All this tedious, time-consuming work will accomplish two things.

First, it will help prove that they are serious about becoming involved in pro-life work. Second, it will put them in a position to ask for help to carry on their work. That is not to say that they can't have a pro-life group without being tax exempt. But if they don't incorporate, their organization is probably never going to grow. They are going to have to reach out to people for financial support. People will expect them to be organized. Good organization shows serious intent.

If this is a political group, they will take a slightly different route, but the process is similar to becoming an educational, charitable organization. Most pro-life groups are educational and have a tax exempt status. Their donors can write off their donations, and the organization does not pay sales tax. Here are some tips on setting up a 501(c)(3) tax exempt organization.

It is wise to hire or confer with a lawyer. It is usually not difficult to find a lawyer among pro-life friends or through a pro-life friend. Lawyers are busy and can seldom spend much time working on this project, but legal expertise will help get a new group started, even though much of the work can be done without a lawyer. The lawyer will need your help answering the questions asked on the legal forms.

We know some determined, patient laymen who filed the necessary forms and got approval without using a lawyer, but it saves grief to have a lawyer help file the documents.

The officers of the new organization will have to provide the Internal Revenue Service with much factual information, the most time-consuming of which will be bylaws and articles of incorporation.

The Internal Revenue Service prints an instruction manual entitled, "Application for Recognition of Exemption under Section 501(c)(3) of the Internal Revenue Code", which can be obtained from any IRS office. This booklet, called "Package 1023", explains in detail what steps must be followed to incorporate. The group must draw up bylaws. These will describe various aspects of the organization, such as its purpose, requirements for membership, composition of the board of directors, meetings, officers, executive director, committees, and how contracts, checks, deposits, funds, books, and records will be handled. They will provide for amending, altering, or repealing these bylaws.

In addition to filing this application for tax exemption, the officers will need to become familiar with state laws and duties regarding charitable organizations. Contact the office of the state's attorney general for this information.

The new organization will have to file yearly tax returns (Form 990) with the Treasury Department. Since these forms require detailed information about the group's sources of income and how it was expended, bookkeeping must be accurate and complete from the very beginning in order to avoid problems at tax filing time. If the organization is going to be active enough to require rented office space, with perhaps one or more full- or part-time paid employees, the guidance and help of an accountant may be necessary.

According to legislation passed by Congress in 1983, tax exempt corporations are required to pay Social Security taxes and must deduct them from their employees' wages, even if they only have one employee. This entails added expense and bookwork.

In addition, it is important to become familiar with state and federal retailers' occupation tax rules for persons engaged in non-profit services.

These are bare-bone guidelines on setting up a tax exempt pro-life organization, but they indicate that there is a lot of work to do to become an official agency. Getting incorporated won't happen overnight. It may require numerous visits to the IRS office to answer questions and explain statements. Even after the organization gets clearance, it is on probation for several years.

It is wise to get to know the IRS investigator and go to him with each new question and problem. There may be quite a few of these before the whole process is completed.

43 SET UP A PREGNANCY HELP OFFICE

Pro-life activists have found that their greatest asset when doing street counseling outside clinics is a crisis pregnancy help center. Ideally, it should be near enough to the clinic that the young woman, once dissuaded from having an abortion, can get immediate help.

Experienced sidewalk counselors report that if you have to drive across town to reach a pregnancy aid center, some women who would otherwise be open to your help will not want to get into your car. This is understandable. They don't know who you are. Most likely, they have heard strange stories about pro-life people. They may wonder what you have in store for them. Thus, having to drive them to a pregnancy help center is not as effective as having one nearby that they can walk to.

Many pregnancy help offices are strategically set up in the same areas as abortion clinics and as close to the clinics as possible. Where there is an abortion clinic in an office building, pro-lifers can find space in the same building. That office gives you added advantages of access to the parking lot, the halls, and lobby, so you can more easily talk to women heading for the abortion clinic. A workable plan is to get enough money to pay the rent for one month and make the escrow payment (usually an additional month's rent), then challenge your supporters to help your pregnancy help office remain in the building.

The pregnancy help office should be staffed during regular business hours and whenever the abortion clinic is in operation. There should always be at least two people there: a counselor, who can talk to the young women and handle pregnancy tests, and someone to handle the phone. You need a private room for counseling, one without people walking in and out and interrupting you. You should have comfortable quarters in a decent location. You will need volunteers or paid employees who are faithful and responsible and can be trusted to show up on time. They must realize the seriousness of the work they are doing.

Most pregnancy help offices stock a variety of literature, such as leaflets, magazines, and books. They give them free to the young women visiting them. There are many good books and articles on fetal development. There are excellent slide presentations on fetal development and the methods of abortion. One of the best we have viewed is at the Aid for Women office in Chicago, where they counsel clients in both English and Spanish.

You should keep a list of doctors in the community who do not do abortions, and give this list to the young couples. You should supply names of doctors who will give prenatal care and even offer a delivery at no charge for women who cannot pay. You will have to know your area well, so that you will be able to suggest the location of a doctor's office that will be convenient to her.

The mechanics of setting up a pregnancy help office are similar to the mechanics of setting up a pro-life office. Go about it systematically and carefully. Do the ground work and try to get community support. You will need it. Get incorporated as soon as possible. You must convince people that if they give money to your organization it will be doing the work they want it to do.

The abortionists would like for the public to believe that there are only a few people who want abortion stopped and who want babies saved. That is not true. There are millions of people who support the pro-life effort. They just can't do the work themselves. But they want you to do it, and they are willing to help you financially and occasionally by volunteering their services. You must convince them that helping you will help women and their unborn children.

44 GATHER EVIDENCE AGAINST THE ABORTIONISTS

In Chicago we began gathering evidence against the abortionists very early, quite by accident. We knew some of the doctors who had been doing abortions when they were illegal. We also knew some ministers who ran a clergy consultation service. When abortion was illegal, they had been sending women to New York and even to Europe. They were so eager to be "good" clergy, helping women kill their unborn babies, that they had begun advertising this illegal service. We found out who they were and learned who the doctors were who had supported them. We also knew doctors who had been active in establishing the National Association for the Repeal of Abortion Laws (NARAL), and we knew some of the people who were involved in what became known as the Religious Coalition for Abortion Rights (RCAR).

Some of these abortionists had been around for a long time, so that, when abortion became legal, they were already notorious. All we had to do was follow their activities as they hung their shingles on the front door instead of in the back alley. Also, there were a lot of strange coincidences that helped us understand what was happening inside the clinics. We kept running into people who worked in the clinics and were disgusted with what they saw and decided to give us this information.

One young woman called me and said, "I'm working in an abortion clinic and its driving me crazy. But I think instead of quitting I should stay and maybe help you." We used to meet at a restaurant near the clinic, and she would give me literature and forms and tell me what problems they were having. I learned who worked there and what each person did. She told me that one day the health inspectors were at the clinic and the doctors were operating on a woman who was bleeding badly. They thought they might have to call an ambulance to take her to the hospital, but they didn't want an ambulance to pull up while the inspectors were there. The inspectors passed them by.

Another woman called to say that at the clinic where she worked, the doctor had performed an abortion on a young girl who was well into her second or possibly third trimester of pregnancy. The baby was large, and they were having difficulty getting it out. They had to crush the

171

baby's head and she had seen more blood and baby parts than she could stand. She told us that when she saw its face, she walked out. Now she wanted to do anything she could to help the pro-life movement.

An orderly called our office to tell us that he had watched a baby slowly die after an abortion, and that he had seen at least one live baby disposed of in an incinerator. It had been at the bottom of a plastic bag, and he noticed that it was still moving when the bag was put into the furnace.

One of the most useful devices in gathering evidence is to attract an evidence-gathering agency to come in and assist you. That was part of our rationale in encouraging the *Chicago Sun-Times* to research its "Abortion Profiteers" series that ran for twenty consecutive days.

It was a real victory for pro-life to get a pro-abortion newspaper that ran nearly a page of abortion ads each issue to investigate the abortion clinics with manpower we could never have afforded. Here was an editorially pro-abortion newspaper doing our job for us. I still claim that pro-life efforts were mainly responsible for the "Abortion Profiteers" front page series on the deplorable conditions of the abortion clinics in Chicago. I had interested a young reporter at the *Sun-Times* in the information that had been coming into our office from inside the clinics.

One day when I could not work at the office because of construction going on there, I called the reporter and suggested that I bring my information to the *Sun-Times* offices. I had notes on meetings with abortion clinic workers and tapes of these interviews. He said to come over. He had been trying to get the editors interested in a doing a series on abortion. I don't know the specifics on his efforts, but I met with him and Pam Zekman, a *Sun-Times* investigative reporter at that time.

Zekman acted bored, but from time to time would copy portions of my file. She assured me that they were not doing an investigation for reasons of promoting the pro-life position, but because they thought it was a good story. I was advised not to say anything about it, or acknowledge that I had any part in it. I told them I would continue sending information.

There was a six-month silence. I had met with them in April and the series began in November. It was a very extensive series and was widely read. Not all of it was helpful to pro-life, but most of it was, because it supported what we had been trying to show through our own investigations: that legal abortion is no safer than back-alley abortion, that abortion is done primarily for profit, and that it is a dirty and corrupt business. That is what the "Abortion Profiteers" series proved. We sent copies of it to many people who were arguing that legal abortion was safe. Here is a summary of the series:

It began on Sunday, November 12, 1978. The first front-page headline (every issue started on the front page with a banner headline) said: "The Abortion Profiteers", with a sub-head, "Making a Killing in Michigan Avenue Clinics". The drawing that would accompany the series was of a surgeon masked and aproned, with his arms folded and a table with stirrups in the background. The caption read, "Some are pregnant; some are not. Most will be sold abortions."

What followed were stories of greed, pain, dirty operating rooms, double charging, and death. "Life on the abortion assembly line: grim, grisly, and greedy", one headline read. "Meet the profiteers: men who profit from women's pain", and "State will hit abortion clinics". Five abortionists were pictured on one page. Each article, three and four pages long, ended with a teaser announcing the story to appear the next day. "Abortion mill bosses cut corners on care", "State to act on abortion clinics". Editorials and letters to the editors commenting on the series began appearing.

Other headlines read, "The abortion lottery", "Women take chances with 'tryout' doctors", and "Abortion as a game of chance". One headline stated, "Patient recalls: 'I was just a guinea pig.' " A box story on Dr. Ming Kow Hah called him a "physician of pain", and another headline blared, "Abortion without anesthetic: 'sadistic' ". A cartoon of a doctor keeping score on his apron had the caption, "Doctors race each other in abortion derby".

Throughout November the stories followed in grim sequence: "Nurse to aide: 'Fake that pulse!' " and at the end of the first week: "Prove Michigan Avenue abortion clinic death".

The writers' pro-abortion bias showed through during the investigation. One headline among the gore assured readers, "Abortion peril greater before legalization", with a photograph of the open grave of a woman aborted illegally. Several endorsements of the series came from "good" abortion groups like Planned Parenthood and the National Abortion Federation, saying the series would clean up the industry.

With a two-column banner headline, "12 dead after abortions in State's walk-in clinics", the editors must have forgotten they had run a story on how bad abortions were before legalization. Reports told of kickbacks, a Detroit doctor who took late abortions that the Chicago abortionists didn't want, and a story on performing abortions on non-pregnant women: "Pregnant or not—women given abortions".

Sun-Times reporters and Beter Government Association workers had gone into clinics with male urine and gotten positive pregnancy reports.

By the middle of the second week, the story had become so negative that a chapter on a "clean" clinic was needed. It appeared under the headline, "Found: safe, compassionate care", and featured a benign, smiling abortion clinic operator who had cooperated with the *Sun-Times* investigators. She told them how a "proper" abortuary should be run.

Two stories were presented against the pro-life movement. "The politics of abortion—a big business", tried hard to show how fighting abortion was profitable. It failed. Then a sinister spy story ran under the headline, "The inside story of the City's pro-life movement".

When I picked up the paper the morning this "inside" story ran, a light went on in my memory. Before I even saw the photograph of our pro-life group inside an abortion clinic hallway and my own picture under the headline, "For 'babies who have died'—his mission", I knew this was about us. I suddenly realized Pamela Warrick, author of the article, was Pamela Warren, a young volunteer who accompanied us on every pro-life adventure for six weeks, then vanished. This was the tall young lady who never let us drop her off at home, but always "near the Wabash Street bridge". The Wabash Street bridge is where the *Chicago Sun-Times* is prominently located.

Pam "Warren" Warrick was in a photograph with our group, looking uncomfortably out of place. I swallowed hard and read. The story was good. Just as I finished, I got a call from Tom Roeser, chairman of our board, from O'Hare Airport. "What do you think?" he asked. I detected enthusiasm. "I don't think it will hurt us", I suggested. "Hurt us! It's a million dollars worth of free publicity." Tom was right. It *was* good publicity, and while we lost a few members for "un-Christian acts", our stock went way up. I reprinted portions of the article and got nasty letters from *Sun-Times* lawyers threatening to sue me for quoting myself from articles they had printed without getting *my* permission! It would have been an interesting case.

The series ended less dramatically than it had begun, with reports on more investigations and how abortions were now banned in clinics that didn't comply with health regulations.

Much good came out of the series. It was useful in getting legislators to enact restrictions on abortion clinics. We bought four thousand reprints and sent them across the country to stimulate similar investigations and encourage more stringent clinic regulations in other cities. But one of the best things that came from the series was the death blow it dealt to the platitude, "Legal abortion is safe abortion". Anyone who pulled out that cliché had to face the inevitable question, And what about the 'Abortion Profiteers' series?"

Gathering evidence takes a lot of imagination. Pro-lifers constantly call our office and ask if they do abortions at one hospital or another. "Why don't you call them and find out?" we tell them.

"Can I?" they say. "Could I call and ask them?"

"Yes. How do you think we find out?"

Many people could gather evidence if they really wanted to and if they used a little imagination. Simply call an abortion clinic and ask them what you want to know. They will tell you everything you need to know—the times you can come in, the cost, even advice on how to look out for the pro-lifers. Much evidence can be gathered from the abortionists by expressing concern, interest, or need. Ask lots of questions, keep them talking, and keep files on what you learn.

If the clinics have any lawsuits or any litigation pending against them, you can find this out at the courthouse. The names of the doctors, the hospitals they are affiliated with, plus other names will all be a matter of public record.

You can also get information from tax forms and drivers' licenses (both public records). Tax records will tell you who owns the clinic who profits from it, the doctors who get paid, and paid employees. Use these public documents. Become familiar with the inside of your county courthouse, your statehouse, the federal building, and the IRS office. You will be amazed at what you can find there.

Happy hunting!

45 FILE SUIT AGAINST THE ABORTIONISTS

The abortionists learned long ago that they could scare off some pro-lifers by filing lawsuits against them for picketing, harassment, disorderly conduct, and trespassing. In some instances these have worked. They have scared some pro-lifers into inaction.

One question I am often asked when conducting a picket or demonstration is, "Can they sue us for this?" Yes, they probably can, if they want the hassle, the expense, and the trouble of proving their case. They can always sue. But they know that you can also sue them. If their case isn't strong, there is the possibility that you will file charges of malicious prosecution or false arrest against them. Lawsuits are often used as clubs with which to ward off each other. Frequently, the mere threat of a lawsuit will terrify a person.

I remember the first time I ran into this problem. I had telephoned the mother of a young woman who was running an abortion clinic but had died in a parachute jump. I called the mother because rumor had it that pro-lifers were saying nasty things about the dead daughter and were harassing the family. I knew this was not true. I called to extend my condolences and assure the mother that pro-life people were not making harassing calls. The mother listened quietly, but during the conversation someone shouted into the phone, "We're going to sue you for harassing my mother!" and hung up. The next day at the office I heard my secretary on the phone saying, "It's spelled S-C-H-E-I-D-L-E-R, Joseph. Yes, he is the executive director." She hung up. I asked nervously, "Who was that?" She rattled off the name of a law firm and said they were calling to get the correct spelling of my name. I panicked. I had never before encountered this. I could see my house and property and the kids' college educations going out the window. I would possibly spend years in jail and all because I had called to offer someone my condolences.

It was a ploy. My lawyer told me not to worry, since I had not harassed anyone. Nothing happened. Since then I have received so many letters and calls from law firms that it has become routine, but they still make me nervous.

However, you can file genuine suits against the abortionists and you can do it successfully. At one of our sit-ins in Chicago, five of our people were maced by a woman who worked at the clinic. There was no reason for her to attack us. Our people weren't doing anything. They were being peaceful. She approached and sprayed mace in their faces, and we had to take three of them to the hospital. We filed suit and after several trips to court, she was found guilty and had to pay costs. Later we learned that the clinic fired her.

If you believe you have a sound, supportable case against an abortionist for assault, forceful restraint, battery, libel, or any other criminal act against you or other pro-lifers, call a good pro-life lawyer and explain your case to him. You may be surprised to learn how many rights we still have. And we had better protect them, because the abortionists and their supporters are trying hard to deny us these rights. They are now talking about creating laws against what they call "emotional harassment". This would mean that pro-lifers could not approach women on the sidewalk and try to dissuade them from having abortions. They are calling our plans "conspiracies to deny women their constitutional rights to reproductive freedom". There are pro-abortion legislators right now who will even try to label a book like this "inflammatory".

It never seems to occur to these abortion supporters that their efforts to protect a woman's so-called right to kill unborn children may constitute a conspiracy to deny pro-life citizens *their* First Amendment rights to free speech, assembly, and redress of grievances. These new laws would harass us, and violate our clearly protected Constitutional rights. We can *find* our rights in the documents that established this republic. They can nowhere find a right to abortion.

Resource:

Kevin Sherlock has written a comprehensive study on researching the abortion industry. It includes chapters on finding out who the local abortionists are, researching malpractice cases, finding out if your abortionist has a criminal record, getting information on abortion hospitals, finding out who owns the corporation that owns the abortion mill, and much more. Order this book, the *Abortion Reseach Guide*, at $5.00 per copy from: Mr. Sherlock, 12526 Wixom, No. Hollywood, CA 91605.

46 HELP A COUPLE FIND A BABY FOR ADOPTION

The number of couples in this country who would like to adopt a child but cannot find one is estimated to be in the millions. Even though newspapers publish articles about the difficulty of adopting children, they skirt the fact that 1.7 million babies a year are murdered through abortion. That, of course, is one reason for the scarcity of children available for adoption.

Pro-lifers receive many calls from couples who are desperate to adopt. Some say they will do anything to get a child. On occasion we have suggested that they come out with us to the clinics and talk a couple going for an abortion into carrying the baby to term for them. Few couples have the courage to do this. They say they will do anything for a baby except the one thing that may work for them. They become frightened, or decide it isn't proper. They prefer to let our sidewalk counselors save a baby and then call them to come and get it.

But a few couples have gone to abortion clinics, talked to those going in, and tried to dissuade a woman from killing her baby by offering to become her child's adoptive parents.

One case stands out vividly. A woman called our office to say she and her husband had tried to adopt a baby for ten years. They were unable to have a baby of their own. They were on a number of waiting lists, but nothing had come through. They were afraid they were getting to be too old to adopt, so they asked us for help. I suggested that they come to the clinic on a Saturday and pick out their baby's parents.

The woman hesitated for a moment, but then decided to try. I told her to meet me at 8:30 in the morning at the clinic, the time the women begin to arrive. I arrived early and parked. I saw a young couple talking in the car ahead of me. When they got out I followed them to the clinic and asked them if they were contemplating abortion. They said they were. I asked them to consider having the baby and giving it to a couple who were desperate for a child.

The man said they wanted the abortion. I continued to follow them. The man became irritated, started calling me names, then pushed his girlfriend ahead of him into the clinic. She seemed willing to discuss the

178

matter, but the boyfriend would not let me talk to her. He was pressuring her into this abortion. I referred to him throughout our conversation as "Dad".

Five minutes after the couple went into the clinic, the prospective adoptive couple arrived. I went to meet them and told them about the couple who had gone in for the abortion. I said if they had the nerve they could go in the clinic and talk to them. There weren't many people there yet. I described the couple to them. The guard would think my friends were just going in for an abortion.

I pretended to be trying to talk them out of an abortion. The guard opened the door. They went in as if they had an appointment. They recognized the couple from my description and tried to convince them to have their baby. They were inside for fifteen minutes when the police arrived—three squads and some plainclothesmen. They went into the clinic.

There was some commotion and five minutes later the police and my friends emerged. There was a lot of yelling. My friends looked confused and frightened. A woman from the clinic said it was my fault, that they were working for me. The guard was furious. But the couple was allowed to go free.

I asked them what happened. They said they had recognized the couple and were talking to the woman when the man became irritated and called the police. I told them they might as well stay and do sidewalk counseling; that there would be thirty more couples coming to the clinic. They might find a couple willing to give up their baby for adoption. They decided to stay.

They were a little nervous because the police were still there, but I explained the situation to the police, who then left. We stayed about an hour.

Later, I received a call from Greg Morrow, a street counselor, saying that shortly after we left, the couple we had confronted came out of the clinic and told him they had decided against the abortion. All the commotion made them wonder if they were doing the right thing. They were going to go through with the pregnancy. The baby's life was saved through our interest in them and their child. We gave the child a value the parents had not recognized. My friends didn't get a baby, but they saved a life.

I don't know of any couple who has actually found a child to adopt by stopping an abortion. But it will happen someday. I suggest that more childless couples have the courage to do what my friends did. I recommend it because one way to save life is to bring a couple with an unwanted child into contact with a couple who want that child.

A more routine way to help a couple find a child for adoption is to ask young women you talk out of abortion if they would consider giving their baby up for adoption. The timing is important. A great deal of tact must be used. You don't want to sound insistent or give the impression that the only reason you wanted them to forego abortion is to supply some friends with a child.

Whatever your approach, and however you succeed, as soon as you believe the young woman wants to relinquish the child, it is important to get in touch with a professional group that handles adoptions.

Never recommend adoption as the first and only option. Some young women should keep their babies, even as single parents. Some probably should not. But the person looking for a baby for adoption is probably not the best judge of that situation.

For information on arranging an adoption and a directory of adoption agencies contact:

NATIONAL COMMITTEE FOR
ADOPTION
   1346 Connecticut Ave., NW
   Suite 326
   Washington, DC 20036

47 USE "INFLAMMATORY RHETORIC"

As a former journalism instructor of the "old school" of objective reporting, I have always believed in using accurate, factual descriptions and definitions. That is why abortion is referred to throughout this book as "killing", and why the unborn child is called a "baby", and why a pregnant woman or girl is called a "mother". These are accurate, on-target words for the reality of what we are describing.

But to the abortionists, these are all examples of "inflammatory rhetoric". The abortionists prefer to disguise the reality of what they are engaged in by using vague, evasive words and phrases. They have to mask the monstrosity of abortion. They refer to the child as "fetal tissue" or merely the "P.O.C." (product of conception). It doesn't sound as barbaric, they reason, to remove fetal tissue, as it does to dismember a live human baby. It is easier to "interrupt" a "problem pregnancy" than it is to "kill" a new human life.

Abortionists thrive on such euphemisms and weasel words. Like things that creep around in the dark, they hate to have the bright light of truth shine on their activities. Many chafe at being called "abortionists", even though they may spend the greater part of their medical "practice" cutting up, salting out, or otherwise destroying human life.

Many abortionists are embarrassed to admit their involvement in abortion, and they wish to keep that phase of their practice quiet. It is important for pro-life activists to take every opportunity to broadcast the fact that Dr. So-and-So violates his oath to protect life. It is important to associate them in the public eye with their profession.

Samples of other "inflammatory rhetoric" that pro-lifers must use at appropriate times to counter pro-abortion jargon are: "holocaust", for America's abortion culture, "abortuary" or "death camp", to describe the abortion clinic, "abortifacient", for pills and IUDs, "fornication", for sex outside of marriage, "adultery", for "having an affair".

When to use these terms and when *not* to use them is important. It is not *always* wise to use the strongest word. It takes prudence to know when to refrain. The overuse or improper use of inflammatory rhetoric can damage its effectiveness. To refer at all times to "murderer" and "baby killer" when speaking of an abortionist becomes tedious and makes one look like a fanatic.

Inflammatory rhetoric must be used with discretion. Do not always use the strongest terms or you will dilute their force when they are most needed. Inflammatory rhetoric is best used for emphasis. Other accurate but less descriptive terms should be used in most discourse, interviews, talks, and writing. A constant litany of inflammatory terms distracts an audience from the main point of a talk. It may lead them to believe anger and revenge motivate the speaker.

The abortionists consider nearly any reference to the reality of abortion, pregnancy, and reproduction that doesn't fit their description as "inflammatory", just as they regard nearly any form of pro-life activity as "harassment" or "terrorism".

But then, people who kill babies for a living are not going to be particularly accurate in describing their trade, or our efforts to shut down that industry.

48 USE PICTURES, SIGNS, AND EFFIGIES

There is a Chinese proverb that says, "One picture is worth ten thousand words." Most people say "one thousand words", but the Chinese say ten thousand, apparently wanting to make it clear that a picture has an enormous impact on people. They are right.

Throughout history, pictures have been used to teach. The windows in Chartres Cathedral in France tell the entire biblical story. The Egyptians used pictures in their writing. The Greeks used statues to tell stories. Frequently stories were told on columns and friezes at the tops of buildings. Even today, in most of our government buildings, we see pictures of groups of people doing important things to maintain our freedoms. These graphics convey not only the story itself, but the importance of the event, and the rightness of the philosophy behind it. It is only appropriate that pro-life activists, whose subject, the unborn, cannot be seen, educate through the use of pictures, photographs, and drawings in order for others to understand the plight of the unseen victim of abortion.

Pro-lifers, from the beginning of the movement, have used pictures of the developing unborn child as well as pictures of aborted babies. More recently, they have used color blow-ups, which are very effective. When we take these pictures to the clinics, more irritation is shown by clinic personnel than when we arrive without pictures. These pictures have a profound effect on the women and their husbands or boyfriends going into the abortion clinic. When they see a photograph of what is about to happen to their child or a photograph of what their child looks like, some stop to talk, and some are even turned back from the abortion. We indicate on the pictures the stage of fetal development that is represented, and the stage of the pregnancy when the child was aborted.

I remember an angry young man who was determined that his girlfriend would have an abortion. He mocked me for trying to show them pictures of what they were about to do. I pointed to the picture of a suction abortion. You could identify the arms, legs, and rib cage of a baby and I said, "This is a picture of your child." He said he didn't want to look at any pictures and he tried to shield his girlfriend from seeing them. He said that he had made up his mind, and that he didn't care about the ''brat''. The picture didn't seem to have any effect on him, and they went into the abortion clinic. I never found out if the girlfriend had an abortion or not, but someday he may remember the picture of the dismembered baby, and it may help prevent him from getting involved in a second abortion.

Where do you get these pictures? Some pro-life publishers offer blow-ups of the abortion pictures. The number of such resource organizations is growing, and we have listed the addresses of some of these at the end of this chapter. You can make your own photographs. We made color photographs from our slides of fetal development and abortion. It was not expensive because we made several dozen copies of each. We had six pictures of fetal development and six of abortion. We trimmed them so that they fit snugly into a man's wallet. If you carry a set everywhere with you, in your wallet or purse, you can be ready if the subject of abortion comes up to supplement your arguments with these photographs. You never know when these ''ten thousand words'' might save some lives.

If you are on a television talk show where they let you show pictures, you can use these photographs. Instruct the station personnel to tape them on a board and have the camera close in on them for a tight shot. They will fill the screen just as nicely as if they were blown up pictures or slides.

Use pictures at your pickets. People can't resist looking at them. Put them in the window if you have an office on ground level. Use them on radio talk shows too. Pull the pictures out and show them to the host. His response may be to describe the pictures to his listeners. From this description you can launch into a description of the method of abortion that caused this baby's death. It's possible to get even a hostile host to comment on the pictures. Never hesitate, while describing abortions on a radio show, to take the pictures out and drop them in front of the host. If he calls them emotional and disgusting, agree with him. Abortion is emotional and disgusting.

Pictures are very effective on leaflets. We printed over one hundred thousand leaflets with the American holocaust pictures on them and handed them out one January 22nd. The pictures and descriptions encouraged a lot of people to join our organization. They were outraged and wanted to do something to fight abortion.

Use pictures on posters. One time we used the ''basket baby'' photograph on a thousand posters and, using a mixture of Elmer's glue and wallpaper paste, put these on lamp posts all over the city. The poster said "Abortion Kills Babies", but the picture was the attention getter.

Pictures can also be used on billboards or pasted on the sides of buildings. There are many ways to use them, but you have to be courageous enough to take some flak. There will always be someone, even within the movement itself, objecting to "sensationalism". They want to stop abortions but are afraid to show people what abortion is. Abortion is an ugly business. Pictures of dead babies are "emotional". They are supposed to be.

One time the board of directors of an organization I belonged to voted not to use the picture of the basket babies. I thought this was a bad decision, so I continued to use it. One of the board members saw the picture at our booth at a health fair at City Hall, rushed to the booth, and tore it down. Everyone standing near thought he was pro-abortion. The nurse tending the booth was amazed to learn that he was pro-life. A few minutes after he tore it down, the mayor of Chicago, Richard J. Daley, visited our booth, and a photograph was taken of him there. It appeared on the front page of the newspaper. Where the basket babies photograph had been, there was a blank space. Thousands of people across the nation saw a picture of the mayor visiting a pro-life booth but without a picture of what abortion is. I'm glad I was not responsible for taking down that picture. I never stopped using it, because it was that picture that brought me into the pro-life movement.

This same rationale—the need to convey the message that abortion is killing real people—is behind the use of signs and slogans which use only a few words to get the larger message across. "Abortion Kills Babies", "Abortion Is Murder", "Stop Abortion", "Choose Life": these slogans can be used on bumper stickers, posters, billboards, letters. They have an important purpose: they make people think. Many people assume that because abortion is legal it must be right and that the Supreme Court could not make a grave mistake. They are wrong, but many people have accepted it.

Our pictures, signs, and slogans remind them that a lot of people don't accept abortion. They think it is murder, and believe it should be stopped. There are people fighting it. They refuse to go along with the status quo, and will express their ideas every way they can.

We frequently get suggestions from pro-lifers for stickers, decals, and buttons. We send these ideas on to the companies that manufacture these items. Almost any good idea can be used on a sticker, decal, tape, or button to spread the message that abortion is the killing of a human being. Never underestimate the value of these devices. Some people think they are corny and ineffectual, but they are wrong. Wearing the Precious Feet lapel pin is the source of many pro-life conversations. Dozens of strangers ask about the Precious Feet. I always carry a pocketful of these pins on trips and hand these out to people who show interest in the one I wear. I have made friends by having the Rose for Life on my lapel.

Symbols, signs, and pictures get through to people like nothing else can. Think of the effect symbols in your own life have on you—the Stars and Stripes, the swastika, the skull and crossbones, a railroad crossing sign, a photograph of your mother, a crucifix.

Don't underestimate the value of pictures, signs, and symbols. When the pro-life victory is finally won, these simple devices will have had a place of honor in helping win that victory.

In discussing visual aids, one can't forget the effigy. This is the figure of a particular individual or sometimes an individual who represents a group, movement, or philosophy. We have found the effigy to be effective if done well because it is so compelling. Use of the effigy always gets media attention.

In Chicago, we have used effigies to represent federal judges who strike down restrictive abortion laws or otherwise take the pro-abortion side in subverting pro-life efforts or advancing the cause of Planned Parenthood and the other pro-abortion groups.

Going against the advice of our lawyers who tell us not to picket federal judges because they might resent it and give us unfavorable judgments, we have picketed half a dozen judges to embarrass them and break the long-standing tradition of judicial immunity. Our pickets of judges and the use of their effigies always draws an enthusiastic crowd.

We make sketches of pro-abortion judges during the court proceedings and make a habit of carrying them in effigy with their crime printed clearly on a yoke around their necks. A photograph of one such judicial effigy appeared on the front page of the *Chicago Tribune*.

You can order pictures from:

HAYES PUBLISHING CO.
  6034 Hamilton Ave.
  Cincinnati, OH 45224

ABBOTSWOOD PRESS
  P.O. Box 1724
  La Jolla, CA 92038

DOCUMENTED PHOTOS
OF THE
ABORTION HOLOCAUST

Autopsies being performed on forty-three of the 17,000 victims.

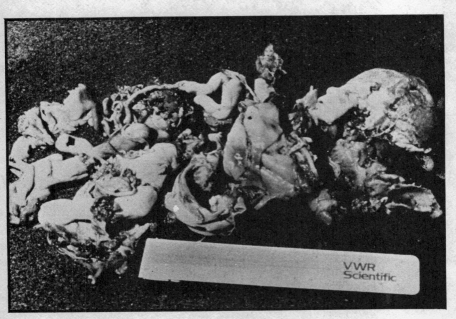

GIRL—25−28 weeks, 1 lb. 15 oz. Salt poison, massive hemorrhaging.

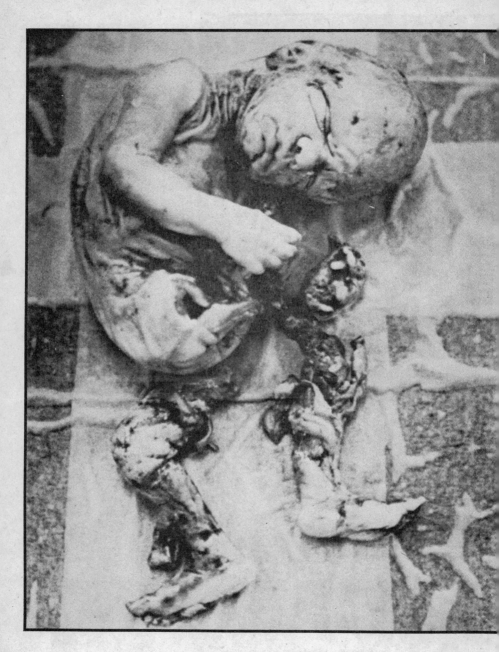

BOY—27−29 weeks, 2 lbs. Death by dismemberment.

BOY—15 oz. Death by total dismemberment.

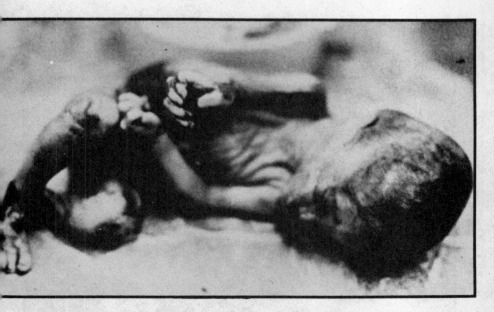

BOY—22–23 weeks, 1 lb. 5 oz. Salt poisoning.

Death by saline poison.

BOY—20−22 weeks, 320 grams weight. Death by total dismemberment.

49 GRAFFITI

Graffiti are drawn or written designs or inscriptions. It doesn't matter where they are, but we think generally of graffiti scrawled on walls, sidewalks, or subway trains. Pro-lifers, like most citizens, are opposed to writing or painting on walls, buildings, or sidewalks. Sloppy graffiti indicate a sloppy, disorganized mind. Orderly people dislike seeing public property vandalized. But graffiti can be used properly, and when they are, they can be effective.

When you do decide to use graffiti, you must use prudence and good taste and maintain a sense of decor. And you have to consider carefully beforehand what you are going to say.

If someone writes on a statue or building, no matter what he says, he is going to make people angry. He is defacing property. He hurts his cause when he does this. We must categorically discourage and object to the use of graffiti on property when damage is caused.

The only objects that are fair game for graffiti are temporary structures, such as construction sites, ad spaces that have not been rented, posts, and poles that already customarily serve this purpose. Even then, you have to consider whether you might be violating somebody's rights. The best location for graffiti is where we already find them, where the abortionists have already written their graffiti.

Graffiti should be neat, orderly, and concise. Some groups use carefully designed stencils—cut-out letters that can be spray-painted onto a variety of surfaces.

All of us have been offended by sloppy, unplanned, unartistic graffiti that give a bad connotation and demean what the person has to say. There are occasions and places where graffiti are workable and effective. But it is best not to put graffiti on abortion clinic walls because, over and above property damage, the message could help people find the abortion clinic they are looking for. If they see a building with "They Kill Babies Here" painted on it, that will telegraph a message to them that they have come to the address they are looking for. That frustrates our efforts to stop abortions. Also, writing on abortion property gives the abortionist ammunition to use against us. They will use the "attack"

191

on them to gain the sympathy of the community and the press. It may also give the police an added reason for making or threatening an arrest.

But graffiti used in a neutral zone can be very effective when the message is direct, straightforward, and in good taste. They should always be neatly done and something you and other pro-lifers don't have to be ashamed of.

In Chicago, we had a number of "graffiti wars" at one construction site. Our signs said "Abortion Is Murder" and "Abortion Kills Babies". Some abortionists came by and rubbed out most of the wording on our signs and added some of their own, making it read "Illegal Abortion Kills Women". The pro-lifers went back and rubbed out "Illegal" and "Women", and added "Babies". It was an interesting battle, as people watched the progressing graffiti war. I don't think a great deal was accomplished by the battle, but it kept a lot of people interested in seeing who was in the ascendancy from day to day, and who got the last word before the fence was torn down.

Although many pro-lifers are not enthusiastic about the use of graffiti, we should recognize that there is a time and place for them. We have cautioned prudence and good taste in using them, and the question to ask is whether their use will help or hinder the cause of the unborn. If you cannot answer with certainty that the grafitti will do more good than harm, do something else. But keep the option available.

50 SET UP A SIMULATED TALK SHOW

Several years ago The National Right to Life Convention presented a television workshop. It was well done. It gave us the impression we were in a real studio and that a television station had come to the convention to get our views. Nothing was done to discourage this notion as we joined panels and talked about the pro-life movement. Then we were invited to view what we had said, and only then did we learn that this was a simulated situation and was not going to air publicly.

While it was only a private workshop with private viewings, it was useful in showing us how we had answered the question, whether we gave all the information we could, and whether we had convinced the audience. Some of the participants were excellent, some were pretty poor, but everyone learned. Several of us decided this would be a good program to adopt and offer at other pro-life gatherings.

All that is needed is a video camera, a television set, an engineer, a platform, and some chairs, along with people who are good-natured enough to take a little criticism. Since that convention, the League has been offering a workshop called "TV and You". People usually respond positively to it. Those requesting the workshop provide a video camera on a tripod and a television set, so that the tape can be played back immediately after it has been made, and the participants can judge it. Somebody who is knowledgeable about video equipment should be on hand. Have a large television screen handy, because you are going to play back the taped interviews afterward so that the whole audience can participate in the workshop. A talk show situation is simulated. Five chairs are used. Four are for the guests and one is in the center for the moderator. A table is placed in front of the moderator. Lots of light is needed for a good picture on the screen. All of the participants should be seated on a slightly raised area or platform. "The studio" can be set up nearly anywhere. At one convention we used a corner of a restaurant.

The host conducts the entire program. One of his first tasks is to pick four people out of the audience to sit with him on the platform. He asks them their names and occupations, and writes these down in their seating order. He introduces each participant and calls each by name throughout the interview. He begins by asking each one a difficult question. After fifteen minutes of interviewing each participant, with care taken to balance the time so that each person gets a chance to respond to at least one question, he dismisses the group and asks them to return to their seats in the audience.

All of this is done before an audience, many of whom are going to be taking part as participants.

Next, the engineer rewinds the tape and shows the entire interview on television. The host stops the tape whenever he comes to a critical point. What he is looking for in these responses is whether those interviewed clarify their position, give enough factual information, whether they presume knowledge that the audience may not have, are able to satisfy the questioner with a direct and strong answer, and give a thorough answer.

We have found, while conducting these workshops, that most people know the basic pro-life answers. They know the sequence of the development of the unborn child and they know all the major methods of abortion. They know the arguments against having an abortion for rape and deformity. They know the danger of abortions to women. But they have a tendency to answer briefly and to answer only the question asked. Often they fail to expand the answer to include additional information. Many forget that when they are on a talk show or in a debate, they need to use all the time they can get. They have to use every opportunity to expand their answers. If the host asks, "When does human life begin?" many will simply just say "at the moment of fertilization" and let it drop.

They should talk about the eighteen medical textbooks submitted to the U.S. Supreme Court in a Missouri case pointing out that these texts make it clear that life begins at the moment of conception. They should talk about the overwhelming evidence given before the Senate sub-committee hearings on abortion, in which seven out of eight doctors present confirmed the fact that life begins at conception. The eighth doctor, an abortionist, said he didn't know when life begins.

They could explain the national and international documents defending the unborn child from the moment of conception, such as the United Nations' Declaration on the Rights of the Child and the American Convention of Human Rights. They might explain the oaths that doctors have traditionally taken confirming their belief that life begins at conception and swearing not to cause an abortion. They should drive their point home so that by the end, there is no question left as to when human life begins.

We have found too often that in these workshops people say yes or no to a question and no more. They should *never* say yes or no in a discussion, but expand on their answer as much as possible, giving overwhelming evidence of their knowledge of the subject and settling the issue in the minds of many of their listeners.

Many have out-of-date information. In these simulated talk show situations it is important to bring up current events—a news item appearing in the paper that day, something dealing with the life issues in Congress recently, or something happening in the movement itself. We quiz them on this new event to find out if they are keeping up to date. A bit of current information can liven up a drab discussion.

In conducting a simulated talk show, you should work closely with the audience. Give first option to criticize the segment just filmed to the people interviewed. They are frequently the best critics of themselves, because often they don't feel satisfied with their presentation. They will usually point out what they could have done better and will accurately point out their shortcomings.

The instructor must be careful during the workshop not to be too easy on the participants or to smooth over their mistakes. He is not there to tell them how good they are, or even to make them feel confident. He is a teacher, prepared to develop them into good pro-life spokesmen. He must be frank about their performances, but he must also be kind and exercise a sense of humor.

In one of these workshops a very talented young man who had his own radio talk show floundered and became embarrassed when he appeared on camera. It was necessary to point out his weaknesses before an audience made up of many who had heard him host his own talk show. He was an excellent host, but he needed improvement as a guest.

The purposes of the simulated talk show are to bring out the weaknesses and strengths of the speakers and to let them learn from each other. It also gives the audience a chance to become part of a talk show situation. Primarily, though, it helps develop speakers for the pro-life cause and helps them get over their first case of stage fright. For many, the simulated program seems like the real thing. They appear before a live audience. They know they are going to be questioned. They are under the lights and under pressure. They experience that first fear that sometimes paralyzes an individual, makes him want the show to be

over, and prompts him to give yes and no answers. By the end of the
workshop, many of the participants are relaxed and enjoying it.

We don't know how many participants eventually get on talk shows
to discuss the pro-life issue, but we do know that their enthusiasm after
such a workshop is often the catalyst some need to accept an invitation
to go public with the pro-life message.

For your next pro-life convention consider a simulated talk show and
give your members an opportunity to learn from this experience. You
will probably find, among other things, that it is a whole lot of fun.

51 USE PRESSURE

The use of pressure can be an effective means of getting what you want. There are two main kinds of pressure. There is overt, obvious pressure, as when a boss tells an employee he will lose his job if he doesn't conform to the rules. That is used frequently to force someone to comply with the will of another. There is also a subtle type of pressure, an indication of certain consequences, such as loss of business from pro-lifers, if changes are not made.

What we are discussing here is the subtle variety of pressure directed not so much against the abortionists as against organizations and individuals supportive of abortion.

The pressure we are discussing here is not a threat. It merely lets people know that you and other pro-lifers will not have dealings with anyone who supports abortion in any way at all. For instance, you can let your doctor know that if he gives abortion referrals or does anything to promote abortion, you will go elsewhere for your medical services and will also tell his patients about his abortion connection. If your druggist dispenses abortifacient drugs or devices, you might let him know that there are other druggists you will go to instead who don't dispense these abortifacients.

We have used this kind of pressure to get ads out of newspapers, circulars, and theater bills. We got an abortion ad out of a theater bill by suggesting that we would ask our friends not to go to any theaters belonging to the chain if ads for an abortion clinic were not dropped. We used persuasion to encourage newspaper employees to pressure the ad department into dropping its abortion ads. These are legitimate means of getting what you want.

Persistent, subtle pressure can be used in nearly any situation where there is a lack of cooperation with the pro-life effort or cooperation with the abortion effort. It may provide just the right amount of leverage needed to effect a change. Even when it does not work, it will cause agitation and uncertainty as to whether the pressure will continue, increase, or be withdrawn.

Pro-lifers have pressured building owners into not renting space to pro-abortion agencies. They have pressured pro-abortionists into dropping efforts to stop pro-life legislation. They have pressured doctors into getting out of the abortion business. They have pressured the administrators of Catholic hospitals to pressure doctors to give up their abortion practices. They let the administrators know that they would picket the hospitals during visiting hours if these doctors remained on staff while engaged in abortion elsewhere.

It may sometimes be necessary to pressure fellow pro-lifers into becoming more involved in the movement. Laying "guilt trips" on less active members by pointing out the achievements of other pro-lifers can revitalize a lethargic group—or it can simply make them hostile. Sometimes it takes finesse to use pressure without causing offense, especially if you are dealing with friends. But if you are careful, it is worth the effort.

With the opposition, you must be careful that pressure will not cause them to become more adamant, to become more entrenched in their resolve. Pressure must include a promise, based on a kind of personal regret. "We really have no choice in this matter. If you insist on supporting abortion, we simply can't continue doing business with you. And we will have to tell our friends about your unfortunate abortion involvement. It's too bad things turned out this way; we're sorry." The approach suggesting a dilemma can be more effective than a frontal attack like: "You are pro-abortion. We're going to boycott you and put you out of business." That can have the opposite of the desired effect by entrenching your opponent in his pro-abortion stand.

I don't recommend the use of threats. Let your adversary know what your intentions are, but without promising that you are going to carry them out. Let them know, for instance, that it is your intention to close their clinic. Say, "We intend to close this clinic" or "We will do everything in our power to close this clinic." But a straightforward threat, "We are going to close this clinic", may not be possible to carry out. It will leave you with an unfulfilled ambition. Your failure may be used against you.

But if you have had a part in closing down some clinics, perhaps the statement, "We are going to close this clinic", simply expresses a determination to repeat what you have already done. They may suspect that if things work for you as they have in the past, you will do just what you say you will, close them down.

Use pressure when and where it seems appropriate and where there is the prospect of its succeeding. Do not make threats, especially any that would suggest you intend to use violence. That would not only backfire, but it could damage the cause of the unborn child. Keep in mind that we want everything we do to work together in a legal, orderly way to close down the abortion industry.

52 STUDY DRUG COMPANY REPORTS

Pro-lifers should receive as much literature as possible from the opposition, even from the so-called neutral agencies such as drug companies that play a role in abortion. You should receive their reports.

When you read them, you will discover that some things they are working on are designed to destroy human subjects. UpJohn Pharmaceutical has been working on prostaglandin F2 alpha and prostaglandin E2 in both suppository and injection form for a number of years, and it was still doing so at the time this book was written. These drugs are used for abortions. Their reports have indicated how successful their experiments are and how well the products are progressing. They want their stockholders and product users to look to them for leadership. They can be very matter-of-fact when talking to their shareholders and customers about the products they produce, but they give a different slant on these developments to the public.

If you go to Kalamazoo, Michigan, to visit the UpJohn Company plant you will get the impression that you are in a church. Everyone is so polite and loving. They don't like abortions at all, they will tell you. They wish nobody ever had to have them. But after all, it is legal, they will say, and since some women are going to have them, UpJohn wants to help make them as safe as possible. Thus, they have developed several different drugs that cause abortion in the second and third trimesters.

They don't really care what the application does to a live, developing baby. It is the woman's decision, it is legal, and they try simply to do what is best for the woman. Descriptions of aborted babies have no perceptible effect on them. There is almost no way to reach them except by promising to do everything in your power, so long as they are involved in the business of killing unborn babies, to hurt their business. As long as UpJohn continues to develop these life-destroying drugs, boycotting all their products is presently the best weapon we have to encourage them to get out of the abortion trade. One pro-life group has printed a list of alternative products to buy instead of UpJohn products. We have printed a copy of this list at the end of this chapter.

You should read the literature from the medical associations, from the obstetricians and gynecologists, and from the scientific community to know what they are doing in the area of genetics and eugenics and what plans they are concocting for a "brave, new world". What is startling in these journals is the cold treatment they give life and death and the utter lack of regard they have for human life. It is a plaything to them, something for them to toy with, a means to an end. It is as though they would like to force the soul out of man and keep only the shell, so that they could have a totally physical being subject to their wishes. They treat people like robots.

If you ever studied the conditions in the Third Reich you found that the German companies that supplied killing materials were also matter-of-fact about it. They even advertised!

Killing is a business today in America, thanks to the U.S. Supreme Court. Drug company literature is typical promotional literature. People need to realize this, even though the facts may shock them. UpJohn's advertisements of its lethal prostaglandins are much like the advertisements for a new vitamin. They sound that innocent.

If you are not getting the drug company reports you are missing not only valuable but revealing information.

Here are the addresses of some drug companies and related organizations:

OB.-GYN. NEWS
 12230 Wilkins Ave.
 Rockville, MD 20852

THE JOURNAL OF THE AMERICAN
MEDICAL ASSOC.
American Medical Assoc.
Circulation and Fulfillment Div.
 535 N. Dearborn St.
 Chicago, IL 60610

AMERICAN MEDICAL NEWS
 535 N. Dearborn St.
 Chicago, IL 60610

ABBOTT LABS
 Abbott Park
 North Chicago, IL 60064

MILES PHARMACEUTICALS DIV.
 Miles Laboratories, Inc.
 400 Morgan Ln.
 West Haven, CT 06516

PARKE-DAVIS DIV.
Warner-Lambert Co.
 201 Tabor Rd.
 Morris Plains, NJ 07950

PFIZER LABORATORIES
 235 East 42nd St.
 New York, NY 10017

ROCHE PRODUCTS, INC.
 Manati, Puerto Rico 00701

SCHERING CORP.
 P.O. Box 280
 Maplewood, NJ 07040

ELI LILLY & CO.
  307 E. McCarty St.
  Indianapolis, IN 46285

MEAD JOHNSON & CO.
  2404 Pennsylvania St.
  Evansville, IN 47721

MERCK, SHARP, & DOHM
  P.O. Box 2000
  Rahway, NJ 07065

G. D. SEARLE & CO.
  4711 Golf Rd.
  Skokie, IL 60076

SYNTEX LABORATORIES, INC.
  3401 Hillview Ave.
  Palo Alto, CA 94304

THE UPJOHN CO.
  7171 Portage Rd.
  Kalamazoo, MI 49001

UpJohn is manufacturing various prostaglandins for second trimester abortions. There is also evidence that these compounds have been employed in first trimester abortions and the possibility exists for self-administered abortions in the home.

Many drug companies have products comparable to UpJohn's. *Please do not support a company whose profits support the destruction of innocent lives.*

CARRYING OUT A BOYCOTT WITH A WALLET CARD

In an effort to persuade the UpJohn company to discontinue its manufacture and research on the abortifacient drug, Prostaglandin for second trimester abortions, one pro-life group issued this wallet card suggesting alternative products that could be purchased instead of UpJohn products.

UPJOHN & ABORTION

UPJOHN is manufacturing various prostaglandins for second trimester abortions. There is also evidence where these compounds have been employed in first trimester abortions and the possibility exists for self-administered abortions in the home.

Many drug companies have comparable products. **PLEASE DO NOT SUPPORT A COMPANY WHOSE PROFITS SUPPORT THE DESTRUCTION OF INNOCENT LIVES.** The list provided will serve as a guide to alternate products. Consult with your physician or pharmacist for further information.

Keep this in your wallet for reference.

KRTL 10/84

UPJOHN PRODUCTS	OTHER PRODUCTS
Adeflor	VidaylinF/PolyViFlor
Adeflor M	Stuartnatal/Pramet FA
Cleocin	other antibiotic
Cleocin Topical	EryDerm
Cheracol	Robitussin/Triaminic
E-Mycin	EES/EryTab
Halcion	Dalmane/Restoril
Kaopectate	Donnagel
Lincocin	other antibiotic
Loniten	other blood pressure med.
Micronase	Diabeta
Motrin	Rufen
Mycitracin	Neosporin
Nuprin	Advil
Orinase	generic available
Panmycin	Achromycin/Tetracycline
Provera	Aygestin
Pyroxate	other cold remedies
Sig Tab	Optilets M 500
Tolinase	generic available
Unicaps	Dayalets/One A Day
Unicap M	Optilets M 500
Unicap T	Optilets 500
Unicap Chewable	Vidaylin Chewable
Xanax	Tranxene/Valium

Available in quantity from Kalamazoo Right to Life, Inc., 609 So. Burdick, Suite 203, Kalamazoo, MI 49007, (616) 345−7164.

53 USE PRIVATE DETECTIVES

Pro-lifers need to employ many different means and strategies in order to save lives. There may come a time in your pro-life work when you need to hire a private detective to get information you cannot secure in any other way.

A classic case in which a pro-life group hired a private detective was in an effort by pro-lifers to find a young black girl and her mother in order to try to talk them out of an abortion. The case came out of Madison, Wisconsin, where a pro-abortionist went to the newspapers with a story about an eleven-year-old girl from Chicago who was going to have an abortion at Madison General Hospital. She needed financial help to pay for the abortion. The abortionist thought a sympathetic story about the girl's plight would bring in money—about $1500 was needed—to help pay her hospital costs.

We learned about the planned abortion and called the hospital in Madison to say we would come up and picket if they performed the abortion. Later, we discovered that the girl was not going to have the abortion in Madison. We presumed she was going to have it in Chicago, where she had first scheduled it. We tried to find out who she was, so we could talk her out of the abortion and get her help.

We could not discover her identity so we contacted the abortionist who had released the story. She wouldn't talk. We could not find out through the newspaper or the Madison hospital either. Since we were running out of time, we contacted an attorney who employs private detectives in his practice, and asked him for the name of a detective. I called the man he recommended.

The detective said he believed he could find the girl within twenty-four hours. He wanted a two hundred dollar retainer and sixty dollars an hour. The fee sounded high, but I thought it was worth it. He thought it would take eight working hours and cost six hundred dollars, a small price for saving a human life. It actually took him four days to locate the girl, but he gave us a break on the cost.

The detective became personally involved in what we were doing. He seemed to admire our determination to search out a young woman, who was a stranger to us, to keep her from having an abortion.

He told us later that his amazement at our interest in the girl was reflected by the mother when she found out that we had gone to all this trouble to find her. She was impressed, but also angry. But it was an education for all of us—an education we could not have gotten any other way.

We have had other occasions when we have wanted to use a private detective, occasions when we have been deterred by the cost but not the morality of it. We see nothing wrong in getting outside help to save a baby's life and a young woman's dignity. No one would cry "invasion of privacy" if we hired a detective to find someone to give her an inheritance. The secular press would praise that action. But if we try to save a life, we are violators of privacy and commit a detestable crime.

There will probably be other times when we will call upon the services of private investigators, since they have access to documents and methods of investigation that we don't have. They also have the time, the expertise, and the contacts we lack to do the job adequately.

When we are serious about the work we do, we are open to the use of experts in the investigation field to get us the information we need to save lives.

For more on the story of the detective and the young pregnant girl, read the account in Chapter 11 on the use of the media. We never found out what happened to the girl and her baby. After we had found her and talked several times to her mother, we decided that we had done all that was possible to prevent the abortion.

During our last discussion with her mother we were assured that the young woman had *not* had an abortion. But the mother also told us that her daughter was not pregnant. Had she ever been? Had she miscarried? We will never know.

54 EXPOSE THE ABORTIONISTS' LIES

A favorite challenge of pro-life activists is to expose the abortionists' lies in discussions and debates. They lie about the victim they abort. A human life is present in the womb and they know it. From talking with them and attending their conventions, we know that they know that life begins at the beginning and that abortion takes a human life. They have found it useless to deny science, biology, common sense, experience, history, and law in order to deceive the public about the humanity of the unborn child, so they admit that this is human life. But they won't admit that it is valuable human life.

They lie about the safety of abortion. They manufacture arguments to try to prove that abortion is safer than childbirth. They know this is not true. When they argue that abortion is safer than childbirth, they are talking about first trimester abortions. They compare three months during which a healthy young woman gets an abortion with a one-year period in which women of all ages and physical condition may suffer injury or death. (''Childbirth'' includes also the three month period after birth.) They compare a three month period in which a normally healthy, young woman has an abortion with a twelve month period for a woman who may be sick, may have had difficult deliveries, or may die from a number of causes, including abortion. They ignore the fact that women who are crippled by abortion don't go back to the abortion clinic to report it. They go to their family doctor, to a hospital, or to the morgue. If they die of infection or internal hemorrhaging, this is not attributed to the abortion on the death certificate. The cause of death will be listed as peritonitis or internal hemorrhaging, rather than abortion.

They lie about the Catholic Church's position on abortion, saying that the Church condemned abortion only in the last century and that before 1866 it was allowed. Abortion was never allowed by the Catholic Church. It was always considered a serious sin. It was condemned in the *Didache*, a second-century Church document, and has always been cause for automatic excommunication in the Church's canon law. Even though the Church has never condoned abortion, abortionists cite a few theologians who speculated about when insoulment takes place, and they claim that such speculation represents the teaching of the Catholic Church. But the teaching authority of the Church is *not* and *never has been* vested in theologians. They serve in an advisory capacity only, and they are often wrong. This is proved by a case concerning a pro-abortion ad placed in the *New York Times* by Catholic theologians and religious. The ad claimed there is a "diversity of teaching" about abortion in the Catholic Church. But the authentic teaching authority of the Church said this was not true, and these theologians and religious risked expulsion from their orders unless they retracted their statements.

Abortionists lie about the number of people who support abortion. They cite polls that ask people if they would allow abortion in extreme cases, such as when the mother's life is in danger, then they use the results to claim that ninety percent of Americans favor abortion on demand. A poll published in *Newsweek* in January 1985, however, showed a clear majority of Americans (fifty-five percent to thirty-three percent) wished to have laws prohibiting abortion except in cases of rape, incest, and pregnancies that actually threaten the mother's life. Nevertheless, abortionists insist that nearly everyone supports abortion, and that Americans want it to remain legal.

We must use sound, convincing evidence to expose their lies. We need up-to-date statistics, the results of accurate polls, and solid facts so that we can contradict the abortionists' shallow arguments.

For instance, when you are on a talk show with an abortionist and someone calls in to ask when human life begins, you should have your convincing argument ready. You might say: "When we attend the abortionists' meetings, we find from their talks that they know perfectly well that they are aborting a human being. During their lectures we have to keep reminding ourselves that we are at an abortion meeting and not a pro-life gathering, because they use so many of the same terms we do in speaking of the unborn child. They know that starting at fertilization a new, unique individual human being exists and that abortion stops that life."

Tell your audience that you have talked with dozens of abortionists about this matter and that you have yet to meet one who does *not* know that in an abortion he destroys a human life. You might relate some of your discussions with doctors and how their experiences with abortion have convinced them of the humanity of the unborn, and how several doctors have admitted that they know when they perform an abortion they are "killing a fellow human being". Such personal experiences from the enemy are valuable in converting your listeners to pro-life.

Quote some abortionists or former abortionists like Dr. Bernard Nathanson, Magda Denes, and others who have written on abortion and who have said that the term they hear and sometimes use in describing abortion is "murder" or "killing". Women admit that they have murdered their baby, and doctors know that during an abortion someone is always "killed".

The only reason doctors perform abortions is that they are profitable. They may claim that they do them out of a concern for women, and if you bring up the fact that they become rich by doing abortions you will stir up a hornet's nest. But you will be accurate. Remind your listeners that many abortionists perform abortions while not using the proper medication, and that many clinics do not do proper pathology reports.

Use all the information you have to make the abortionists look bad, to expose them as charlatans in the business of killing. You don't have to talk about a particular doctor, and generally should not, but you may refer to abortionists in general. It is easy to find abortionists who have been responsible for the deaths of women through botched abortions. And it is easy to find abortionists who run unsanitary, disorganized clinics. When abortion proponents say that abortion has to be legal so that it will be safe, you can point out that it is often less safe when it is legal than it was when it was illegal. Since abortionists do not have to worry about being exposed to the law, they can be less careful.

Throughout the abortion debate the attitude to maintain is one of calm, matter-of-fact self-confidence; the pro-life debater knows he is not going to be rattled and that he is not going to be asked a question he can't answer. He is not going to be put on the spot because he has the answers; he has the advantage of having truth, logic, and reason on his side. The abortionists are the ones who should be worried and concerned that they are going to come off looking bad. The pro-lifer will look good because, to reasonable people, he is defending human life. The abortionists are defending the killing of innocent children, an action impossible to defend. They base their arguments on the weaknesses and perversions of human nature. Pro-lifers use the highest human aspirations and an appeal to absolute values.

Pro-lifers should never be afraid to debate the abortionists. We have everything going for us, if we do our homework and use the facts. Exposing the abortionists' lies is an important part of our work. We should take every opportunity to do it. It is really rather fun.

55 HOW TO RATTLE YOUR OPPONENT

As mentioned earlier, we expose the abortionists by pointing out the exaggerations, lies, and weakness of their arguments. The effect of this exposure is to rattle them and to make them angry. It forces them to become defensive. It is important to put them on the defensive and to make them try to excuse what they are doing by arguing that abortion is a "necessary evil". Frequently, the best way to prove your own point, that abortion is a dangerous, dirty business, is to use the abortionists' own statements.

If you use only pro-life statements and pro-life arguments and quote only pro-life authorities, the abortionists will counter that you are expressing a biased opinion. But if you quote their own doctors, their own authorities, even some former abortionists who are now on our side, your opponent will have a more difficult time countering you. Dr. Bernard Nathanson, author of *Aborting America* and *The Abortion Papers* is a convert to pro-life and very quotable. Still pro-abortion, Magda Denes wrote a graphic portrait of abortion, *In Necessity and Sorrow: Life and Death in an Abortion Hospital*.

Using the abortionists' statements to defend the pro-life position is the best defense at our disposal. That is why it is important to read carefully everything we can get our hands on that the abortionists have written. They often make bold and damning statements. They are their own worst enemies. When they talk among themselves, they frequently express their problems and uncertainty, a variety of personal concerns, and their ambivalence about doing abortions. That is why it is important to attend their meetings and read their literature. You can get your best arguments against abortion from the abortionists. Using their own statements against them rattles them and is the best method we have of making them look bad.

Once, on a radio program in Chicago, I was debating a Catholic feminist who was saying that abortion has little adverse effect on women and that women do not have to accept burdens they feel are difficult to cope with. She made what she thought was a strong argument for abortion. To her, pregnancy was often only an unwanted, unplanned condition that was better gotten rid of.

At one point, her arguments were so firmly based on personal convenience and selfishness that I asked why these conditions couldn't apply also to an already born, but inconvenient, child or an elderly person who required much care. She fell into the trap. She said that nobody should have to accept an unwanted burden that interfered with personal happiness and a chosen life style.

I don't believe she intended to make so sweeping a statement, and she tried to qualify her answer so that it wouldn't sound so heartless. But I pursued the "logic" of her abortion argument and it had to include eliminating the handicapped and the incapacitated elderly. Her argument on eliminating the elderly encouraged our previously lackluster host to challenge her. She became angry, turned away from the host and out of range of the microphone. It was bizarre, facing an opponent who was so angry that she refused to talk.

Of course, it was a field day for pro-life. I had the remainder of the program to myself. She did turn back to the microphone for a closing comment, but she had lost a good portion of her air time.

One listener, who tuned in the program on his way to the airport, told me that he nearly missed his flight, trying to stay with the program as long as he could to find out what happened to the angry pro-abortion lady. He wondered if she had left the studio. In a sense she had.

56 KEEP THE ABORTIONISTS OUT OF YOUR COMMUNITY

Keeping the abortionists out of your community is not an easy task anywhere, and it is especially difficult if you live in a big city like Chicago, with more than two dozen abortion clinics, a dozen hospitals that do abortions, and many doctors' offices where abortions are performed every day. Yet in some areas of the country there are towns where nobody does abortions or even makes referrals and where doctors are committed to healing.

But even in these communities, the word may go out that someone is moving in to set up an abortion clinic or that the doctors at the local hospital want to start performing abortions there. Countering such developments requires a massive educational program on the part of local pro-lifers. If the effort to educate the community has not already begun, *you* will have to begin it so that there will be an anti-abortion atmosphere in that locale.

If there had been such a hostile attitude toward abortion throughout the country at the time *Roe v. Wade* was being considered by the Supreme Court, perhaps abortion never would have been legalized. But so many people were uneducated about abortion that appeals from the so-called women's rights groups, and a prevailing attitude that democracy requires us to allow others to do things we wouldn't do ourselves, won the day for the abortionists.

At the local level you must develop an educational program that concentrates on the unborn child as an unseen victim. It is essential that this victim becomes a real person in the mind of the community. The more the unborn is acknowledged, the less tolerant the community will be of taking that person's life.

It is a great tragedy that thousands of us were not working on such an educational project years ago. If we had taken our cue back in the 1960s when the abortionists began efforts to legalize abortion on the state level and when so-called "clergy consultation services" organized to send women out of the country for "therapeutic" abortions, how much better off we would be today. If we had used the April 1965 article in *Life* magazine, the story complete with Nillson's photography of the

211

humanity of the unborn child, we would have been ahead of the enemy. *Life* started out this article by saying that human life does not begin at birth but nine months prior, at fertilization. If we had made copies of that article and spread it far and wide, we could have done what they did in Ireland and that is attach an amendment to the constitution forbidding abortion.

But we did not do that, or anything close to it. While the abortionists were working to push the cause for legal abortion, we were not pushing our cause to protect the unborn child or even to get his humanity recognized. As a consequence of our negligence, abortion is now common. But in areas where it is not fully established, we can still keep it out with education. It is much easier to keep abortion out of a community than it is to try to get it out after it is established there. If you learn that an abortion clinic is coming into your community, you are obliged to try to keep it out.

One of the most effective projects you can undertake to keep abortion out is to try to get the pastors of every church in your area to give sermons against abortion. Try to get permission to distribute literature outside the churches, to put items in the church bulletins, even convince pastors to allow you to present talks or slide-shows at their churches.

The abortionists complain that pro-life has a natural constituency: the believing communities of Christians who are strong in faith and can be a powerful force for fighting abortion. The abortionists do not have this source of strength. No truly God-fearing Christian is "pro-abortion". If we had every Christian church in the community fighting abortion, the fight would spill over to non-churchgoers who often look to the church for leadership in moral matters. If, through the churches, we established in the community a basic respect for life, we would be miles ahead in the fight against legal abortion.

Another pro-life project is to make it clear to real estate agencies in your community that if an abortion clinic moves into one of their buildings, they are going to have problems. They will lose old tenants and be unable to attract new ones. Their building will be picketed because of the abortion clinic it houses. On a regular basis there will be people outside their building on the sidewalks, trying to keep patients from going into the abortion clinic. This picketing will interfere with other businesses in the building.

There are many things that can be done in the community to create a hostile attitude toward abortion and abortion providers. You should use all of them: ads in the local newspaper, radio talk shows, leaflets at the high schools. Your effort to keep abortion providers out should be a total effort.

You must also reach your community leaders and your local politicians. Urge passage of local zoning ordinances prohibiting such facilities within your community's boundaries. Let those holding office or running for office know that they are being watched, to see how they respond to voters' requests for help in keeping the abortionists out. Stage rallies and demonstrations to create public awareness of what will happen if an abortion clinic is established in the community. Public officials are sensitive to the voters' wishes, especially in smaller communities. They will be more willing to come out against a clinic before it is approved if they see a large, vocal community organization active in protesting against it.

Ask your pastors and other church leaders to call on the mayor or the village board members or town council to find out where they stand on the issue and to let them know that your church will not tolerate an abortion clinic in the community. Back up these private meetings with mass attendance at city council meetings. Your chances of success in your fight against abortion are greater before a clinic is established in your community than after it is entrenched. Take advantage of the fact that a clinic hasn't been set up there yet. The rest of us wish we still had the opportunity to keep the abortionists out.

57 CONDUCT A BLITZ

The blitz is a brief visit to an abortion clinic or other anti-life office or establishment. It is a most useful pro-life activity. It is done quickly.

From four to ten pro-lifers enter the abortion clinic waiting room as a group, introduce themselves, and talk to the people who are sitting around. They take a little time simply to make their presence known, to feel at ease, and to get the feel of the place. Then they place pro-life literature in the various magazines that are lying about and pick up copies of the material the clinic has available, and replace it with pro-life literature. They talk to the young women sitting there.

When blitzing an abortion clinic, pro-lifers strike up conversations with the women waiting for abortions, discuss their decision, and explain why pro-lifers are interested in them. They ask if they can help them or give them information. Some of the blitzers will try to dissuade the women from going through with their abortions and will try to talk them out of accepting dangerous information.

While the blitz is taking place, some people will be upset. Those in charge of the clinic immediately identify the pro-lifers as invaders. They will call the director, order the blitzers to leave, and call the police.

The pro-lifers then tell the clinic personnel what they are doing there—trying to stop the killing of innocent children. The pro-lifers ask the abortionists questions about the work they do.

The pro-life attitude should be one of peaceful concern: for the people who run the clinic, for the people who perform the abortions and give misinformation, for the victims of anti-life propaganda, for the women seeking abortions, and above all, for the babies who are about to be killed. The blitzers, during the brief time they are in the facility, are there to help.

They stay as long as they can, talking to people and looking through the literature, until it is time for the police to arrive. If they wish, they may wait until the police enter the clinic or office and then take orders from them. And they should make it clear to the people who run the facility that they do not take orders from those who kill unborn children or give advice and counsel that corrupts individuals and ruins lives. The group should let the abortionists know that they cannot intimidate them or force them to leave before they are ready.

After the police arrive the blitzers stay and talk to them and explain what they are doing in the clinic. When the police order them to leave, the blitzers may do so in an orderly manner, while making it clear that they will return, because they believe it is important to try to prevent people from being exploited by the abortionists.

If the police tell them not to blitz again, the pro-life leader will remind the police that they have a right to visit abortion facilities to express their views. The police may advise the blitzers that when the clinic personnel order them to leave, they are obliged to do so. The blitzers should tell them that they prefer to wait until they are given orders by the police.

If the blitz has the effect they want and they wish to avoid a confrontation with the police, the pro-lifers may simply walk out and invite everyone in the clinic to come with them. They will tell the clients that they don't have to go through with an abortion, and that they can get real help from the pro-lifers.

If an abortion provider approaches in a hostile manner, the pro-lifers warn him that if he touches them or if he continues to close in, they will file charges of assault, or assault and battery. The pro-lifers do not touch anyone.

Those carrying out a blitz should not have to submit to any physical violence, nor will they cause any violence. Care should be taken not to damage anything during the blitz. It is proper to take free literature available to visitors, but not to damage property—even publications or notices on the bulletin board.

After the confrontation with the abortionist, they walk out and head for another abortion facility. In this way, a small group of pro-life activists can carry out a series of blitzes in a single morning.

Blitzes can strengthen the local pro-life effort. In a community where pro-lifers have never been inside an abortion clinic, the blitz can give them knowledge, encouragement, strength, and confidence.

I have observed people during a blitz becoming comfortable in a foreign atmosphere. Seeing the inside of an abortion clinic, talking to counselors, and getting a feel for the arrangement of the clinic give the group renewed determination for future activities. Since many blitzes can be carried out in sequence, the group experiences a string of victories in a short time. In Chicago, we carried out eleven blitzes by a single group one morning.

There need be no arrests, as a group goes from one establishment to another, blitzing, educating, showing concern for the situation these unfortunate women are in, and saving lives.

Blitzes, properly planned and carried out calmly, are one of the most powerful tools pro-lifers have for saving lives, educating the public, and demoralizing the enemy.

58 THE BULLHORN

The bullhorn is a useful pro-life tool. There is something awesome about the magnified voice. It has a chilling effect on people. If you are driving along the street or highway and hear an amplified voice say, "Pull over!" you know that somebody means business. The police use loudspeakers on their squad cars for traffic and crowd control. They are used at major sporting events. The magnified voice helps keep order. Even when the Supreme Court police told us we could not use a bullhorn at our picket of the Court in 1983, they allowed us to use it to control the crowd.

An adequate bullhorn is the little gray model from Radio Shack. It uses eight size AA batteries, has good volume, and a volume control dial. It can be carried in a briefcase. It is useful to have three of them. When you get to a demonstration, give two bullhorns to the marshals, putting them at each end of the line of march and use a bullhorn yourself to conduct the march. It is effective for leading the group in chants and songs and for announcing the march program.

Every pro-life activist should have a bullhorn. Even though you may have only a small group picketing, if you use a bullhorn, everyone in the area will know you are present and that your group is serious about what it is doing. When you talk to your group with a bullhorn you keep their attention. Across the country, pro-life activists are using bullhorns for all of their public activities. Just a few pro-lifers armed with bullhorns have been able to counter successfully much larger pro-abortion gatherings.

The activist must be familiar with the city ordinances dealing with the use of amplification devices. There are generally no laws against use of a bullhorn in a commercial area during daylight hours. You may run into trouble at night or in residential areas during daytime hours. As a rule, when in doubt, simply use the bullhorn and find out what the authorities say about it. If you are told by the police that you cannot use it, ask to see the ordinance. We were told in one district that we could not use a bullhorn so we went to the police station with the complaining officer to check out the ordinance. We found that there was no ordinance against using it. So we returned and continued using it with police approval.

In some cases, we have been told that if we use the bullhorn we will be arrested. In these rare cases we have put it aside and used it as a symbol. At a picket of an abortion mill in Norfolk, Virginia, when the police told us we could not use a bullhorn, we placed it on a mock grave site we had constructed. Photographs of the picket used in the newspapers showed the grave site with the bullhorn sitting there, indicating that our freedom of speech had been aborted. It was symbolic of our being prohibited from speaking out. Abortion clinics are allowed to kill children for profit, yet we were not allowed to give directions, lead the protestors in prayer, or tell the people passing by why we were picketing.

In Fargo, North Dakota, we were ordered not to use the bullhorn, and we asked to see the ordinance. The officer drove us to the police station and showed us several pages of regulations, but he did not fully convince us that a hand-held bullhorn was illegal. When we continued to use it, an arrest was made and the bullhorn was confiscated. It took six weeks to get it back.

The bullhorn has other uses besides picketing. We have used it in crowds to find people. Once we saw a well-known pro-life journalist in Washington, D.C. walking at a rapid pace two blocks ahead of our group. We could not catch up with him, so we employed the bullhorn. "Paul Fisher", I called. Paul did a doubletake, and waited for us to catch up with him. He took us to lunch in the Senate dining room and we gave him a story.

59 THE EVIDENCE (BRAG BOOK)

If your pro-life group is directly involved in counseling women out of abortion at the clinic door or if you participate in counseling at one of the four thousand crisis pregnancy centers in the United States, you probably have already begun to accumulate a collection of photographs of the babies you have saved from abortion.

In the course of follow-up contacts with the young women you have dissuaded from abortion, you will develop a keen interest in the pregnancy, and as the time of delivery gets closer, you will offer help and encouragement. Along with this involvement there often develops a sense of "parenting" the child you helped save from abortion. There is no greater reward for the pro-life counselor than to see the object of that concern safely brought to term. Often the parents will give the counselor a photograph of the baby. There are thousands of such photographs being carried in wallets and purses of pro-lifers all over America.

It is an excellent testimonial to the effectiveness of pro-life street counseling to gather a collection of these photographs into an album and make it available to the public when the opportunity arises.

When ABC-TV "News Nightline" visited the Pro-Life Action League offices to tape a program on abortion, the League called in eight sidewalk counselors who work in front of clinics in Chicago. Besides discussing their work at the abortion clinics (very little of which was used on the program) the counselors presented a photograph album filled with pictures of children they had saved from abortion. The cameraman filmed the book page by page as Marian Masella described its contents and described how the children pictured in the album had been rescued.

This book was bold testimony to the effectiveness of the pro-life street counselors' work. Dozens of bright faces—babies in their mothers' arms or propped up on pillows—looking out at a jaded press. We had hoped they would be shown to the often ignorant, callous public, but these pictures never made the "Nightline" program. Pictures of damaged abortion clinics were shown, with broad hints of pro-life violence. But the work pro-lifers do in saving the lives of thousands of children was ignored, just as the violence to human life that goes on inside the abortion clinics was virtually ignored.

But occasions may arise when a Brag Book will be used. We advise that such an album of survivors be maintained by every activist pro-life group. Ask all your counselors to get two pictures of the babies they have saved from abortion. One of these could be donated for the album. It is inconvenient to gather them for the album and then to have to return them. Provide a brief description with each photograph, giving the date the mother was talked out of abortion, the clinic, the circumstances, the date of the baby's birth, and whether the parents kept the child or put it up for adoption. The information is, of course, kept confidential.

A page of these pictures can be used as a visual for a fund-raising project in which you point out to prospective supporters that this is the result of your efforts, and this is the kind of program they will be supporting with their contributions.

It may also be used as a handout at churches and schools in a bid to recruit street counselors. Such a flyer could be effective as a handout to women going into the abortion clinic, though generally more hard-hitting tactics are better used at this late stage. (See Chapter 1, "Sidewalk Counseling".)

Whenever you use these pictures publicly, you should get written permission for their use from both parents or from the mother if there is only one known parent.

60 GET INFORMATION FROM LICENSE PLATES

Every car is required to have license plates and there is information on them that can be useful to pro-lifers. If you see someone drive up to an abortion clinic and park in a space that says, ''Reserved'', it's possible that the owner of the car is on the staff or is the doctor who does the abortions.

You can use license plate numbers to track down a lot of information. All you need to do is call the license bureau or get someone to call for you, perhaps a friendly police officer or a lawyer, and let them know that you need information from the license number. You can get the name and the address of the owner of the vehicle. In some states it will cost a dollar or two to get this information.

The best arrangement is to have a friend in the traffic division or in the Secretary of State's office. Ordinarily, if you call up the license bureau with a license number and ask for the name and address of the owner, you will get a runaround and may have a hard time getting it. But if you know someone in the Secretary of State's office who has a legitimate reason for getting the information, you can contact that person. With a little effort, you will always be able to find someone who will get you the name and address of a vehicle owner.

You may find out that the vehicle is not registered to the person who was driving it, but you may still learn some interesting facts. We discovered that a person entering the clinic was driving a car belonging to the owner of the building that housed the clinic. Sometimes the owner of the car will be associated with clinic personnel, but will be someone you had not suspected was part of the operation. There is a lot of information to be gleaned from a license plate, and there is nothing illegal about finding out who the car belongs to. If someone hit your car and drove off and you managed to get his license number, you would be able to find out who he is and where he lives. It is a useful and effective way of finding out who people are. You want to know who the doctor and the clinic staff are so that you can send them letters and picket their homes. (See Chapter 37, ''Picket the Abortionists' Homes''.)

It can also be useful to check license plates simply to find out where the clinic's clients are coming from. Are most of them from out of town or even out of state? Much useful information can be obtained through license plate numbers, and we strongly urge pro-lifers to become proficient in getting information in this way.

61 INSERT MATERIAL IN NEWSPAPERS AND MAGAZINES

When we speak here of inserting pro-life material into newspapers and magazines we do not mean buying advertising space. Chapter 8 is all about that. What we are talking about here is the insertion of pre-printed material into magazines and newspapers that will then be picked up and read by people who can benefit from the information.

When we go into an abortion clinic to blitz, we always take literature with us. Lying around on the tables and in racks are various magazines the women and their boyfriends leaf through as people do in any doctor's office. We insert our literature in these. We quickly open the magazine to a center page and insert a flyer such as ''Life or Death'' or some other material that tells about the dangers of abortion or the development of the unborn child. The more professional this material appears, the more it is going to seem a part of the publication they are reading. If you have a four-color enamel insert of a single sheet you can slip it into the magazine and the reader will turn to it like a page of the magazine, believing at first that it is a part of the magazine. This won't cause as much of a stir as if it is a sloppily printed piece that is obviously a planted insert.

This method of spreading the pro-life message is effective to use in hairdressers', barbers', doctors', and dentists' offices. If you have a few extra minutes while waiting in these offices, insert literature in magazines or newspapers there. It takes only a moment, and it can be done unobtrusively. While you are leafing through a magazine, simply slide a page into it. People will come across it later and may read it. Get into the habit of carrying inserts with you so that you will have them ready when you need them.

Here is another idea some have used: when you buy the newspaper from a dispenser you open the door by depositing coins. While the door is open, you can slip inserts into all the newspapers in the dispenser. Open each paper halfway and slip your insert in between the pages. If it is professional material, people will get the impression that it is an advertisement. It takes a pocketful of change to get the machines open, but once open you have access to a number of newspapers for making insertions. People buying the newspaper will be getting more fact and more news for their money.

Use your imagination in getting your pro-life literature out to the public. Don't hesitate to accept an offer to have your literature sent out in another organization's mailing. Pro-lifers frequently contact one another when they have special projects to promote. Your literature can be sent out with pro-life newspapers, magazines, and book lists.

But you need not be dependent just on pro-lifers to disperse your literature. If you have a friend who does mass mailings, ask if he would be willing to insert some of your information in a package on general issues. Wherever you can get the pro-life message out, do it. In this book we have chapters on billboards, leafleting, and a number of other methods of dispensing information on the pro-life issue to an uninformed public. Use these devices, too.

We have to resort to using methods that may seem unusual and bizarre because the abortion story is not getting out to the public through the electronic and print media in an honest, unbiased way, because the media are for the most part prejudiced against the unborn and favor abortion. The late Francis A. Schaeffer was right on target when he said in a 1982 interview with the *Chicago Tribune*, "There has been a fundamental shift in this country, one in which Bible-believing Christians face a hidden censorship in the media." Often that censorship isn't even hidden. So pro-lifers must use their wits in devising a variety of means and methods to get the truth of abortion out to the public through the media.

62 USE SOUND EFFECTS (WHISTLES, HORNS, MUSIC) AT THE ABORTIONISTS' RALLIES

When you are conducting a counter-demonstration against the abortionists, it is helpful to have a variety of sound effects in your possession that may be employed while they are giving their talks or singing their pro-abortion songs.

Once, we attended an abortion rally in the Daley Center in Chicago, where the abortionists had scheduled several singers and speakers. They drew a crowd of about one hundred. We did not have that many people. We had heard about the rally on the radio shortly before it was to start. But we had bought a gross of whistles. They were little Adean pipes and each played eight notes. With our twelve people, we gathered around the periphery of the abortion rally.

It was a Saturday afternoon and there were many children and young people out sightseeing, so we told a number of them that, if they would stand by and blow the whistles with us on cue, they could keep the whistles. All they had to do was stay a while and blow the whistles when we asked them to. We attracted about thirty or forty teenagers and children. Most of them didn't understand what the rally was about, but they wanted the whistles. You could actually play melodies on them. They made a shrill, piercing sound.

As the members of the abortion crowd started their talks, we told the young people to start blowing their whistles.

They made a shrill, disorganized sound with many different pitches. We also had two young women with guitars. When the abortionists shortened their talks because of our whistle-blowing, they called on their entertainers to get the abortion crowd singing. As soon as they started singing, our guitarists started playing a fast song with with a beat that threw them off. The abortionists quit playing the dirge and started a peppy jazz-type number. Our guitarists started playing a slow ballad. We began singing. As a result of these actions, the abortionists abbreviated their program.

No media had come to cover their rally, so they broke up early and began to leave. As they were leaving we noticed a television van pull up across the street. Carrying the few signs we had brought with us, we cut across the plaza to the van. The TV crew saw us with our large banners professing the right to life of unborn children. They took pictures of our group. The reporter said they had been told there was an abortion rally. We told them that the group had disbanded, but we would be happy to do an interview. We stole the only coverage the abortionists would have gotten and were able to get our message to the public. Our sound effects had worked.

Other sound effects you can use to advantage are tape recordings. Some groups have used recordings of a baby crying, the whir of a suction machine, the baby's heartbeat, and pro-life songs. These can be used outside the clinic and amplified to the desired volume. The tape of the baby's heartbeat is very effective. A group in Akron, Ohio taped a child screaming, "Mommy!" It echoes and reverberates, having a chilling effect on the "mommies" going in to have their babies killed. Some groups have considered having a sound recording of a woman screaming from pain. They would play this in front of the clinic to indicate to women what they are getting into.

At rallies we have used tape recordings of inspirational music. At a protest at a Catholic seminary where a notorious pro-abortion doctor was being honored as an outstanding citizen by a group of priests, we played a recording of the Gregorian Chant "Dies Irae" (Day of Wrath), from the Mass for the Dead. We also played the "Misereri Mei Deus" (Have Mercy on Me, O God). We played these on a tape recorder and amplified them through our bullhorn. It was interesting to watch the faces of the priests as they arrived to honor the pro-abortion doctor and had to run the gauntlet of pro-lifers while this traditional chant from the funeral Mass echoed through the seminary grounds.

It is effective, during a march, to have a recording of a group such as the Mormon Tabernacle Choir singing the "Battle Hymn of the Republic". Such music can have a powerful effect at any rally, march, picket, or demonstration.

With a little planning, you can have sound effects that augment your program, add a flair to your march, give a note of professionalism to your event, and help achieve the spirit you want. At the same time, good sound effects can cause distress to the abortionists. We encourage more use of good sound effects at pro-life events.

63 WOMEN EXPLOITED BY ABORTION (WEBA)

Testimonials are always of great value in selling a product, a philosophy, or way of life. Testimonials from people who have had real life experiences in an area being considered are of even greater value.

Early in the pro-life movement, it became clear to some pro-life leaders that the best people to speak out against abortion would be the women who had been involved in abortion—women who had had abortions themselves or had a close encounter with abortion. While we were running ads in the *Chicago Sun-Times* and the *Chicago Daily News*, we began getting telephone calls and letters from women who had had abortions. They were responding to these ads, which simply told about the dangers of abortion and the humanity of the unborn.

We decided it would be helpful to get them in touch with one another, so we asked each if she would like to come to our office to meet other women who had had abortions. Most agreed. They had an inspiring get-together, one which seemed to benefit all of them. For several it was a real boon, something that they badly needed. Out of that meeting came Women Exploited (WE), a group of women scarred by abortion. It was not a large group at first, less than a dozen, but it began to grow and out of that group came a much larger organization, WEBA—Women Exploited by Abortion. This organization, which has grown rapidly, now has chapters in cities throughout the United States.

Laurie Nelson of Chicago founded WE. Laurie had had an abortion with the help of Planned Parenthood and was very unhappy about it. She felt that she had been pressured into making a quick decision. She found no one at Planned Parenthood or at the abortion clinic to try to talk her out of it or to give her both sides of the story. She had gone to Planned Parenthood to get the referral and was encouraged by them to have the abortion. They even phoned her from time to time to make certain she went through with it.

She said she felt tremendous pressure to have the abortion and afterwards she felt remorse, physical pain, and mental anguish, the natural consequences of having her unborn baby killed. She wanted to do something to make amends and to keep other women from feeling the grief and pain she felt. She wanted to talk to other women and to dissuade them from going through the same experience. For several years, Laurie went to abortion clinics to do sidewalk counseling. Later, she went into full-time counseling, with a group called Aid for Women, advising women against abortion.

Nancy Jo Mann, of Des Moines, Iowa, had a similar experience with abortion, but it took her longer to channel the regret and remorse she felt into helping others. She started WEBA, Women Exploited by Abortion. She has been on a number of television programs and has spoken at many pro-life rallies and conventions. She has had a powerful influence on women contemplating abortion.

Women who have had abortions and now regret them are coming out into the open more and more. There seems to be less reticence to talk about abortion and to admit that one has committed a serious sin. Through Christ's healing power, many of these women are being drawn back into religion and a proper relationship with God, and when they have been healed and forgiven, many feel an obligation to speak out against abortion. We see women like Linda Tuttle, Brey Keaton, Lorijo Nerad, Kathy Demma, and Pat Morris, all members of WEBA, admitting their abortions and trying to help other women avoid making the mistake they made.

When you discover a good spokesman who seems to have her life together after an abortion and is willing to talk about it, ask her if she will go on a talk show or do an interview. Suggest that she call a reporter and say that when the abortionists claim that a million and a half women each year vote with their bodies in favor of abortion, she happens to be one of the many who have had abortions and vote against it. These women are the best ones to speak out against abortion because they know what it has done to them physically and psychologically. They can tell women about the devastating aspects of abortion and can draw others into the movement.

On a talk show in Kansas City we discussed Women Exploited by Abortion, and after the show our office received dozens of letters from women who had had abortions and wanted to contact organizations from which they could receive help in dealing with post-abortion trauma. Wherever the program aired, the same thing happened. Women called in to relate stories of traumatic abortions. They wanted to find a group not just to help them but to help them help other women. There is a need among many women who have had abortions and have repented to expiate for the sin and try to make up for the loss. One way to make up for the loss of one's child is to help prevent another woman from destroying hers.

The time is coming when there will be organizations of men exploited by abortion, men who have been drawn into supporting an abortion, or have even encouraged an abortion, but later regretted the part they played in destroying their child.

We have met many men who suffer from involvement in abortion. There was a group in Chicago called Fathers United against Abortion with a few members. Not many men wanted to admit that they brought a young woman to an abortion clinic. They didn't seem to have the kind of energy needed to organize a program to help other men. But we think the time is coming when repentent men, sick over their part in abortion, will form a national organization much like WEBA. When that time comes, we will add another chapter to our book. We believe young men are out there, about to respond to the grace of conversion.

It may inspire them to take action if they look at the tremendous work done by people like Dr. Bernard Nathanson, formerly an abortionist, but now on the pro-life circuit explaining the evils of abortion and revealing how the abortion culture was promoted and abortion legalized through deception, exaggeration, lying, and courting of the media. Nathanson's books, *Aborting America* and *The Abortion Papers: Inside the Abortion Mentality* and the film he narrates, *The Silent Scream*, are valuable resources that support the message of WEBA that abortion is a violent exploitation.

We must be bold in asking people with special knowledge and experience to use it in the abortion battle. It is sometimes difficult to talk them into exposing their dark secrets. We convinced Linda Tuttle during a picket of an abortion clinic in Kansas City that it would be helpful to the cause if she went public with her abortion. It took a great deal of courage and spiritual help, but she went public and became a very convincing speaker for pro-life.

Don't be afraid to ask people to speak out. Don't force them, but try to convince them that their testimony may be helpful to the unborn and to other women exploited by abortion. And if you want to see an abortion provider panic, just mention the word "WEBA".

64 LEAVE A MESSAGE FOR THE ABORTIONIST

Most abortion clinics have an after-hours telephone message service. The message is recorded, as they don't want to miss a single customer. Since they are so eager for calls, many pro-lifers call the abortion clinics in the evening, after the abortionists have gone home, and leave a message. They have a page of slogans and facts about abortion complications and statements that women have made about their abortions. They read these statements over the phone, onto the recorder.

They tell them, for instance, that one out of every ten women having abortions is sterilized by the abortion, that the baby's heart begins to beat at three-and-a-half weeks after conception. They quote from Dr. Bernard Nathanson's book *The Abortion Papers* on the dishonesty of abortionists. They and their friends fill up the tape with these and other statements.

Someone at each clinic has to listen to the entire tape at the beginning of each workday, because, squeezed in among all the pro-life messages, may be some business for them. They cannot afford to ignore the tape or rush through it. We know this, because we once had an answering machine that recorded messages and it was always filled up with statements, strange music, and things abortionists had phoned in. After a while, we decided it was not necessary to tape record messages since most of our calls were from friends calling to relay some information we could get during working hours. Calls from girls who needed help nearly always came during the day when we were at the office. When the machine finally broke down, we didn't replace it.

But the abortionists have to take recorded calls from women and girls seeking abortions. So pro-lifers occasionally fill up these tapes with messages about the crime of abortion and other informative statements. It is not necessary to make insulting remarks, and never leave a threatening message. The strictly educational ones will irritate the abortionists enough and also use up their tape. If a girl is calling to leave a message, the tape may run out and consequently, she will have a little more time to reconsider her abortion decision.

When pro-lifers are not picketing or counseling at the clinics or doing other pro-life work, they often go through the list of abortion clinic ads in the phone book; then they call up the clinics and leave long, informative messages. If they happen to get a live person on the phone, they simply engage in conversation.

65 THE DEPOSITION: HOW TO MAKE IT BACKFIRE

From time to time, pro-lifers will be drawn into legal actions and will be required, by court order, to submit to a deposition. A deposition is a matter to be considered seriously. It is nothing but a request, but it is backed by a court order. If you refuse to submit to a deposition, you must be prepared to pay the penalty. It could be a fine or even imprisonment.

The deposition is requested by a law firm and ordered by a judge. It will specify the matter at hand and tell you where and at what time to appear. It will advise you to bring your attorney and suggest that you be prepared to spend a day answering questions. The deposition becomes a part of the official court record.

You never really know what the attorneys will ask you so you must be prepared for almost anything. Your attorney will help you anticipate questions so that you will know how to answer them.

The lawyers taking a deposition are digging for information. Consequently, do not give them any information voluntarily. Answer questions as directly and briefly as possible. If they ask you something that you don't know, the answer to give them is, "I don't know", "I can't recall", or "I can't remember". If you have only a little information, give that and stop; don't volunteer anything you are not specifically asked. Don't volunteer your feelings, emotions, observations, suspicions. Don't act as though you are certain of something if you aren't. Don't be afraid to say, "I think", or "As I recall". Don't give out information as being absolute if it is not. A deposition can be used against you and your friends in a suit, and it *will* be if they discover any damaging information.

A deposition is a search warrant for everything in your past relating to this case. Through it they hope to help their client defeat you and your friends.

When you are submitting voluntarily to a deposition, you certainly cannot lie because you are under oath during the deposition. What you can do in a deposition is embarrass the opposition by boldly citing facts they may not want to hear. You can educate them through the deposition. During a deposition by attorneys representing Planned

Parenthood, I mentioned, whenever opportune, that one reason I picketed abortion clinics was that Planned Parenthood's foundress, Margaret Sanger, had once said that the most merciful thing a large family can do for its smallest member is to kill it. She meant that abortion is a boon to the newborn of a large family. I read that into the deposition. They didn't like it.

It is useful to make statements like, "I can't understand your question. The way you phrase it makes no sense to me", or "I don't know how you expect me to answer that." Let everyone present know that you feel contempt for what these attorneys are doing. They are working for people who believe in killing innocent children. You have contempt, not for the legal process or the use of the deposition, but for people who assist the abortionists.

A law firm that accepts abortionists as clients evidences a lack of moral rectitude. The contempt you feel for them may be manifested in your attitude. Let them know that you are cooperating with them under pressure, and that you do not respect their client. You may say things that clearly convey that message in your deposition.

The deposition in many cases is not of much value. Frequently, it is used to find out if there are grounds for drawing you into the case or to discover the extent of your involvement in the case.

The depositions I have taken have been educational. It is interesting to follow their line of questioning to see if you can figure out what they are trying to get at. Frequently, I have observed that the opponent's attorneys are frustrated in their efforts to get the evidence they want against a pro-life client. They are counting on a deposition to help them. When you are called upon to submit to a deposition, find an excuse to postpone it. Eventually, however, you will have to give the deposition because you are under court order and to refuse would put you in contempt of court. You may, however, go before the court to show cause why you should not give it. When you give the deposition though, remember that the less you say, the better.

66 CALL THEIR BLUFF: THE LEGAL THREAT

Into nearly every pro-lifer's life as an activist there will come a legal threat. It may be a phone call from a law firm or, more likely, a letter on very impressive stationery with a long list of names at the top. It will say that, on behalf of its client, the firm of such and such wishes to notify you that if you ever do such and such again, legal action will be taken, or they will not hesitate to take legal action, or something to that effect. It is probably a ploy—a shallow threat of legal action if you continue doing something they don't want you to do.

Many pro-life activists have received letters like this or have been contacted by phone. The phone call sometimes promises a letter, but the warning letter rarely follows. These are methods of intimidation aimed at scaring you into complying with their wishes.

The first time this happens it will concern you. Many pro-lifers have been stopped in their tracks by a phone call or threatening letter from a law firm. It is, unfortunately, all that is needed to stop some pro-lifers from doing good and useful work. This is a shame. People have been stopped from picketing, leafleting, and even from counseling because a law firm retained by an abortionist gave them a call or sent them a letter. The reaction was just what they wanted. If a threat can scare the pro-lifers off, the abortionists win their battles cheaply.

Whenever you get such a threat, you should contact your attorney immediately, read him the letter, and send him a copy of it. He will be able to appraise the situation adequately. If it is an obvious ploy, he will be able to tell you so and put your mind at ease. He has probably sent letters like that himself at the request of a client. Sometimes they work. More often they don't.

One summer we received a letter from an attorney in St. Louis saying that if we pursued an action we were contemplating in southern Illinois, legal action would be taken against us. They were trying to stop us from coming to Granite City, Illinois, to picket their client's abortion clinic.

I called my attorney who said that it sounded like a classic bluff, but that I should be careful. I went ahead with my plans, and while I was at their client's abortion clinic, I took the letter out, read it to the press and then set it on fire. The lawyer who had sent the letter was standing in the clinic doorway. He recognized the letter and noted my attitude toward it. Burning his letter in front of the press notified him and the public that I thought very little of his threat. I had called his bluff, and there was nothing he could do about it.

Another "legal" letter said that we would be sued if we pursued a certain course of action. I read the letter over my Newsline to let my listeners know that we had received a threat from the abortionists and that it was of no consequence to us. That was the last we heard from them.

We used the same technique when we were ordered to turn over some private files during a deposition. Rather than comply with the order, I announced on the Newsline that certain confidences made to me would become public information at the insistence of a pro-abortion attorney. I gave the lawyers' names and the name of the judge who ordered the deposition. I made this public because I knew they wanted to scare us and I wanted to let them know that we were not scared. They never pursued their demand.

Usually, when we have called the abortionists' bluff on a legal threat, they have not followed through. Even if they do, it does not mean they have any grounds for a suit or that they could win it. More than likely, even the deposition will be useless to them.

There is a lot of bluffing in the legal arena. Lawyers have their jokes about this. So don't collapse under legal threats. They are not frightening, and you can fight a legal challenge, whether it is real or feigned, if you have a good lawyer and are secure in your position. Take the threat and throw it back at them.

Or, write them a letter: "If you continue your threats, my attorneys will take appropriate action." There are some penalties for misuse of the legal process, and they know it. Don't let them scare you. Call their bluff.

67 COUNTER CHARGE FOR FALSE ARRESTS

If you are a pro-life activist out on the front lines at the clinics, sooner or later you are going to be threatened with arrest. The police are going to be called and you are going to be charged with anything from inciting a riot or mob action to disorderly conduct or even trespassing.

Before the clinic operators call the police they are going to *threaten* to call the police. When the police finally arrive, the abortionists will file a charge against you and swear to the fact that you did something illegal. You may be arrested on a totally false charge. It is good to let the police officer know that you are not guilty of what you are being charged with and that there is the possibility that if you are charged, booked, and incarcerated, then later found innocent, you will file a suit of your own for false arrest or malicious prosecution. You should challenge the motives for your arrest and let the arresting officer know that you are taking the charges very seriously.

If you are told by the police that you cannot do something, and you do not believe there is an ordinance against it, challenge the officer to show you the ordinance. The police will frequently, for their own convenience, tell you that you cannot do something that may be perfectly legal. They have a great variety of charges they can level against a person, some of which are very broad, such as "disorderly conduct" or "loitering". You might have to let them know that you are not ignorant of the law. Remind them, for instance, that if you are not picketing, but sidewalk counseling, you do not have to keep moving. If you are not carrying a picket sign, you don't have to be moving because you are not picketing. The police frequently tell pro-lifers that they cannot use a bullhorn, even when there is no ordinance against it or when they are well within the laws that govern the time of day or the zone the clinic is in. Tell them that you want to see the ordinance governing this situation.

You have rights. You have a right to free speech, a right to assemble, a right to express your beliefs, a right to encourage people not to do evil things. You have many rights under the Constitution that may be casually violated for the sake of peace or for what others see as order. So counter their charges and orders wherever possible. Do it politely, but firmly.

It is important for us as pro-life activists to be well read in this area of the law so that we can speak knowledgeably. It does not hurt, in instances where there is considerable harassment by the police or clinic guards, to have a lawyer come with you to the clinic to speak on your behalf.

Do not always take the police officers' decisions as final. And do file charges if you are arrested falsely or are charged falsely. Talk to your lawyer about the possibility of filing charges for violation of your basic constitutional rights. You may win. And if you don't, you will at least inconvenience the abortionists by requiring them to use their lawyers and their money, as well as the time they wasted in court.

The abortionists have been having a field day for the past several years taking the pro-lifers to court, having them arrested, fined, even imprisoned. Stalwart pro-life activists like John Ryan of St. Louis have spent months in jail for sidewalk counseling because abortionists had gotten injunctions against it. Literally hundreds of pro-lifers, doing nothing more sinister than trying to save lives and consciences by talking women out of abortion, have been arrested, tried, and found guilty by "born again" Christian judges who argue that we cannot have anarchy and we must save lives by "changing the laws".

Many of these arrests and even convictions are unconstitutional, and they must be challenged in the courts. Arbitrary arrests may be violations of the constitutional rights to free speech and assembly. Hasty, overboard injunctions against pro-life pickets and sidewalk counselors need to be challenged and a public cry of outrage raised.

We believe that, in time, pro-life attorneys will win enough of these challenges in court to send a message to the abortion providers, their attorneys and pro-abortion judges: that unconstitutional harassment will not be tolerated. Many such cases are being pursued on a regular basis. If you think you have a case of an overboard, unconstitutional action against you or your organization, contact a local pro-life attorney or get in touch with one of these law firms for legal help.

CATHOLIC LEAGUE FOR
RELIGIOUS AND CIVIL RIGHTS
   1100 West Wells St.
   Milwaukee, WI 53233

THE RUTHERFORD INSTITUTE
   P.O. Box 510
   Manassas, VA 22110

FREE SPEECH ADVOCATES
Box 815
Notre Dame, IN 46556
or
c/o T. Pat Monaghan
New Hope, KY 40052

68 GO NATIONAL: JOIN THE ACTIVIST NETWORK

In May 1984 an unprecedented event took place in Ft. Lauderdale, Florida. It was the first national activist convention ever held. It attracted more than six hundred people and most of the nation's activist leaders.

The highlight of the four-day convention for many was a massive picket at a local abortion clinic and the saving of two babies' lives. The demonstration, filmed for the "MacNeil/Lehrer Report", was the largest and best organized that clinic operator Barbara Zeitlin had ever seen.

Out of this national activist convention came some very good things, the most significant of which was the development of a national plan of action. Several late-night meetings of seasoned activists resulted in the development of a core group, a tentative program, and a decision to close abortion clinics through more effective counseling, frequent pickets and demonstrations, sit-ins, national days of rescue, better training programs, use of clinic coverts, and the development of many other powerful techniques and programs.

It was agreed that there should be a network of agencies to coordinate these activities, and regional directors would be appointed to see that activist groups in their areas carried out the programs. All of the directors agreed that if action called for civil disobedience of a non-violent and peaceful nature, they would take part in such action and risk arrest.

At the National Right-to-Life Convention in Kansas City, Missouri, a month later, many of these leaders met again to formulate a six-month program to feature one national activity each month. These included blitzes of abortion clinics, picketing of doctors' and clinic operators' homes, vigils, demonstrations at rallies of pro-abortion political candidates, a national day of rescue through sidewalk counseling and marches to abortion clinics, and a national day of amnesty for the unborn, during which efforts would be made to close down as many abortion clinics across the country as possible.

To prove that a day of amnesty was feasible, a demonstration was held the day after the meeting at a Kansas City abortion clinic operated by Planned Parenthood. Word of the large demonstration leaked out the night before, and all six of Kansas City's abortion clinics closed down for the day, Saturday, May 6, 1984.

The existence of a national program of activism concerned the abortionists who had become accustomed to only random picketing and sidewalk counseling. The increased, organized activity also cost them in the hiring of guards, posting of signs, and paying of legal fees as the number of arrests and lawsuits, generally made to harass pro-lifers, increased dramatically.

But if the activist program disturbed the abortionists, it gave a new enthusiasm to pro-life activists. It was encouraging to know that during an all-night vigil, other pro-lifers were holding this same vigil all across the nation.

The enthusiasm of the activist leadership was encouraging to all who attended the meetings. More than eighty activists attended one after-hours meeting in Kansas City. The attendance read like a ''Who's Who'' of Pro-Life Activism.

John Ryan of St. Louis, who up to that time had spent five months in jail for repeated invasions of abortion clinics, told the gathering, ''The abortion clinic door holds no meaning for me''. Joan Andrews and Ann O'Brien, also arrested and imprisoned for six months, told of their prison experiences. (All were later arrested again and given additional prison sentences.)

Franky Schaeffer, in addressing the banquet crowd at the closing ceremony, spoke forcefully on behalf of the activist branch of the movement and called for relentless picketing until abortion clinics are shut down. His talk solidified the activist agenda and upset the moderates. His stirring talk was a worthy send-off to a growing, determined activist arm of the movement.

Activisim is essential to the eventual success of the movement. Writers such as Professor Charles Rice have said that the old pro-life movement is dead, while prayer and activism constitute the new effort. Political writers such as Thomas Roeser have pointed out that activism will eventually give the movement the political clout it must have to influence Congress and political leaders and give the movement the credibility it needs to attain its demands.

Activism, as Moral Majority's Cal Thomas has pointed out, is a means of getting attention from a hostile press. Former columnist Patrick Buchanan and other pro-life writers have praised activism and encouraged pro-lifers to join the ranks of the street fighters for the cause of life.

Roeser wrote in a liberal publication, the *Chicago Reader*, that America is a country where the liberal and moderate establishment wants nothing so much as to be left alone to enjoy its rich heritage, its easy living, and its comfort born of compromise. The activist in any cause keeps jabbing at the soft underbelly of the complacent giant who will, eventually, if only to get rid of the disturbance, grant the pesky request. Without this constant jabbing there will be no change, Roeser says.

It would be a shame, after reading a guidebook on activism such as this, for pro-life readers not to become a part of the national activist network. It would in fact be criminal to remain a moderate in the face of such a crisis as abortion.

Advantages to joining the national activist network are both physical and psychological. The physical advantages include receiving routine directives on national activities and communications telling of programs that have worked well and explaining why. It provides for association with national activist leaders at regional and national gatherings and an exchange of media accounts. There is also the realization that every major activity done at home is being multiplied across the country.

Among the psychological benefits are the certainty that women are being dissuaded from abortion and their babies' lives saved by your work and that of thousands of other activists working in concert with you. Add to that the knowledge that you are in the prayers of some of the most faithful servants of the Lord, who sacrifice, suffer, and pray for your success just as you are praying for theirs.

You will know also that the abortionists at the headquarters of the National Abortion Federation (NAF) and elsewhere are keeping tabs on your activities and marking your incidents of activism on their charts, then reporting them to the Treasury Department's Bureau of Alcohol, Tobacco, and Firearms, to the Justice Department's Federal Bureau of Investigation, to the House Judiciary Subcommittee on Civil and Constitutional Rights, and to the press. Their helplessness in the face of organized, non-violent direct action is becoming ever more apparent.

A second national activist conference was held in Appleton, Wisconsin April 11–13, 1985, and the fruits of that event will be felt across the country for years to come. Hundreds of pro-life activist leaders pledged a new unity of effort to save the unborn and to educate the public to the injustice of abortion.

Joining this national activist effort is simple. Write to the Pro-Life Action League, 6160 N. Cicero Ave., Suite 210, Chicago, IL 60646, and we'll put you on the activist network list and keep you informed of the national programs. The rest is up to you.

69 CREATE AN IMAGE: THE ABORTION FIGHTER

It is important for pro-lifers to do their own public relations work. Pro-lifers, in general, do not get much media attention, and pro-life activists not only do not get much attention, but they often get little understanding or support even from other pro-lifers. Each pro-life group has to take care of itself in the publicity field. Each right-to-life group works for its own survival, even while its members work together for a common goal.

As a rule, if you want recognition, you will have to blow your own horn. You do this by playing up the projects you undertake that are successful, and bragging about your accomplishments and those of the people you work with. This helps establish a good public image.

Issue lots of press releases, give advance notice of your activities, call the media before every important event, call other pro-life groups to tell them what you are doing, and ask them to join you. Try to form loose coalitions with other pro-life groups. But remember that you will have to do most of the public relations work for yourself.

When a group of your people stage a sit-in and get arrested, cheer them when they come out of the clinic, praise them in your comments to the press, and give them awards at your banquet. In your annual awards program, dedicate a page to people who have been arrested. Give a "Dirty Dozen Award" to people who have done something that is feisty and that helped to create an atmosphere of enthusiastic activism. At an awards banquet in Appleton, Wisconsin, "Project Save Our Babies" awards featuring a jailor's ring with five brass keys were given as the "Jailed for Life" awards to eighteen pro-lifers who had been arrested and put in jail briefly for picketing and sidewalk counseling at the local abortion clinic.

If someone refers to you or your organization with a term that you like, call yourself by that term. Fr. Charles Fiore, O.P., and I were called the "Green Berets" of the pro-life movement in a column by Patrick Buchanan, talking about the kind of feisty activity for which our organization—then Friends for Life—had become known. The Green Beret title grew out of our opposition to the Archbishop of Chicago, the late John Cardinal Cody, who would not cooperate with us in trying to get Planned Parenthood out of the United Way fund drive. We challenged him and worked with Protestant groups to get Planned Parenthood dropped. Buchanan called us Green Berets for fighting aggressively for what we believed in.

Other titles can be used to your advantage. If they call you a "hit man", "hired gun", or worse, make the most of it and use it to your advantage. Begin your talks by listing the names that have been used to describe you and your work. "Steely-eyed zealot" and "Holy Terror" can be referred to, in a humorous way, to let people know that others see you as an aggressive pro-life activist. Consider these titles compliments, and nothing to be ashamed of. At least they are calling you something. It's better than being ignored.

Don't hesitate to use props in a bold, colorful way: the bullhorn, for instance. Some years ago, when my voice was hoarse from shouting, I bought a cheap Radio Shack bullhorn and now carry it in my briefcase. After a few pictures of me with the bullhorn appeared in newspapers around the country, it became a trademark. Now I take it with me wherever I go.

We have thirty professionally constructed baby caskets that we use on special occasions. We place them on a long purple cloth. This has become symbolic of the pro-life protest of killing children. A "Secret Weapon", as we call it, is a garbage can full of baby dolls with streaks of red paint on them to simulate blood. This device has been adopted by pro-life activist groups across the country. People know you are around when they see your props. They do not soon forget them either.

Some people say pro-life should strive for a respectable, high class image. Perhaps some organizations should. But we don't believe respectability is all that important. What matters is that you are aggressive and effective in your battle against abortion. Are you well-known to the abortionists? Does the press know you? Are you available to other pro-life groups? We believe it doesn't do much good to have a quiet, unheard-of pro-life group that is rarely seen in public. You need to become known and recognized as a force in the community and as someone abortionists must contend with.

Leave your card at the desk of abortion clinics in every town you visit. Leave them a note saying you are in town to organize pro-life activists there to close down the abortion industry. This should conjure up in their minds images of protests and pickets and "trouble" for them. Try to create a strong image in your community and wherever you go. Become known as *the* activist pro-lifers in your community, in your state, even in the nation.

In every town and city we visit, we search for somebody with flair, someone who is not afraid of the abortionists, the media, the police, or his reputation. We look for someone who is not so concerned about his image that he hides his light under a bushel. We look for leaders, and when we find them we urge them to become the activist leaders their communities need. We look for people with ideas, a feel for public relations, an ease with the press, and a great deal of enthusiasm and optimism. Much as we respect those who are plodding, careful, and respectable, we look for those who will keep the image of activism alive in the community.

We think it is important to use public relations techniques, even gimmicks, to keep the issue alive for the public. Someone has to create the image of the abortion fighter as a tireless, aggressive, imaginative, daring, cocksure, and optimistic individual who carefully plans his strategy and accomplishes what he sets out to do.

70 CREATIVE PUBLICITY

Pro-lifers are engaged in a long battle for life. We know that to win we must make the most of every possible opportunity to prove a point about the horror of abortion. This is true even when the opportunity is not apparent. The activist must develop the facility to make the most of what to some seems to be a hopeless situation. We have plenty of chances to practice this. Creative publicity can help. It can be used to capture your opponent's momentum, excite the media, or simply recharge your own batteries. Three stories best help to illustrate the idea.

Several years ago, during a period when absolutely nothing seemed to be working in favor of the pro-life movement, we were trying to stir up enthusiasm with a Mother's Day march to a number of abortion clinics. Despite widespread advertising and countless phone calls, we had a miserable turnout, maybe forty people. It was raining. The paint on our signs was running. Spirits were low. Only one local TV reporter showed up together with her camera crew. At each clinic, we wired a rose to a nearby tree, but we weren't picketing or chanting. The reporter said something to the cameraman about not getting many visuals and looked ready to leave. Our chances of even a mention on the evening news looked grim.

Our next stop was to be a small park, a playground, where the year before we had planted a rose bush. Here we were to say a few words and then disband. I was ahead of the group, walking rather fast. I wanted to make sure that the gate was opened so we could get into the park. When I arrived, there was not a soul in sight, because of the rain. There were no children playing, no one sitting on benches. The park was completely empty.

Then it occurred to me, they wanted a visual. So I went up to the swing set where a row of little horses hung on chains and gave each horse a big push. Then I went to the carousel and ran around with it one or two times so it was moving fast. There was another row of horses on springs, which I began bouncing back and forth. Anything that could move I pushed, swung, or yanked until it was all in motion.

By this time the camera crew arrived and as the reporter approached, she stopped the cameraman and said, "Get that!" He focused on the swinging horses and then, as I noticed later on television, panned out to a broad shot that encompassed the entire park in motion. The reporter came to me and said, "Would you like to comment on your march today?" The camera turned to me. I stood at the entrance to the park with all the toys moving, slowly by now, in the background. I said, "Where are our children? They are dead from abortion. They have all died in abortions. They should be playing here. There should be noises and laughter, but there is only silence. Only their ghosts are here."

The reporter was affected by this. She asked, obviously moved, "Do you ever save any babies through these tactics, these methods you use?" I told her we had just saved one at the last clinic. Some of our counselors had talked to a young woman going into that clinic. They were still talking with her but were pretty certain they had dissuaded her from having the abortion.

The whole segment was used that night on the television news. It was not long, about a minute, but it was one of the first times we had ever received sympathetic coverage. The symbolism of the empty park moving with ghosts did something to the reporter, and her question, "Do you ever save any babies?", was very significant. Reporters rarely ask anything like that. They are most often concerned about women's rights and their being harassed. They don't think about saving babies. The event was a kind of breakthrough, coming at a moment when everything, for that day at least, looked lost.

Another example shows how a creative idea can take the momentum from under pro-life opponents and give it to us. Planned Parenthood was suing a local transit authority to have their pregnancy counseling ads placed on buses and trains. The Pro-Life Action League was named in the suit. We took advantage of the action to argue that if Planned Parenthood could run their ads, we could run ours right beside theirs. Our ads were professionally produced pictures of the American Abortion Holocaust from the discovery in California of 17,000 aborted babies. The pictures were gruesome and the sliced and fragmented bodies of the aborted babies hideous to see. The ads were admitted as evidence to the court, numbered, and in that way made public material. The move was covered by the press and the pictures, which are far too gory and gut-wrenching ever to appear on TV under normal circumstances, were in fact photographed and shown nationwide by Cable News Network.

This produced good results. A woman from Dubuque, Iowa, Sandy Kirkbride, called to say that she had seen the ads on television and asked if she could have one to put up on a billboard she owned in a high traffic area of the city. She ran the ad on the billboard during October and November 1984, just before the election. The billboard itself became a media story and the abortion picture was broadcast again. This exposure was the direct result of following through on the idea to use the pictures as court evidence. It is vital to follow through on publicity ideas. The effect can be far in excess of the original intention.

A final illustration of creative publicity took place in Washington, D.C., at the time of a large pro-life rally. During the rally as an attempt to divert media attention from the pro-lifers, a comparative handful of people from the Religious Coalition for Abortion Rights held a ceremony in a nearby church. The ceremony called ''Rejoice for Choice'' condoned abortion and ostensibly thanked God for the great ''gift'' of abortion. Being prepared for the fact that the media was likely to give this event undue attention, we prepared a banner which we carried to the sanctuary of the church. We unfurled it in front of the TV cameras during the middle of the ceremony. The banner said ''Sacrilege'' in huge, red letters. The statement, which was simple and to the point, made network news across the country. It gave the momentum that the media was prepared to give to the pro-abortion group back to the pro-lifers. It also restored the equilibrium of the pro-life rally, where there were over 70,000 marching for life compared to a few hundred gathered to support ''choice''.

Pro-life publicity is most effective when it reaches abortion supporters on their home turf. Tom Roeser, a Chicago writer, has been extremely effective at placing his pro-life articles in liberal, pro-abortion publications. I recently convinced Arthur Shostak to include an essay I wrote on men involved in abortion in a clearly pro-abortion book he wrote aimed at men whose wives or girlfriends have had or are considering abortions. For years our pro-life group ran a classified ad headlined ''Don't Abort Your Baby'' in the middle of all the ads for abortion clinics in a local newspaper, until the newspaper dropped all of its classified ads for clinics. These approaches reach more people who are less likely to see your pro-life publications. We must reach more people all the time. Creative publicity is important. The more people who see the truth about abortion, the more there are to abhor it. Be creative.

71 THE DIRTY DOZEN

Throughout this book I have referred to groups of pro-life activists who stick together and form the nucleus of an activist program. These pro-lifers have sometimes been called names like the "Dirty Dozen". They are a special group who can be counted on to do the things the average pro-lifer would not want to do or would not feel capable of doing.

Any pro-life leader should be able to find a dozen or so tried and true activists to do the more difficult work. Time and again we have found a dozen people who will come together to sing Christmas carols at the American Civil Liberties Union offices on Christmas Eve or to picket a local newspaper, book publisher, pro-abortion celebrity, or outspoken Planned Parenthood advocate. When you need a quick picket, a dozen people you can count on, rain or shine, night or day, will fill the bill. A dozen people make a decent picket. They can handle a leaflet or conduct a good protest.

Even a major demonstration takes about a dozen experienced leaders: a march leader, marshals, press secretary, bondsman, co-ordinators. No matter what happens, your Dirty Dozen will keep the event running smoothly.

At a picket of a federal judge one day we were able, in a short time, to gather just a dozen people, but, small as it was, the picket was a major success, resulting in a photograph of our group with the judge in effigy that appeared on the front page of the *Chicago Tribune*'s local news section.

Our Dirty Dozen used to go through downtown Chicago sticking up posters on lamp posts and leafleting at train stations and bus stops. There were usually twelve of us, covered with paste and grime. That's how we acquired our name, the "Dirty Dozen". Even though most of the original group moved on, the name remained.

Every activist pro-life group should have its Dirty Dozen. It will expand and thin out; members will come and go. But it is a group that will work hard, can be trusted, will show up when needed, and will do the work that has to be done when it has to be done.

When they have finished an assignment, the group should go out for coffee and discuss what they have just done. They should feel special, because, indeed, they are. They don't mind rolling up their sleeves and going out to do what no one else wants to do. Nothing they do is sinister or wrong, and nothing they do is violent, but everything they do will be special because of their spirit.

Every organization needs its "Dirty Dozen".

72 HAVE FUN

Some people think a grim face is appropriate for their tour of duty as a pro-life activist. But not many keep a grim face very long. It is true that the battle we are fighting is serious, and the evil we are fighting is as great as evil can be. The sin we are fighting is mortal and damnable in the sight of God. A sanction of excommunication has been attached to it by the Catholic Church. There is no room for levity of attitude in our war against abortion.

However, fighting abortion can have its rewards and even some lighter moments. Christ said that in this life there is a hundred-fold return for living according to His teachings, and this is true in the battle against abortion.

We are always aware that we are on the right side of the issue, fighting God's battle and doing His will, and that is a source of great satisfaction.

We are fighting alongside good people. The people in the movement are the best people there are, a veritable communion of saints. These are the people who care about others. They love the helpless unborn and ask no compensation or recognition for their work to save them. We are constantly associating with the elect. It is cause for rejoicing to be in the company of such people. It is true that there are disagreements and differences within the movement. But even allowing for disagreements, we recognize that we are among good people, and we take satisfaction and pleasure in each other's company.

In any unpleasant situation, there is a need to see the humor, incongruities, and strange conflicts that arise, and these occasionally punctuate the tragic aspect of the fight. The human condition is a complex condition from which there is no escape. But on occasion, we can find some humor in standing back to look at it. Sometimes our shortcomings and even our conflicts have a humorous aspect to them. the fact is that we are often thought of in stereotypes, as "little old ladies in tennis shoes", as people who don't wear the latest styles or have the biggest cars and who have too many children. We are not thought of as "the beautiful people". We're mostly common folk, and we accept that image and have a little fun with it. A joke we use in Chicago: "How can you tell a pro-lifer?" Answer: "He's the one who needs a ride."

Most pro-lifers find rallies, conferences, conventions, and seminars to be delightful experiences, even though they deal with a tragic issue. It is good to get together once a year with people whom you enjoy and actually miss when you are away from them. It is an honor to be with people you read about, hear about, and whose activities you admiringly follow.

My first meeting with Franky Schaeffer in a Fort Lauderdale restaurant was something I had been looking forward to for years. He was a powerful force in the pro-life movement, one whose books I had read and whose films I had viewed. Meeting him was a great honor. It has been the same with all the great people I have met. I recall the first time I met Senator Jesse Helms and Congressman Henry Hyde, as well as my first meetings with Nellie Gray, Paul and Judie Brown, Jack and Barbara Wilke, Dr. Mildred Jefferson, and other greats in the pro-life movement. My meeting with Sam Lee in Chicago was a red letter day. I had admired his work in St. Louis for years. It was the same when I met John Ryan and Elasah Drogin. These and hundreds of other meetings with pro-lifers have been joyous occasions.

When you are with people you have worked with, suffered with, and even been arrested with, it is a treat just to go out for pizza and enjoy one another's company. It's a little part of the Lord's hundredfold.

There can even be a little hilarity in marking a special event. After a group of us met in Orlando, Florida, at the National Right to Life Convention, to plan the first national activists' convention, we discovered a poor man's Disney World near the hotel. There was a studio where you could dress up in period costumes and have a group photo taken. The men rifled through the old double-breasted suits and wide-brim hats. The ladies found some vamp outfits from the Twenties, and all of us selected artillery reminiscent of the Capone era. The backdrop was a dingy, over-decorated room with a bottle and deck of cards on the table. We sat for eight photographs. They turned out to be hilarious. They were so good that even the photographer wanted two for advertising his booth. Tom Marzen with his Christmas tree mustache and straw hat posed with a Thomson submachine gun. Nancy Hackell, with a bandana and a cigarette, made a convincing vamp. Priscilla Sanders held a pistol; Dick Amswald held a rifle; Susan McMillan, who couldn't find a gun, sported a sword. I sat in the center with a tommy gun.

The pictures now hang on the walls of pro-life headquarters across the country. We gave them various titles like, "Non-Violent Direct Action, Phase Two" and "The New NRLC Board of Directors". It is a souvenir of those moments when you feel good about your mission and the people you're with and you commemorate it in a special, ridiculous way.

We are in the pro-life movement to put ourselves out of business. The best news we could hear would be that abortion has become illegal, that the clinics have closed, and that the unborn children have laws to protect them. We pray for that. We could then get back to living normal lives and making our living in a nation that does not destroy its posterity.

But while we are in the business of saving lives, we cannot always be somber and serious. We must enjoy our work. We have to enjoy the travel, the get-togethers, conventions, meetings, seminars, pickets, demonstrations, and all the other things we do to save lives, even when this work is fraught with danger and requires sacrifice and hardship. Pro-life Christians know that they are recognized not only by their love for their fellow man, but also for their Christian joy, which surpasses the world's joy. We have to share that joy with one another and, occasionally, just have a rousing good time.

73 WARN THE GARBAGE MAN, "YOU'RE HAULING CORPSES"

This chapter title describes what a group of us did at a Chicago abortion clinic. We were there when the garbage man came to pick up the bags from a dumpster behind the clinic. Someone by the alley saw the truck drive up. Several of us went behind the clinic and asked the garbage man if he realized what he was picking up. He said he knew it was a medical facility. We told him that it was not a medical facility, but an abortion clinic. We strongly suspected they were throwing out what they call "biological waste" which are parts of human bodies, the remains of children they abort at the clinic. We told him that dead bodies should not be treated like garbage.

He was shaken up and didn't know how to respond. Then he said he didn't consider it part of his job to haul away human bodies and that nobody had told him that this was what he would be doing. He stopped loading the truck, removed the bags he had already picked up, and drove off.

Following this success, we decided to see if we couldn't get all the sanitation companies to refuse to pick up garbage from the abortion clinics. Unfortunately, the clinics got to them first. When we called we were told that someone had called them to explain that there were no body parts in the pick up. They had explained that these were sent to a pathology lab, and they assured the sanitation officers that there were no violations of health codes. Only by inspecting the contents of bags could this claim be confirmed or denied, and many dumpsters were padlocked.

We learned that in some cities abortionists have been inconvenienced at least temporarily by companies refusing to pick up their garbage. They have had to hire sanitation companies from far away and have been required to pay higher rates to have their garbage picked up.

This type of action may seem insignificant, but it lets the abortionists know that their activity is so reprehensible that even garbage collectors do not want anything to do with them. The treatment of human beings—literally, throwing other people in the trash—offends decent human beings. It is an education for the abortionists, for the public who hear about it, and for workers who have to face the abortion reality.

This is the kind of activity pro-life activists should investigate on their own; they should use their imaginations and think of other facilities they can contact with similar complaints.

For instance, consider the mailman. The person who delivers mail to abortion clinics knows that some of the letters he delivers contain inquiries about abortion or letters informing the abortionists about new equipment, seminars, meetings, publications from other abortion organizations. How does a decent Christian man or woman feel about transferring such information to an abortion facility? Talk to the mailman and suggest that he ask for a transfer to get off a route that requires him to deliver mail to abortion clinics. He may think that it is not his place to decide what mail should be delivered and what should not, but it is worth your time to ask him to consider this problem. You may find someone to whom abortion is so abhorrent that he would indeed ask for a transfer, and somebody else would be assigned to this route, and then you could start over again working on the new mailman. In Livonia, Michigan, Lynn Mills, a mail carrier, refused to deliver mail to the local abortion clinic. Lynn also happens to be director of the Pro-Life Action League of Livonia.

Consider people who come to the clinic to make repairs, to check the sewer, to install new phones, to put in new lighting. Let all these people know they are servicing a death camp. This can be effective. You never know a person's disposition until you talk to him. You don't know who you might encounter or whose conscience you might touch, but by constantly pointing out the abomination of abortion to those who brush against it, you may find a strong ally who will help you in your efforts to shut down the industry.

74 GET PRO-ABORTION BOOKS AND PORNOGRAPHIC MATERIAL OFF THE SHELVES

Books and magazines that would have shocked our parents—and that would have shocked *us* a few years ago—are now commonplace in bookstores, magazine racks, and public libraries. We have degenerated as a society. We can either tolerate filth and let it saturate our own lives or we can try to change the situation.

If we are determined to change it, part of what we have to do is go into bookstores and libraries and check out the section on family planning, birth control, and abortion. In most bookstores and libraries there is a lot of pro-abortion literature, but few books that speak against abortion are on the shelves.

Cases in point are Dr. Bernard Nathanson's books, *Aborting America* and *The Abortion Papers*. Even though they are excellent books, it is nearly impossible to find them in secular bookstores. Apparently, store owners do not want to stock books that might offend their customers. For nearly every other issue, there are books which present both sides of the argument, but bookstores shy away from books that treat abortion unfavorably. Gradually, though, this is starting to change.

What *you* can do to get pro-life books on the shelves is to start an organized program of phone calls and visits to bookstores, asking for pro-life books you know are available and encouraging the store to stock these. Have others ask for the books by titles. Supply a demand for them.

You can also complain about the books supporting abortion that are on the shelves. Point out their bias and lack of scientific data. There are also some things you can do to neutralize their effect, if you cannot get them off the shelves. Insert pro-life flyers and other literature in them. These pro-life inserts will provide the facts to refute the books' content and recommend good pro-life books.

Protest and picket the bookstores that consistently display a pro-abortion attitude or that traffic in pornography. Years ago, our pro-life group protested a book of photographs depicting sexual activities involving children. We went to the store to complain, talked to the manager, tried to hide the books, and asked people to call the store to complain. One of our demonstrators made a scene at the counter protesting the book.

The book, *Show Me*, got a lot of adverse publicity, but it remained on the shelves. We continued protesting. In time, when Nancy Czerwiec got on the case, she got it enough bad publicity that it was removed from some libraries and even from some bookstores. It was this constant pressure, over a long period of time, which finally got this piece of pornography out of general circulation. That same kind of pressure can be used anywhere, but it works especially well in small communities. If enough people protest and threaten to take their business elsewhere, this pressure can clean-up the book shelves.

Whenever you buy a book or magazine in a drug store, grocery, or bookstore and see that there are publications there that are immoral or pro-abortion, always register a complaint with the owner or manager. If all the stores are equally bad, assess the situation carefully and let their management know that you will not tolerate a vicious attack on morality. Let them know that their promotion of immorality and abortion is a travesty. No businessman wants adverse publicity or picketing in front of his store, so promise him that this is what he will get if the offensive material is not removed. Be persistent.

Try to convert them. Don't be afraid to go into a store and level with the management. Even though abortion and dirty books and magazines are legal, they are immoral and demeaning, and they undermine the moral fiber of the community. Most people know this. Make store owners feel embarrassed to have this kind of trash on their shelves. They may tell you they cannot get rid of it and are forced to sell it. That is not true. They can refuse to sell anything they want and return it to the distributor. In some hard cases, perhaps the best you can do is to get them to put this material out of direct view by moving it to a more remote section of the library or store. You may not have as much influence as you want, but through your protest, you will always accomplish something.

Your credibility in trying to get this material removed is greater if you are familiar with it. Become acquainted with some of the offensive passages, and write letters to the editor of the local newspaper explaining the kind of material the library or store is offering as "literature".

Your letters, talks, pickets, and protests will be the squeaky wheel that gets the oil. If you make a clamor and get the community concerned, you can bring enough pressure to bear on the purveyors of trash to get them to remove it or at least put it under the counter.

You can also work to get ordinances passed against pornography or pressure for the enforcement of laws that already exist governing what can be distributed. Most states already have anti-pornography laws that are simply not enforced. Many municipalities also have laws and ordinances on the books, but pornography may have slipped into the area so subtly and gradually that few realized that objectionable material was passing over into hardcore pornography.

You may have to contact your lawyers or legislators to get legislation drawn up and introduced and to have them help you get new laws or city ordinances passed.

Where you can't get laws passed to regulate the distribution of pro-abortion literature or pornography, try to get these materials removed from your local stores, or at the very least, demand that pro-life and pro-family literature be introduced.

There are other methods that might work when argument has failed. One plan is for a number of people to go into the store, all taking their purchases to the check-out counter and saying: "I notice you sell obscene material here. I'd like you to consider withdrawing it from your shelves." If they say no, the customer leaves his purchases at the counter and walks out. If this happens enough, they may reëvaluate their decision to sell pornographic literature or promote abortion.

Some people who have been offended by what a store is selling have covered up the obscene magazines by putting decent magazines in front of them. If they get caught, they may get a scolding, but by defending their action they influence other customers to protest. When you find that your programs are working, spread the word to other like-minded people.

There is a liquor store in Lincolnwood, Illinois, that sells and promotes pornography. It used to be that when you walked into the store the first thing you saw was a lewd magazine display beside the snack rack. Youngsters who went into the store with their parents were confronted with lascivious pictures. On several occasions, a group of Catholic men went into the store and tried to get the owner to move the pornography away from the entrance. Since he was adamant about leaving it where it was, they told him they would not be shopping there anymore. They asked other customers to relay the same message and spread the word. This was the only tool they had, since local obscenity laws were not enforced. Eventually the magazine rack was moved away from the front door to a less conspicuous place. This was no great victory, but at least the owner took a forward step. They are continuing their effort to convert him.

The same tactics can be used to remove articles promoting abortion and novels that support it. There is not much that can be done at this stage to get these banned, but we can boycott stores where they are sold.

And we can put pro-life books in the library and make sure they stay there. We can let librarians know that we will be checking these books regularly to make certain they don't mysteriously disappear.

If public libraries are going to provide books that support abortion, they must also present the pro-life side, and if they don't, they should be boycotted. Our tax dollars support public libraries. There are hundreds of pro-life books that can be introduced to libraries and they should carry all of these.

We have a list of books that should be donated to the library or that libraries should be compelled to purchase. See Chapter 15 for some of these titles.

75 GET YOUR INFORMATION INTO PROGRAMS, GREETINGS, FLYERS, AND ADS

The opportunity to have the pro-life message printed in a secular publication presents itself from time to time. Sometimes newspaper ad departments will solicit business by calling you to place an ad. Be prepared to deal with these requests. As a not-for-profit organization you might get a cut rate.

The telephone directory has a special section for service agencies, and you should try to get your organization listed there. You may not be able to put a lot of information in your listing, but people will know that there is a pro-life group in the community. You may get your message across in a slogan, such as "Protect the Unborn", or "We're Here to Help Pregnant Mothers", which will indicate the type of work your organization does and the services it offers. You can buy a display ad in the Yellow Pages near your listing, where you will not be so limited in what you say. Often it is advisable to make your ad ambiguous, simply indicating that you deal in problem pregnancies and abortion information or counseling. In this way you attract not only women seeking help in having their babies, but also those contemplating abortion. Use a standard logo and statement to represent your organization, one you can insert into a publication on a moment's notice.

Some newspapers and magazines will run your ad at no cost. *Chicago Magazine*, for instance, runs a quarterly section which lists service agencies free of charge. Seek out these publications and tell other pro-life groups about them.

Appoint several volunteers to be on the look out for opportunities to place your pro-life ads. Also, have these same volunteers on the lookout for the abortionists' publicity. If you can't get the abortion ads out, seek an equal opportunity to use that same medium for your pro-life statement.

In an age of mass communications there is almost no limit to the ways you can get your message to the public. A glance around your own desk will reveal many publicity vehicles: decals of every shape and color, logos on your checks advising against abortion, rubber stamps with brief messages, stickers, program books, pins, and buttons. Christmas cards and cards for special occasions, bookmarks, lapel pins, cloth decals that appear to be sewn on, bumper stickers, stencils, and a whole new market of advertising on radio and television through public service announcements and paid advertisements.

At a demonstration at the Cincinnati City Hall, as our group prepared to enter the building, every demonstrator was handed a badge that said "Pro-Life" in white letters on a red background. The large oval badges were striking. With everyone in the demonstration wearing one on his jacket, the overall effect was one of unity and order.

Every day at our office, we receive pro-life mailings that include flyers, invitations to pro-life events, appeals for money, and numerous announcements. The mailings range from handwritten cards to four-color, professionally-printed pieces, from mimeograph sheets to half-tones on slick, enamel paper. Each has its special appeal and accomplishes some good for the pro-life effort. But the ones that usually accomplish the most good are those that deal directly with the victims, the unborn child and the exploited woman. Whatever medium is used, it is ultimately the subject matter that either wins or loses support for the cause. And we have the most important subject matter in the world—preservation of human life.

76 HAND OUT LEGAL INFORMATION AFTER THE ABORTION

One area in which pro-lifers have often been remiss is in dealing with the woman who has already had an abortion. For a woman who has had an abortion and comes to us depressed and unhappy, we recommend special organizations that she can get in touch with such as Women Exploited by Abortion (WEBA). We also have important work for her to do. She can help other women going into the clinics, by talking them out of having abortions or she can take part in counseling sessions at pregnancy help offices.

But when a woman walks out of any abortion clinic, most pro-lifers tend to shun her. She has rejected the help they offered. She has killed her baby. She is undoubtedly leaving the clinic with ambivalent feelings about what she has just done, but also she is probably experiencing some feeling of relief that she is able simply to *walk* out of the clinic. As a rule, pro-lifers do not know what to say to her.

Sometimes they tell her that if she needs help she should contact WEBA, and they hand her some literature. Or they may tell her they will pray for her.

But there is something very practical that pro-lifers can do. They can tell her that she may have complications from the abortion. The things they told her about complications before she went into the clinic are just as true after she has left. They should approach her, and hand her a leaflet telling her what to do about those complications.

One effective leaflet we use is called "As a Woman You Must Know Your Rights". It states, "If you believe that you did not receive proper information concerning the abortion, if you believe that you have suffered physical, mental, or emotional problems because of this abortion, if you believe that the abortionist lied to you or withheld information about risks or alternatives, you may have the right to sue for money damages!" There are included ten questions that a woman, after she has had an abortion, can ask herself:

1. Did the abortionist take a complete history of your health?
2. Did the doctor give you proper counseling about what to expect, about risks or dangers, about the alternatives to abortion? Were

261

you told that there could be complications? Were you told that you could develop mental problems?

3. Were you told that there are other agencies that would help you if you decided against the abortion? (In other words, were you given an alternative or just a sales pitch?)

4. Were you given general medical instructions to follow after the abortion to allow for a safe recovery? Were you given an emergency number to call if you developed problems? (In other words, did they give you some kind of recourse if complications developed?)

5. Did you sign a consent form that fully explained your rights?

6. Did you feel as if you were treated as a unique individual or just another patient on an assembly line? What made you feel this way? (One of the most common responses from women who have had abortions is that they felt like they were part of a herd of cattle.)

7. Did you have severe pain, severe bleeding, infection, emotional problems after the abortion? Did you go back to the abortionist or to a different doctor? (This would, of course, be after some lapse of time, but something for the woman to keep in mind because it does frequently happen.)

8. Was the abortion clinic clean? Did the doctor wash his hands between patients? Did he examine you at any time after the abortion?

9. If you were more than twenty-two weeks pregnant, were you told that your baby could possibly survive on his own and could be born or aborted alive?

10. Were you given any drugs or medicines without proper instructions about usage or side effects?

Then the brochure gives some very important directives:

If you believe that your rights have been violated, take immediate action. Go to a competent doctor and get a complete physical examination. Phone a complaint to the district attorney. Phone a complaint to the Board of Medical Quality. Phone a complaint to the Health Department. Call a pro-life legal organization which will review the merits of your case and represent you as appropriate.

One abortion clinic, touted as among the better ones in Chicago, has twenty-two malpractice suits pending against it. If we can prompt those women who have complaints about their abortions, about conditions in the clinic, about the doctor, or anything else, to sue, we can, in time, put these clinics out of business. It is important to have a leaflet like this ready to hand women leaving the clinic. The leaflet should be geared to the local scene, having local phone numbers and addresses.

More than one abortion clinic has had to close down due to the burden of multiple malpractice suits. Many more would be closed if pro-lifers systematically, and with persistence, encouraged clinic customers to take them to court.

77 GO AFTER ABORTION FUNDING THROUGH LEGISLATION

On a hot July evening in 1976, in Fanual Hall in Boston, during the National Right-to-Life Convention, a large crowd gathered to greet Representative Henry Hyde, a Republican from Illinois, after the Hyde Amendment had passed for the first time. This amendment to the Department of Health and Human Services and the Labor Department funding bill cut off federal funds for abortion. The crowd was raucous and rollicking as Hyde entered the historic hall.

Bill Baird, Boston abortionist, marched in front of the hall with some women and a styrofoam cross. Upon hearing of the pro-lifers' victory, Baird came into the hall and stalked up and down the upper gallery. There was a rumor that he wanted to file charges against someone. Baird likes to file charges. He got some attention when NRLC president Dr. Mildred Jefferson invited him to come in and sit down.

Probably at no time in its history had the rafters of Fanual Hall resounded like they did that evening. Henry Hyde and his fellow pro-life legislators had inaugurated the beginning of the collapse of the abortion culture. They had attacked the abortionists where it hurts most: in the pocketbook.

During subsequent years, the Hyde Amendment has appeared in different forms, but always it has had the effect of stopping some abortions by cutting off federal funding and has set the stage for the cutoff of state and even county funding for abortion.

The Hyde Amendment made it possible for activists in Chicago to get abortions out of Cook County Hospital. Because there was a federal law allowing states to cut off funding of abortion, County Board President George Dunne decided that, by extension, the county could do the same. At Cook County Hospital, funds were not designated for a particular service. Instead of stopping funds for abortion, then, abortions were simply stopped. The Voluntary Interruption of Pregnancy (V.I.P.) ward was closed. That was one effect of the Hyde Amendment. There were many other good effects.

Pro-lifers in Illinois had helped pass legislation based on the Hyde Amendment but applied to state rather than federal funding of abortion. The Illinois bill was stronger than the Hyde. It had no exceptions. The cutoff passed, but was temporarily enjoined with the help of American Civil Liberties Union (ACLU) attorneys for other pro-abortionists. Ultimately, when the Hyde Amendment was declared constitutional, Illinois' strong law went into effect, and other states began passing legislation to cut off state funding of abortion. Cutting off welfare money to pay for abortions saves an estimated three hundred thousand lives each year.

Legislation to curb abortion is important. Even if at times it seems futile to get a bill passed, even if it seems that we cannot stop many abortions through legislation because the money will always come from somewhere, the fact remains that many who do not have the option of a tax-funded abortion will have to carry their children to term. The woman will decide to take care of this new life rather than have it destroyed with tax dollars.

Pro-lifers must fight to end funding of abortion on every governmental level, including its funding with U.S. money in Third World countries. We must fight to save decent pro-life Americans from passively cooperating in abortion with their tax dollars. It is an outrage for those who abhor abortion to have their money used to pay for it.

One obvious advantage of cutting off government abortion funding is that it reduces the profits of death peddlers. Without government funds, it is difficult for some of them to operate their clinics. One Chicago abortionist reported profits of more than $900,000 in welfare abortions in a single year. In a less profitable year, he reported, he netted only $700,000 for destroying poor women's babies at taxpayers' expense. It is no wonder that pro-lifers' blood sometimes boils.

78 COORDINATE YOUR POLITICAL PICKETS NATIONWIDE

Several years ago, when Senator Edward Kennedy was a presidential hopeful, he was picketed in Chicago with a carefully planned arrangement of signs. Each sign was two-feet square and displayed a single letter. Together, the signs spelled out, "TED KENNEDY IS PRO-ABORTION". The boards were brilliant white and the letters were black and red.

The participants were choreographed to use the cards in such a way that, when the picket marshal cried out, for instance, "Give me a 'T' ", the whole group shouted "T" and the person holding the "T" sign, face-down against his legs, raised it quickly over his head, straight-arm. Then the marshal shouted, "Give me an 'E' ", the crowd shouted "E", and the second person in line held his sign up next to the "T". And so on down the line until one long sign read, "TED KENNEDY IS PRO-ABORTION". This had to be rehearsed so that all the letters were held at the same height, were held close together, were properly spaced, and were in proper sequence.

In Indianapolis, we picketed a dinner honoring Senators Kennedy and Birch Bayh. It was Senator Bayh's birthday, which falls on January 22. Along the street in front of the banquet hall, we spelled out, in the manner described above, "KENNEDY & BAYH VOTE FOR ABORTION". Our line-up stretched half a block and was so impressive that all the television cameras followed the spell-out. As our message developed, those inside the banquet hall came to the windows to watch. We got more attention than the dignitaries inside.

Coordinate several actions to take place simultaneously during a protest or demonstration. For instance, while a large group is outside protesting, the leader can send a few people inside the hall. At an appropriate point in the candidate's talk, they will ask a question about his position on abortion, or simply shout out, "Abortion!" or "What about the unborn babies?" Others planted in the crowd can take up the chant. If these efforts are successful in one community, the leader should call ahead to the next city where the candidate is heading, contact the activist pro-life group there, and describe in detail the methods, techniques, signs, chants, and leaflets used. Recommend that these same techniques, signs, and visuals be used at their demonstration.

This lets the candidate and his entourage know that there is an organized effort by pro-life all across the state or country working for his defeat. The press will also catch on to the fact that the effort to defeat this candidate is well-coordinated. People in a particular locale may not recognize this as a coordinated effort, since most likely they did not attend other rallies, but the important thing is that the candidate will realize it, and the traveling press will begin to see the pattern of planned, coordinated action. Such organization can have a powerful effect on the candidate's campaign.

We used a variation of this in Illinois when Representative John Anderson was running for president in 1980. We followed him on his campaign trail, and Anderson was said to have confided to a friend, that he was greatly disturbed by the concerted effort to keep the abortion issue and his position on it before the public. He had written a fund-raising letter for the National Abortion Rights Action League, and we distributed copies of this at every stop. Another of our "secret weapons" in the Anderson campaign was a little Irish lady, Rosemary Stokes, who met him at nearly every talk to ask him why he had signed a letter to raise money to kill babies. He must have begun to rue the day he put his name on that letter.

In the case of the Kennedy pro-life pickets, by the time Kennedy reached Florida, the fifth stop on his tour, the media were asking him about these protests of his abortion position. This forced him to state publicly that he approved of a woman's right to abortion.

An even better example of the power of organized protest was the picketing of Geraldine Ferraro during the 1984 presidential campaign. Ferraro, vice presidential candidate on the Democratic ticket, claimed to be personally opposed to abortion while speaking out for free choice and carrying a 100 percent pro-abortion record in Congress.

Pro-life activists across the country demonstrated with similar chants, posters, card sections, and slogans. This was so effective that the national press caught on to it midway through the campaign. Reporters such as Bill Peterson, of the *Washington Post*, wrote on the phenomenon, and talk show host Phil Donahue conducted an interview on it, to which he invited the Pro-Life Action League director to defend this action. So successful was the campaign that the National Abortion Rights Action League (NARAL) instigated an investigation by the Federal Election Commission (FEC) of the Pro-Life Action Leage, charging a breach of charter.

It takes organization, planning, and a great deal of cooperation to coordinate pickets with other pro-life groups around the country. But it has a powerful effect on candidates and the press. These demonstrations keep the issue before the public. That, in itself, is a major achievement.

COORDINATING A NATIONAL PROGRAM OF PICKETS

When a nationally known pro-abortionist is traveling through the country, it is effective to let him and the media know that your protest is nationally organized and coordinated. A well-placed directive like this to a few hundred activists will accomplish your goal.

HOW TO COORDINATE POLITICAL PICKETS OF MONDALE-FERRARO

FOR OUTSIDE APPEARANCES

1 Purchase sheets of 3/16" Foamcore or white poster board from your local art supply store. Also, buy water-repellent, quick-drying black paint and a ½" or 1" brush. The message you want to spell out is: FERRARO & FRITZ BACK ABORTION. ("Ferraro" is intentionally named first.) Cut the boards into 25 smaller panels, each measuring approximately 2' by 2'. Cut one of these panels in half and paint an "I" on each one (for the "I's" in "FRITZ" and "ABORTION.") If either of the candidates appears separately in your area, you will have to say he or she "BACKS" abortion, so paint an "S" on another panel. Then paint all the remaining letters, one per panel. Letters should be as large as possible, extending almost to the edge of the board, 5" to 5½" wide, as illustrated.

2 Before chant begins, boards are kept down at foot level, letters facing legs, as shown. Top and bottom should be marked on back side of each board. Be sure to leave a space of one arm length between words. A blank panel is not necessary.

3 When candidates approach, the leader calls out on a megaphone, "Give me an F!" and the first person in line raises his or her letter high <u>overhead</u> and keeps it there until the entire message is spelled out. The letter-holders and all members of the group repeat each letter as soon as it is called out, yelling "F!" "E!" "R!" etc.

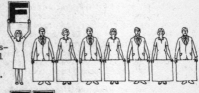

4 The leader continues immediately, "Give me an E!" and the second person raises the "E" up next to the "F". The chant is repeated quickly as the leader calls for the rest of the letters, "R", "R"..."A"..."R"...until the entire message is spelled out. The letter on the front of the board should be indicated in small type on the back to avoid mistakes.

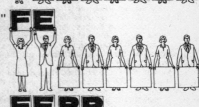

5 After the "N" has been displayed, the leader asks, "What do we say?", to which all respond loudly, "<u>Ferraro and Fritz back abortion</u>!" The leader then begins the chant, "Life yes, abortion no!...Life yes, Ferraro no!...Life yes, abortion no!...Life yes, Fritz no!..."

This photo shows how it's done, but there's no space between "NO" and "O'CONNOR" and too much space between the "L" and "I" in "LIFE." Also, letters are not held above the head for maximum visibility and impact. Watch such details and your demonstration will be effective.

FOR INSIDE APPEARANCES

The campaign to direct attention to Ferraro and Mondale's militant anti-life stands must be brought inside the halls, auditoria, churches and conference rooms as well. Signs large enough to be effective and grab media attention can be carried into such areas and displayed at the appropriate time. The trick is to fold them in half and conceal them in your briefcase or handbag, or under your coat or jacket.

A typical attache case is anywhere from 14" X 9½" to 17" X 11." If you double those measurements, you have a sign 14" X 19" or 17" X 22" and that's big enough to do the job and get the message across. Several signs can be inserted in a case or bag, to be distributed to other pro-lifers inside, so not everyone need carry a case or bag.

To make your folding sign, simply measure your briefcase or handbag to see how large a sign can be put into it. Then double the smaller measurement and cut a sheet of poster board that size. After your message ("FERRARO & FRITZ BACK ABORTION" or some other appropriate statement) has been painted on it as large and bold as possible, turn the board over and cut gently down the middle where you want the fold to be. Be sure to cut only as deep as necessary to enable the board to be folded and still retain its strength. (If you cut too deeply and fear the board may tear, affix clear Scotch tape on the front side over the cut.)

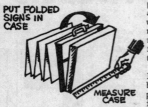

PUT FOLDED SIGNS IN CASE

MEASURE CASE

CUT GENTLY FOR FOLD

If many pro-lifers infiltrate appearances by these pro-abortion candidates and display these signs all at once, while shouting, "Abortion!" whenever they refer to life-related issues, the effect on the speakers as well as the public and media can be great.

It's just as important to bark out, "Abortion!", every time Ferraro or Mondale touch on a life issue as it is to display the signs. Newspaper and TV cameras can ignore the signs, but radio and TV microphones pick up these cries and comments. They cannot be deleted easily without also deleting what the candidates are saying. If these tactics are used consistently across the country by pro-lifers, our message will get the coverage it deserves.

The purpose of this systematic approach to picketing the Democratic national platform is threefold: First, it will become clear to the candidates that there is an organized program of protest when they see the same pattern wherever they go. This will send them a message that pro-life activists are well organized against their platform. These visuals will telegraph to them that there is effective planning behind the scenes. Second, the traveling press follow the candidates wherever they go and will see the pattern in these demonstrations and will eventually question Ferraro and Mondale on their reaction to this "conspiracy." Third, this overt action will keep the abortion issue alive throughout the campaign. When interviewed by the press, we can detail both candidates' abortion stand. Have a statement printed and ready for the press containing their pro-abortion statements. For more unformation, call THE PRO-LIFE ACTION LEAGUE at (312) 777-2900.

Joseph M. Scheidler, Executive Director.

79 THE VALUE OF PETITIONS

Petitions, as a means of effecting change, have less value than many of the other pro-life actions or devices discussed in this book. Some people overrate petitions, while others denigrate them. Their real worth lies somewhere in between.

Petitions are too easy to come by to be of any great value. All that is required is to collect a lot of names and addresses on some sheets of paper. Yet, a large number of these names and addresses often impresses legislators, executives, or committees by conveying the message that there is great interest in the issue at hand and that people have taken a firm stand and are not afraid to publicize their commitment on this issue.

When discussing petitions, it is necessary to point out that if you have a choice between a petition or a personal letter always opt for the letter. You may not always have this choice, though. Petitions are a kind of substitute for letters that won't get written.

While a single letter is better than a page of petitions, and represents thousands of people who feel the same way as the letter writer, most people will not write letters. But they will sign petitions. So, if you have a point to make and want to impress someone with the number backing you, print large numbers of petition blanks and instruct your members to go out and get them filled.

Getting petitions signed is an art in itself. It takes persistence and humility to stand in front of a church or shopping center or to sit at a table or go from car to car to get the pages filled. Some people seem to enjoy it, but most of us do it only because we can't refuse any pro-life request.

A cheerful, open disposition is helpful in getting petitions signed. It is important that petition gatherers not be easily discouraged. Some people will not only refuse to sign petitions, but refuse with insults and arguments. Some even become so incensed at what you represent that they will try to spoil your petition. For the sake of the cause, it is best not to argue with hostile people or take offense at refusals to sign. Some people may not be opposed to your issue, they simply don't sign anything.

When the number of petitions desired has been collected, it is important to present them in the most advantageous way.

Arrangements should be made beforehand with the people or organization to whom the petitions are to be presented, so that they will be on hand to receive them. Also, you can inform the media that you will be making the presentation at a given time and place.

The manner in which you present petitions is important, too. Do it in a way that will enhance the sheets of petitions. In themselves they are not too interesting, but they can be made interesting.

In Pittsburgh a few years ago, People Concerned for the Unborn Child (PCUC) wanted to impress the Governor that large numbers of citizens wanted to stop paying for abortions with tax dollars. They had collected thousands of pages of petitions. They planned to bundle them together and leave them on the Governor's desk.

Our office suggested that instead they tape the sheets together, end to end, and roll them into a thick wheel and present them that way, as we had done in Chicago. They went us one better. They delivered them in a roll, but since the Governor was not in, they began unrolling the petitions in his office, rolled them through the hall, down the staircase, across the rotunda of the Capitol and up the opposite staircase, leaving a seemingly endless ribbon of petitions.

The TV camera crews and newspaper photographers had a heyday taking shots that showed the entire strip leading through the building into the Governor's office.

Another pro-life group had children deliver the petitions. They stacked them in a pile that was taller than the smallest child.

Some have weighed their petitions and played up the "weightiness of the issue" angle.

A statement should always accompany the petitions, with a copy to the person or agency being petitioned and one for the press. If the press does not attend the presentation, write a story for them.

If your petitions accomplish your goal, play up this victory for all it is worth. The publicity will encourage those who worked on the petitions, as well as those who signed them. It will also popularize the petition method.

The petition has some fringe benefits for those who use it wisely. It is a useful method of drawing people into your cause. Signing a petition is a way to make the signer think about the issue you are interested in. It is flattering to some people to be asked to sign a petition. Their interest in your issue may be enhanced by putting their signature down on your petition.

Before you deliver your petitions to their destination, copy all the names and addresses on them. Use them as part of your mailing list.

Don't be too hard on the lowly petition. It has its place in the effort to end abortion.

80 SET UP A PRO-LIFE CONVENTION

A convention is a collection of meetings, workshops, and seminars used as a vehicle for getting pro-lifers together to encourage more pro-life activity. It is also a time for rededication, presentation of new ideas, and learning about other pro-lifers' successes and problems. It is a time to listen to experts in the fields of law, medicine, activism, politics, and legislation. In short, it is an opportunity to expand one's education, learn from the experiences of others, and become recharged in the pro-life effort.

Attending pro-life conventions builds enthusiasm, inspires pro-lifers to do more for the cause of the unborn, and strengthens their determination. Also after finding out what efforts work for others, they can try these programs, projects and methods in their own locales.

But running your own convention takes a lot of planning. You will need a crew of helpers who are known to be dependable. You must find a convention site that is conveniently located and is not going to cost so much that it will be prohibitive for people to attend. You may have to find a place with banquet facilities, and also rooms for out-of-town guests to stay economically.

You will first have to conduct some fund-raising projects to get started on the convention, because you will need money to advertise, send out mailings, pay for programs, and pay to reserve your convention facilities. Some of the bills will have to be paid while you are still preparing for the event. This is why convention planners often give discounts for early registration. That is money in the bank that helps keep them going.

You will need people to arrange entertainment, decorate the tables, schedule the speakers; print the program; pick people up at the airport, bus, or train; sell tickets; select the meal; contact the media; and arrange for dozens of other items that will make your convention a success.

The convention should have a theme and a goal. It should concentrate on some facet of pro-life work, and develop that theme. The theme will tie the parts of the convention together and give it a direction, such as, "Activism: Why It Works".

You may want to present honors at your convention to people who have done outstanding pro-life work. Select your speakers carefully. If you are going to have a keynote address to start out the convention and a banquet speaker to end the convention, these should be people who will be a drawing card for each event, bringing people to the beginning of the convention and holding them to the end or attracting those who might not otherwise come to hear just the traditional pro-life subjects. Invite someone who will draw leaders in the community and have a message that will not only inform and inspire but motivate to action.

The convention can be good publicity for your organization. It can give you a name, establish your place in the community, and acquaint you with the press. People who attend a well-organized, instructive convention frequently become your organization's best supporters. They will return to their communities and discuss your efforts among their friends.

Don't expect a lot of media coverage of your convention, especially if you are in a large city. There are so many conventions going on that pro-life groups usually don't expect much press attention. Still, if you have an outstanding speaker or an unusual series of workshops, you might attract the press. The Americans United for Life Legal Defense Fund (AUL) have a good track record for media coverage. You might bring your main speakers in early to appear on radio and television talk shows. Have them mention your convention or join them yourself on the talk show to announce the details of the convention.

You might also hold a march or demonstration in conjunction with the convention to alert the public to what is going on.

Set up a press room where your speakers can be interviewed and where the media can get press releases, type their stories, and make calls. The press may come to a few workshops, but as a rule they don't attend the entire convention. But they may drop by just to see what is going on if you publicize it well enough.

If your convention does get publicity, the abortionists may try to attract the media, too. At their press conference, they will trot out their platitudes, slogans, and semantics to show that they are the defenders of women's rights, and that you are trying to take these rights away. Such pro-abortion activity can help you. If you are picketed by the abortionists or if they hold a press conference, this introduces the element of conflict into your convention, and conflict draws media attention. It can help your public image and publicize the fact that you are a force in the community.

A convention takes planning, a good staff, a coordinator, a convention chairman, and lots of money. You may have to contact your more wealthy members for money to get the convention off the ground.

Don't be disappointed if your first convention is smaller and less impressive than you had expected. People will profit from it. Few things you do in the pro-life movement are useless. It is better to go ahead with your plans even if you suspect that it won't be as spectacular as you hope. Your first convention rarely will be, and it will also be your hardest. You will make lots of mistakes. Learn from those mistakes, and your second convention will be easier.

Don't overextend yourself by bringing in too many special guests on your first attempt. That will only burden your committee with extra expenses. Try to get speakers to donate their services. Provide them with transportation, room, and board. If you can't afford hotel rooms, ask some of your members to accommodate them in their homes. Most speakers are happy to stay in someone's home and many even prefer this arrangement to a motel room. But always be sure to ask the guests their preference.

Avoid unnecessary expenses for your first convention. Use simple decorations, free entertainment, a low budget meal. Don't go in debt. It is hard to get members enthusiastic about paying off debts.

It is also important to do something that will become a tradition at your convention, such as giving a special award. Create an atmosphere that identifies your organization. Develop a spirit that draws convention-goers into your organization. Make them feel that they are an important part of a great movement—a spirit your speakers can help establish.

The convention can help hold the pro-life movement together in your community. People usually become enthusiastic during a convention and are encouraged to go out and continue their fight for the unborn. The complaint we hear most often at conventions we attend is that the planning committee has not directed sufficient attention to the role of activism in the pro-life movement. We held an activist convention in 1984 and invited activists from all across the country. Even that wasn't as active as we would have liked, but it got the ball rolling, and the next year we got what we had wanted, a 100 percent activist convention. We were in our glory.

81 VIOLENCE: WHY IT WON'T WORK

By violence here we mean a direct, physical attack on some type of facility or the personnel who work there.

There is a small faction within the pro-life movement—just as there is within any movement—who, from time to time, talk about the advisability of stopping abortion by force. We have even heard some who discuss the possibility of the abortion conflict escalating into a "shooting war".

Most of this is just talk. The fact remains, however, that there have been incidents of violence against both pro-life facilities and abortion clinics and offices. Generally, this violence has taken the form of damage to property, although there was also a kidnapping of an abortionist and his wife.

This author has been struck, spit on, pushed, and received innumerable death threats, warnings, insults, and crank calls; he has had his sight damaged, tires slashed, office windows cut with glass-cutters and broken with rocks, and his office painted with roofing tar. Nearly all pro-life activist leaders can cite a similar list of malicious acts. Some pro-life offices have been fire bombed. Pro-life pickets and counselors have had buckets of water thrown on them, have had cars driven toward them at high speeds, have been struck by these cars and with clubs by clinic guards. We have almost all been subjected to a variety of insults and injuries. Few of these incidents ever get reported, since many police departments are reluctant to acknowledge that they happened. There have been very few arrests of abortionists made, and even fewer guilty verdicts handed down.

On the other hand, there are a growing number of highly publicized instances of what appear to be pro-life violence against abortionists and their clinics. The kidnapping of abortionist Hector Zevallos in August 1982 by the so-called "Army of God" was an isolated and unusual incident, allegedly the responsibility of a few zealous anti-abortionists acting independently of any larger group. Zevallos and his wife were released unharmed after eight days, and one of the men implicated in the "conspiracy and attempt to interfere with interstate commerce" was sentenced to thirty years in jail, with twelve more years added to the sentence later.

Another anti-abortionist, admittedly acting alone, was jostled after he entered a New York abortion clinic, spilled gasoline on the property, and set the clinic ablaze. The only one who suffered injury was the anti-abortionist. The building housing the clinic was damaged. In 1984 there was a rash of attacks on abortion clinics, mostly on the East Coast, in Texas, and in Washington State. In these and other cases, the aim seems to have been to curtail abortion by putting the facility out of commission, at least temporarily.

It should be pointed out that the abortionists, in presenting what they believe to be cases of pro-life violence, often lack evidence that the attack was made by pro-life people. And they lump together all kinds of "terrorist tactics" such as telephone calls, pickets, and peaceful sit-ins, in an effort to present a sinister picture of what is in fact *non*-violent pro-life activism.

All of the activist pro-lifers the Pro-Life Action League works with concur with the League's position against violence and its program of *non-violent direct action*. We take our commitment to non-violence seriously, believing that violence on our part would be counter-productive. It is the abortionists who are engaged in routine violence against unborn children (dismemberment, salt poisoning, strangulation) and their mothers (hemorrhage, scarring, infection, sterility). The use of violence could damage the reputation of pro-life activists, while undermining traditional non-violent methods. The use of violence might reinforce the erroneous belief that the end justifies the means, and that evil can be overcome by evil.

Besides, the use of violence probably would not work in the long run. The destruction of an abortion clinic is a temporary solution. New quarters can be found. Putting an abortionist out of commission for a while, as in the 1982 Zevallos kidnapping, did not stop abortions. While we might respect the zeal that would prompt such activities, we do not condone or recommend them.

We have corresponded with Peter Burkin who was implicated in an abortion clinic firebombing in New York. Several of us have visited Don Benny Anderson, who has been sentenced to a federal penitentiary in connection with the 1982 Zevallos kidnapping. We are also in touch with Joseph Grace, implicated in a case of damage to an abortion clinic in Norfolk, Virginia and have visited with Curtis Beseda, implicated in a clinic fire in Everett, Washington. All four men are dedicated to the belief that unborn children's most basic right—the right to life—is being violated by abortion and that daring actions are needed to awaken

Americans to the terrible reality of abortion. But most pro-lifers would say that all four, if guilty, went too far.

What lasting advantage is there to show for the actions they were accused of? Zevallos went back to Hope Clinic to do more abortions; the damaged clinics have reopened or have sent their clients elsewhere. Was the effect these actions had on the image of a movement that condemns violence helpful? While we understand the feelings of anger, outrage, and frustration that likely prompted these and similar actions, we advise pro-lifers not to resort to violent tactics, but to save lives and stop abortions through non-violent, direct action.

Direct action, and even civil disobedience, have an important part to play in winning the pro-life battle. But violence, we believe, does not.

We must point out for the sake of proper perspective, however, that no amount of damage to real estate can equal the violence of taking a single human life. Civilized societies rate the loss of life as far more serious than property damage. But today, in our society, punishment is meted out to those who damage property while those who destroy life are rewarded. It is a sign of the deterioration of our values that much of the national media concentrates on damaged buildings, with pictures of charred real estate, while refusing to present pictures of the human victims who are heartlessly and systematically dismembered and painfully killed inside that real estate.

Pro-lifers are rarely allowed to show on network television the victims of abortion—the real violence of the abortion debate. Yet we have had to watch ad nauseam pictures of damaged buildings carefully panned on America's TV screens, while being directly or indirectly accused of causing the damage.

But we will not play the abortionists' violent game. We plan to win without resorting to violence.

82 GET INTO POLITICS—RUN FOR OFFICE AND FORM A PRO-LIFE PARTY

One of the most effective ways to influence law is to join the legislative bodies that make the laws.

Pro-lifers have recognized from the beginning that having the right people in the right places can get us the laws we need to protect the unborn. Abortion was foisted upon the American public, not by the legislative process which is the way changes are supposed to take place, but by a *fiat* of seven Supreme Court justices.

With the federal courts so powerful that they make laws and impose them on the people, the people have to be even more diligent about electing good politicians in the hope that they will curb the excessive power of the court. Many Americans believe the courts have become so powerful that we are living under a virtual judicial dictatorship.

It is important to elect to our legislatures men and women of principle, representatives who know right from wrong, who understand good and evil, and who will stand fast by what they believe. Governments are all about people. Abraham Lincoln called ours a government "of the people, by the people, and for the people", and he said that as such it would not perish. If it is truly of, by, and for the people, it will not perish because it will be good government.

But this will happen only if our elected officials understand what people are, human beings from the moment of conception, and that the right to life comes from God, not from the state, and that this right must be protected from beginning to end. Anyone who aspires to public office but has the notion that some people are expendable and can be legally exterminated is not fit for public service. Such an individual is an enemy of the people and must be kept out of government.

It is vitally important that those who approve of the killing of unborn children or the elderly or the handicapped not be in positions of influence. They disqualify themselves from the legislature, the judicial system, or the executive branch. People who lack right moral principles and who cannot see the evil of destroying human life, experimenting on humans, or permitting promiscuity, who vote to promote pornography and homosexuality, have no business in public office. Only those who have sound moral principles and adhere to guidelines based on a Judeo-Christian ethic and the natural law should represent the people.

It is not easy to run for office—or even to know what office to run for, for that matter. There is a great deal of red tape involved in getting the necessary signatures, getting on the ballot, getting endorsements from the right people, and getting elected. Today it usually takes a great deal of money to run for nearly any office and certainly for high public office. But pro-lifers must run for office, and some are doing it. Whenever a solid pro-life person believes he can spare the time and effort and can make the expenditures, he owes it to society to run for office: and to run to win.

Consider some of the opportunities made available to the person running for office: the opportunity to reach the public with the pro-life message, giving people a better understanding of what pro-life is all about, explaining what an injustice abortion is and the damage it is doing to society. Consider how many times Congressman Henry Hyde, in his capacity as an elected official, has been called upon to appear on talk shows and newscasts, where he relays the message to the nation that it is human life which is destroyed in abortion. Hyde's graphic statements are well known to most pro-lifers, but they startle the less informed with their precision, as when he talks about the "inconvenient, pre-born child". How many times Hyde has made it clear that there is a human being, inconvenient to someone, who has to suffer the ultimate penalty, death. Consider the opportunities Ellen McCormack had when she ran for president, and think of other pro-lifers who are not afraid to make public their support of human life.

Most of us have seen pro-lifers running for public office who were afraid to bring up the abortion issue, arguing that it might lose them votes. It is sad how some candidates fudge on the pro-life issue, but are outspoken on every *other* issue. Any candidate worthy of public service should be willing to take a strong stand on pro-life and let the people know where he stands.

No one should be ashamed of defending the unborn nor be ambivalent about taking a stand for life. Some candidates explain that the pro-lifers know they are pro-life, but they don't tell anyone else because they are afraid of losing the liberal vote. This strategy may work in some cases, but a candidate should also consider that his silence on abortion may lose him sympathetic pro-life voters who don't know his strategy. A candidate is only fit for public office when he stands up for the principles he believes in.

If you decide to run for public office, run to win. There is a need for more pro-lifers to run for office or to be more directly involved in the campaigns of pro-life candidates.

A problem arises when two pro-life candidates run against each other in a primary race and a pro-abortion candidate will run against one of them in the final election. You must determine which pro-life candidate is more open about his pro-life stand and which has the best possibility of winning. You should back one of them. It may even be worth the effort to try to talk one of the pro-life candidates out of running.

If there is no pro-life candidate running, you have a problem. If two abortionists are running, generally vote out the incumbent and let the new candidate win. The incumbent will have prestige and his tenure will have garnered him committee chairmanships. Vote him out of office and start with someone who has less clout. Even if he is not good on our issue, a new office holder will generally be easier to work with than an incumbent. You are also punishing the incumbent by letting him know that you worked for his defeat because he used his office to promote abortion. Voters should also consider the candidate's affiliation with other office holders who may be favorable to our position and could influence him on a particular bill.

There can be some complicated situations in politics. For suggestions on working for pro-life candidates and defeating pro-abortion ones, stay in touch with your local or state pro-life political organization or one of the national agencies listed at the end of this chapter.

In the state of New York there is a pro-life party. Some say that this doesn't do much good for the movement, but those who established it point out several advantages: your party can carry five to seven percent of the total vote and, if it is a close election, a deal can be made with one of the candidates to bring a promise of pro-life support if the pro-life party will swing its votes his way. You can also take votes away from a pro-abortion candidate to let him know that you are not going to tolerate his support of abortion. Another advantage of having a pro-life party is the increased access to the media your candidate will have. Pro-life activist Art O'Brien, of Garden City, New York, said a new world of media interest opened up for him when he ran for a local office as a pro-life candidate. He was able to introduce the abortion issue on many media outlets that he had not formerly had access to.

For information on starting a pro-life party or seeing how a pro-life party functions, along with its advantages and disadvantages, see the list of political action committees at the end of this chapter.

Politics is a vital area of pro-life concern and always will be. Even if the movement gets a pro-life amendment throughout the states, pro-lifers will still need to have legislators on their side to fight abortionists' efforts to make exceptions and erode the law.

Pro-life has always considered a politician's statement that he is personally opposed to abortion but cannot impose his morality on others to be the worst kind of political hypocrisy. We have picketed and challenged such candidates as Edward Kennedy and Geraldine Ferraro, both of whom profess to be Catholic, although they have consistently voted for pro-abortion legislation and against pro-life bills.

In 1984, during the presidential campaign, national attention was focused on the abortion issue because of the selection of a "Catholic", Geraldine Ferraro, as the Democratic party's vice-presidential nominee. Like Senators Kennedy, Moynihan, and others, she claimed to be a good Catholic. She said she wouldn't have an abortion herself, but she thought it would be wrong to deny this "right" to others.

Important elements in the angry debate that ensued when politicians claimed they could vote for abortion and remain good Catholics were the strong statements of Archbishop John J. O'Connor of New York. He left little doubt about where politicians stand when they claim to be Catholics while rejecting the Church's condemnation of abortion:

> We fail to see how office holders can escape their responsibility in this grave matter. Particularly we fail to see the logic of those who contend: I'm personally opposed to abortion, but I will not impose my personal views on others. That position is radically inconsistent because a third party's right is at stake.

> Archbishop John J. O'Connor
> New York
> (*National Catholic Reporter*
> August 17, 1984, p. 8)

I do not see how a Catholic in conscience could vote for an individual explicitly expressing himself or herself as favoring abortion. As far as I can see, there is no way. I don't see how it can be justified. It seems to me that if you maintain that you're "pro-choice", then you have to say you approve abortion if it is chosen. So that makes you pro-abortion. It's a very crucial question for voters.

> Archbishop John J. O'Connor
> New York
> (*Wanderer*, July 5, 1984, p. 1)

Catholic legislators are fortunate to have the guidance of the teaching Church on moral questions. But confusion is being caused by the Catholic legislator who says that he or she is personally against abortion and who then votes for abortion legislation and accepts money from abortionist groups. The bishops rightly expect a Catholic legislator to have a developed, informed, sensitive, Catholic sense of what is morally right or wrong. The Catholic knows that morality is not determined by democratic vote, but ultimately by God's law. The most fundamental issue facing the legislators today is the abortion question, whether human life in the womb has a right to exist, to be born, to live out its span of years. A legislator should not dodge the issue. I do not understand how in good conscience any legislator could be in favor of abortion if he or she admits that medical science has shown that human life exists from conception and that the legislator has a duty to protect all human life. It would also be unprincipled for a legislator to adopt a pro-abortion stance simply because in our contemporary American society there are more votes and money coming from pro-abortion forces. A third approach of a legislator, particularly a Catholic one, is to separate a personal opposition to abortion from his legislative stance. The usual terminology is: "I am personally opposed to abortion, but I will not let my personal beliefs influence how I vote." I see this approach as lacking in both logic and courage, as irresponsible and even dangerous. The pro-choice Catholic legislator is, in my judgment, neither logical nor theological. Such a legislator is not showing the courage of his convictions. For a Catholic to follow his conscience in an amoral society such as ours means great sacrifice. Heroism is sometimes called for in holding to what is morally right. The bishops should rightly look to Catholic legislators to be principled and strong in fighting for the right to life and dignity of all God's sons and daughters. It is no exercise of civil liberty to destroy one's own or another's unborn child. And the bishops are rightly dismayed by Catholic legislators who, in a position to uphold human life, are tolerant or passive before the horrendous moral evil that is abortion.

Most Rev. John F. Whealon
Hartford, Connecticut
August 10, 1984

Catholics must demand a categorical commitment from candidates on their opposition to the funding of abortion and their intent to make it illegal. If they refuse to commit themselves or put you off by stating that while they are "personally opposed" to it, they must listen to other voices in their constituency or prefer to leave women to decide for themselves whether to abort or not, then you cannot in conscience vote for these candidates. To do so would be to cooperate seriously in perpetuating this horrible crime, which will eventually draw down divine punishment on our nation.

Catholic Bishops of Iowa

We call upon all in public office and positions of authority to oppose legalized abortion by support of a constitutional amendment. We plead with them to lead the struggle against abortion in our State and Nation. We urge them to stand up for the sacredness of every human life. We urge them to advocate legislation to inhibit and eliminate the killing of unborn children.

The Catholic Bishops of New York

Political Action Committees:

NEW YORK STATE RIGHT-TO-LIFE
PARTY
  P.O. Box 865
  Rome, NY 13440

NATIONAL PRO-LIFE POLITICAL
ACTION COMMITTEE
  7777 Leesburg Pike
  Suite 305
  Falls Church, VA 22043

LIFE AMENDMENT POLITICAL
ACTION COMMITTEE, INC.
  P.O. Box 1983
  Garrisonville, VA 22463

NATIONAL CONSERVATIVE
POLITICAL ACTION COMMITTEE
  1001 Prince St.
  Alexandria, VA 22314

THE AD HOC COMMITTEE IN
DEFENSE OF LIFE
  810 National Press Bldg.
  Washington, D.C. 20045

83 HOW TO DEAL WITH THE POLICE

Dealing with the police will always be an element of the pro-life activist movement because we are going to be out on the streets and in the clinics and involved in what are potential conflict situations. At most of our demonstrations, marches, pickets, sit-ins, and blitzes there will be police on hand. It is important to have a standard plan for dealing with them.

The first rule to keep in mind is that we are not fighting the police. We are fighting the Supreme Court's 1973 ruling on abortion. We are fighting the law insofar as it is bad law, but we are not fighting law enforcers or those who are supposed to keep order. Consequently, we do not represent a threat to society or to law and order. We are trying to improve society and make it better for people to live in. We are trying to protect lives, and this is essentially what laws are supposed to do.

Most police departments have mottos to the effect that they serve and protect the public. Their work is to protect the rights, property, and lives of individuals. Abortion-on-demand has not negated all our rights. Pro-lifers still have the right to free assembly, to march and picket, to pass out information, and to talk to others. People still have a right to be given free information and to receive it.

We can rightly tell the police that we are doing the same things they are pledged to do—that is, serve and protect. We are trying to protect the unborn child. We are trying to serve the pregnant woman. The relationship with the police should be, as far as possible, a positive one. Before a demonstration or picket, call the police and tell them where you are going to be, at what time your activity will begin, and how long it will last. Make it a rule that before any public event, you call the police. Don't call them before a sit-in, blitz, or sidewalk counseling, however, because you don't want to tip off the abortionists that you are coming. But let them know about all your public activities and ask them for protection.

Always carry a pocketful of personal name cards and give them to the police commander or officer in charge. If they ask who is in charge of the demonstration, come forward and tell them who you are and assure them that you know the rules you are supposed to follow. Tell them you intend to obey the laws. Try not to be contentious. Some police are belligerent and will start giving orders. If the orders are reasonable, such as that a picket must keep moving, must not block the entrance to the building, and must not block the sidewalk, then listen patiently and accept their orders. Even though you know these rules, it is better to listen and assure the police that you intend to abide by their rules and keep order.

You must be wary, however, of being commanded to obey rules that don't exist. The police are there to preserve order and they would be happier if there were no conflict at all. They would be happier still if you were not there to begin with. Sometimes they will be hostile simply because you are making their day more difficult than it would be otherwise. Sometimes they may bring to work with them a bad disposition or personal problems.

But don't let them make up rules that curtail your rights. If you doubt that an order is backed by a law or ordinance, ask the officer to cite the law or ask him if you may check to see if he is correct. Tell him you will obey the law, but you do not want to be told to obey laws that are not on the books. The police will usually cooperate with your request to see the law.

In the final analysis, the police have a responsibility to preserve order, but they will generally not hinder you if you conduct yourselves properly. If you challenge them imprudently or disrespectfully, you may run into trouble and on some occasions the police will charge you with breaking the law, even when you have not. Even in this case, remain polite and respectful.

Policemen, too, can be educated to the facts on abortion. Never pass up an opportunity to show them the pictures of what is going on inside the clinic you are picketing. It is better to have them on your side than fighting you, and it helps if they understand the reason you are there. More often than not, the police are sympathetic to our cause and give us considerable latitude in conducting our marches and demonstrations. Only a few are strongly sympathetic to the abortion clinic operators or have only one thought in mind—to lock us up. But these are few and far between.

The pro-life police officer is in a quandry, knowing that our presence at the clinic is saving lives and that when we are removed the killing commences. He feels trapped between his "duty" to uphold the law and the need to stop abortions. Rarely will an officer risk losing his job by not performing this duty to remove us. But there are some things he can do to help us while carrying out his orders.

If the clinic is in rented space, he can delay arrest by insisting that the owner of the property and not the abortion clinic administrator file the complaint. He can take time to try to convince the picketers to leave peacefully. He can begin the arrests slowly, taking only one or two picketers at a time. He can try to negotiate between the picketers and the clinic administration.

In a St. Louis clinic sit-in the police were able to take six hours to finalize the arrests, by which time the clinic was closed. No abortions had been performed.

At the jail a friendly police officer can help the pro-lifers by recommending that fingerprinting and photographs be waived and by expediting the booking process.

Even knowing that there is a friendly officer is comfort to the arrestees, especially those experiencing first arrest. Activists who have been arrested can add their experiences to the list of tactics a pro-life police officer can use, and the accounts of friendly police are long and interesting. Someday a book should be compiled relating these efforts. It would be fascinating reading.

84 KNOW THE ABORTIONISTS' PUBLIC RECORD

Two of the most rewarding benefits of researching medical malpractice suits against abortionists are the ultimate rescue of the unborn child and the protection of the health of the mother. By giving summaries of these complaints against the abortionists to women contemplating abortion, we expose the so-called safe, legal abortion for what it is—a myth and a cruel hoax.

In Chicago, we found dozens of malpractice suits on file at the Cook County Circuit Court against the very clinics that were glossed over in the famous *Chicago Sun-Times* "Abortion Profiteers" exposé of the Chicago abortion industry. Of course, we also have copies of the suits against the clinics that were exposed in that series. By handing out these copies of lawsuits, we help the woman about to enter the abortion clinic to realize, through the tragic experience of other women, that there is a real threat to her health and even to her life. If we can get a woman interested in the damage an abortion can do to her, we may have an opening for a conversation with her about her decision and turn her away from the abortion clinic.

A woman going into an abortion clinic is concerned about her health. She has set aside the value and rights of the child and even her own spiritual well-being, but she is still interested in coming out of the clinic alive. If you can convince her first and foremost that this abortion clinic is a dangerous place, you have your foot in the door.

There are some excellent books, such as Ann Saltenburger's *Every Woman Has a Right to Know the Dangers of Legal Abortion*, which recount the case histories of women who have suffered serious physical consequences from abortion. *Ministering to Abortion's Aftermath*, by Bill and Sue Banks relates the psychological and emotional scars that linger afterward.

How can you find records of a particular clinic or doctor? This can take considerable research. One of the first things to do is check the records in the county buildings. Investigate the law file docket of medical malpractice suits and ask the person in charge of the computer index to advise you of the file number of the abortionist. Give the name of the doctor, if you know it, or the clinic. If you don't know the name of the doctor, you will find that out by getting the file on the clinic. Check the names of the defendants in the case. If a computer isn't used, then refer to the alphabetical index of defendants. The names will show up if there are any cases. Write down the docket number and present that to the person at the law file counter. You can then make copies of these files. It may cost you a dime or so a page, but you are going to want to have a good copy for your use at the clinics.

You will also find legal papers in this law file docket, such as the subpoenas that were issued to get the defendant in court. There will be answers to the interrogatories or depositions, and there will be other information that may be useful to copy for your own files. Remember, this is all public information. You should also ask for a computer printout of the case summary to date.

This is going to cost you about a dollar, but if you give them the docket number of the case which you already have, they will run off a printout of the case. That will give you the disposition of the case, the judge's ruling, the final entries, whether the case was dismissed from prosecution, whether it was dismissed through an agreement, or whether it went on to judgment. There will be a lot of useful information and it may help you find some friendly witnesses or even possibly an attorney whom you may want to contact for further information.

While you are at it, and since you have their names, you might as well look up other matters concerning the abortionists, such as whether they have divorce suits pending against them or whether they are involved in other legal procedures. Perhaps they have been involved in consumer fraud. In Chicago, we found out that an abortionist was using federal money to pay his employees. Following his trial his clinic was closed down, and he was sentenced to two years in a federal penitentiary. It is not only the malpractice suits you are looking for, but anything that might help ferret out illegal activities.

In doing this sort of thing, it is important to be systematic and careful. You may want the assistance of a lawyer, and you may wish to hire a secretary to help you set up your files.

You should have a thorough understanding of your state constitution, the election process, how a bill goes through the legislative process to become law, and the various departments in your state government. You will need a handbook on your state government which you can get from the Secretary of State's office, or from any elected official. You will want to know the state statutes that apply to abortion. You will also need to know the statutes that apply to doctors and those that apply to the public health department.

You will need to study the sections on criminal law, regulation of professions and occupations, public health, and safety in your state constitution. And you will want to be in touch with your pro-life state legislators.

The Secretary of State can be helpful to you in obtaining the names and addresses of corporations, including abortion clinics, which are registered agents, and also in giving you the names of their corporate officers. It is helpful to visit the corporation department of the Secretary of State's office in your city or, if you can, in the state capitol. You can be straightforward in your investigation since you are dealing with public documents.

A publication that will be very useful to you is a certified list of domestic and foreign corporations for any given year. This usually comes in a booklet, that is available free of charge. This list will also include not-for-profit organizations such as Planned Parenthood.

Contact your Attorney General's office for free legal assistance and guidance with any problems regarding charitable trusts and solicitations, consumer fraud, and environmental violations, such as the disposal of the products of abortions.

The disposal of aborted babies has frequently been a problem. Some clinics use a garbage disposal, while some throw the aborted babies away with gauze and other expendable items. This is a matter that should be checked out, because there are laws regulating the disposal of "biological waste". Check with your state Department of Public Health to get a list of the licensed ambulatory surgical facilities. This will include abortion clinics and give the regulations dealing with abortion clinics.

Know your state laws regarding the operation of free-standing clinics. Contact the director of the Department of Public Health, the Consumer Health Protection Agency, or any health regulation facility, and ask them about abortion clinic regulations. Contact the agency dealing with women, infants, and children. Also, you should be in touch with the Department of Public Aid in your city or state. Ask them about the abortionists. Are there cases of medical fraud? The Department of Public Aid is responsible for administering programs locally, and they should be aware of clinic conditions in their area.

Contact the Department of Registration and Education, and especially its medical investigations division. Here you will be able to obtain advice on the current state laws that apply to the licensing of doctors. Get information and records of disciplinary actions that have been taken against any abortionists for any given period of time. You should also be able to get documentation from them regarding medical malpractice suits against abortionists. Look to this organization for follow-up on anything you may have already obtained involving the abortionists.

Abortionists sometimes discuss, at their meetings, complications and problems that arise at the clinics, but which aren't revealed by their records. At the National Abortion Federation Convention in New Orleans in April 1983, for instance, high complication rates were discussed in one of their workshops. Cindy Pierson, of Women Care in San Diego, said the complication rate went as high as eight percent on some days. Phillip Stubblefield, a doctor and member of the National Abortion Federation, remarked that the possibility of major visceral injury is always present in an abortion, and that it is possible to come close to killing a patient. These people know how dangerous abortion can be. If they are so aware of the dangers, we should be carefully watching for those occasions when the danger becomes a reality.

It should be obvious that it is essential to establish close contact with the departments in the state government that deal with the lives of citizens, including the unborn.

Get to know your public library. It is a good resource for the study of abortion and allied subjects, with its directories of special interest such as the *Ayer Directory of Publications*, published annually by William J. Luedke in Philadelphia, and the *Directory of Medical Specialists*. Check out the publications of the various medical societies.

Your local medical society will have the names and addresses of local doctors and their hospital connections. Frequently, it gives their telephone numbers. Telephone directories in your public library will have the names and telephone numbers of doctors all over the country. The *Encyclopedia of Associations* lists national and international organizations of social welfare, health, trade, business, and government. Under "Choice", for instance, it might have the Association of Planned Parenthood Physicians, Planned Parenthood Federation of America, Human Life and National Family Foundation, Scientists for Life, and others. Usually, it gives organizations' addresses, phone numbers, the directors' names, their conventions, and their publications. And don't overlook your public library's out-of-town newspapers, general periodicals, and microfilms indexed by subject.

When I first learned of the Supreme Court's abortion ruling, I wanted to get some quick background on the issue. I had not been paying close attention to the abortion debate. I went to the Chicago Public Library and looked under "Abortion" in the *Reader's Guide to Periodical Literature*. I began reading back issues of *Time* and *Newsweek* from the late 60s to see what changes had occurred that led us to such a sweeping decision. It became clear that there had been a big push for abortion for quite a while. The news magazines had not taken a neutral stand, but had been in favor of liberal abortion. They argued that anti-abortion laws needed "reforming".

It was interesting to see how the stage had been set for legal abortion. The June 1967 issues of various newspapers reported that the American Medical Association had relaxed its abortion stand. Newspapers and magazines debated the issue hotly but almost always with a pro-abortion slant, leaving the reader with the impression that laws against abortion were outdated and unjust. States where abortion had been legalized were held up as models to be emulated.

The push for abortion was apparent in most of these articles. Abortion was in the process of being legalized, and much of the press was helping the process along. It was fascinating to see the media bias and observe their prejudice. One writer saw abortion as a political issue, another as a religious issue. The abortion "right" came about carefully orchestrated. It had been coming for fifteen years before it arrived in January 1973 as the "law of the land". Since then the secular press has made a gallant effort to keep it "safe and legal".

The government publication department in your local library is an invaluable resource. You can get their records on information services. There is staff available to instruct you on the use of the indexes, assist you with computers in locating information, and refer you to resources outside the library. They also have a loan policy. Government publications can be used only on location, but most documents will be loaned on request to libraries affiliated with your local library. Many of the indexes of government publications, such as the *Congressional Record* and the *Federal Register*, are available in on-line formats in the computer reference center. There is usually a copying service available for a fee.

It is important to be aggressive in your research. Find someone to help you. Even if the person is not particularly friendly, he has an obligation to help you. You don't have to tell him which side of the issue you are on. Ask for directions and learn how the system works, so that you can get the information you need.

The information is there. All we have to do is dig it out.

85 GET RID OF BENCH ADS AND OTHER ABORTION PROMOTIONAL DEVICES

Difficult as it is to believe, abortionists consider the destructon of life through abortion just another business venture. They know that it pays to advertise, and do so in the Yellow Pages with big two-color display ads. They advertise in the newspapers and even in programs designed for teen concerts. They sell abortion on radio and television. From time to time, you will see their posters in train stations, on billboards, and on ad benches. Pro-lifers find this advertising intolerable since it leads women to places where they can have their children murdered, and perhaps have their own reproductive futures ended. So pro-lifers do not take kindly to it.

But there are ways to neutralize this advertising or get it removed. First, start with the company doing the advertising. Call them or write a letter letting them know that this advertising is reprehensible, that it causes conflict in the community, and indicates that the company has taken a pro-abortion position. The advertisers will almost always reply that they don't endorse the products they advertise. So make it clear to them that they are not advertising just another product. They are advertising abortion. The fact that they are willing to accept the advertisement indicates that they endorse abortion. Perhaps, when they understand your concern, they will offer to advertise the opposing view. Tell them that you would not think of using their advertising facilities so long as they advertise abortion. Your primary effort must be to get them to drop the ads and to agree not to support either side of the issue. You must decide first, however, before turning down their offer of advertising, whether your ads would be of such great benefit that they would neutralize the abortion ads.

Our decision has generally been to convince the advertising agency, whenever possible, not to advertise for either side. For one thing, we cannot afford to pay for advertising as easily as the abortionists can. We never hesitate in our dealings with an agency that advertises for the abortionists, to agree not to press them to advertise for pro-life, if they will agree to drop the abortion ads. If they do not agree, we let them know that their abortion ads are so offensive that we fear the more militant pro-life groups will make certain that the advertising doesn't remain in place.

There was once an especially odious case in Chicago where a Catholic advertiser accepted advertising from a notorious abortion clinic, placing the ads on benches at bus stops near high schools.

When the Pro-Life Action League learned about these benches, we contacted the ad agency and talked with the owner. We told him of our concern for the young women who saw these abortion ads on their way to school. We told them the reputation of the clinic, and what kind of people ran it. We talked about the immorality and dangers of abortion.

He said he agreed with us, that he was opposed to abortion and had three children of his own. His brother was a priest. But, he said he had a contract with the abortion clinic. We asked him why he had signed a contract with an abortion clinic in the first place, and he said that at the time he did not know they performed abortions. He assumed it was just a medical facility. We told him that since they had deceived him, he could break the contract. He refused.

Next we issued a press release explaining that a Catholic layman was running seventeen abortion ads near high schools, some of them Catholic. We said that the ads would not be profitable to him if pro-life readers would encourage other advertisers not to rent his ad benches. We called some companies whose ads appeared on his benches and several of them registered complaints and promised to discontinue their ads.

A report informed our office that someone in the neighborhoods where the benches were had obliterated the telephone numbers and name of the clinic on the benches. The ad benches were not paying off for the abortion company. When the defaced ads were repainted by the ad bench company they were almost immediately painted over again by irate citizens. After this second effort, the abortion ads on the benches were not replaced.

The same thing had happened before when the Chicago Transit Authority (CTA) had advertised for an abortion clinic at their train stations. They found that these ads were routinely obliterated and their riders were not able to read the phone number or the address of the abortion facility.

There always seems to be a group of determined, persistent pro-lifers who make sure that abortion advertising of this type is rendered ineffective. The upshot is that the abortion clinic administrators as well as the advertizers come to realize it is a waste of time and money to advertise through this method. A determined segment of the public does not approve of exploiting women through abortion nor destroying human life.

Even though the Pro-Life Action League neither condones nor encourages violence or vandalism, it is indulgent toward those who would render abortion advertising harmless and paint over an abortion ad that promotes violence against a human being. The violence of abortion is far more serious than the obliterating of a sign.

While perpetrators of vandalism must be willing to accept the consequences of their act, in a real sense their actions may be more than an option. For many these actions constitute a moral obligation.

86 SPECIAL CLINIC CLOSING PROGRAMS: PROJECT JERICHO, THREE MONTH BLITZ, AND OTHERS

As the pro-life movemnent becomes more aggresive, and activism becomes the rule instead of the exception, pro-life groups are designing elaborate programs with the direct object of saving human lives. These programs are doing just that.

One such program is Project Jericho, an on-going plan of active sidewalk counseling and intense picketing, which is being used successfully in Tempe, Arizona, and elsewhere.

One of the organizers, John Jakubczyk, notified our office of this program in July 1983, describing it in detail. The basic concept is to get local church groups committed to picketing abortion clinics on a regular basis. Each group is responsible for being at the clinic one day a week. Each group provides its own signs. Each group has a schedule of who will come to the clinic on a particular day. Those scheduled are responsible to appear that day or must arrange substitutes in case they are unable to come. The project coordinator is responsible for encouraging groups in the area to participate in the program and for speaking to pastors. These coordinators are also responsible for training volunteers. The emphasis is on local churches addressing the abortion tragedy in their *own* neighborhoods.

The coordinator begins by seeking an appointment with individual church leaders in order to set up meetings to speak with members about going to the clinics. Other pro-life work will be necessary, painting signs, making phone calls to remind people of their commitment. The coordinator provides counselors to train volunteers as sidewalk counselors.

Project Jericho incorporates picketing every day the clinic is open to make the public aware of the evil of abortion. Picketing is scheduled three times a day—morning, noon, afternoon. There is a regular turnover of picketers. A few people do not have to spend long periods at the clinic. Other pro-lifers reinforce the counselors each day during the clinic's peak hours.

Project Jericho encourages educational activities and suggests working with existing pro-life groups to strengthen or rebuild them. Its

297

purpose is to revitalize pro-life leadership in the community and rekindle enthusiasm among those who have never had a unified method of stopping abortion.

Project Jericho is based on three Scriptural references: Jeremiah 1:17—19, Proverbs 24:11—12, and Ezekiel 33:9—10.

> But do you gird your loins
>> stand up and tell them
>> all that I command you.
> Be not crushed on their account,
>> as though I would leave you crushed
>>> before them;
> For it is I this day
>> who have made you a fortified city,
> A pillar of iron, a wall of brass,
>> against the whole land:
> Against Judah's kings and princes,
>> against its priests and people
> They will fight against you, but not
>> prevail over you,
>> for I am with you to deliver you,
>> says the Lord. (Jeremiah 1:17—19)

> Rescue those who are being dragged to death
>> and from those tottering to execution withdraw not.
> If you say, "I know not this man!"
>> does not he who tests hearts
>> perceive it?
> He who guards your life knows it,
>> and he will repay each one according
>>> to his deeds. (Proverbs 24:11—12)

> Son of man I have appointed you
>> as sentry to the House of Israel.
> When you hear a word from my mouth,
>> warn them in my name.
> But if you warn the wicked man,
>> trying to turn him from his way,
>> and he refuses to turn from his way,
>> he shall die for his guilt,
>> but you shall save yourself.
> As for you, son of man,
>> speak to the house of Israel:
> You people say,

> "Our crimes and our sins weigh us down;
> we are rotting away because of them.
> How can we survive?" (Ezekiel 33:7–10)

By obeying the word of God, the Jews brought down the walls of Jericho. By our listening to God's command, the walls of legal abortion will suffer the same fate.

Each participating church group has a team captain, responsible for ten individuals. Each individual is committed to a picketing time slot once a week. The team leader contacts each team member and confirms the picketing time. If a member of the team is not able to show up at the time indicated, the captain helps him find another time and selects a substitute for the open time slot. The captain reports to the group commander weekly to tell him the number of pickets that week and to report any problems brought to his attention. The captain is directly responsible to the group commander. The captain is responsible for seeing that the picket is conducted in an orderly manner. And he leads his group in prayer. Problems are reported to the chairman and the committee attorney. The captain provides the placards. There are as many captains as there are churches represented in the operation.

In the ideal Jericho project there are eighteen captains. The commander is responsible for three captains. He gets information on the number of people who picketed during each of the time slots and takes reports on the effectiveness of the counseling and picketing. The group commander is directly responsible to the Jericho committee. There are six group commanders, each over three parishes. One of these is the group coordinator. The Jericho committee is a coalition of pro-life organizations.

Picketers and counselors sign up for times they will be at the clinics. If someone cannot show up he will get a substitute at once.

The police are contacted to discuss pro-lifers' rights to picket and counsel and pass out literature. In an Arizona case, the question arose as to whether a pro-life defendant had a right to be on clinic property. The judge found that under the First Amendment, pro-life picketers were entitled, not only to hand out literature, but to enter the parking lot and premises to communicate with clinic clients. This case should be used by pro-lifers being told that they cannot be in the parking lot because it is private property. Highlights of the case are included at the end of this chapter.

Those planning "Jericho" enterprises should have legal counsel and expect legal harassment even though picketers and counselors are acting out of moral conviction and under First Amendment protection.

Attorneys should examine possible federal actions against police and abortion clinics that use the courts and lawsuits to harass pro-lifers and attempt to intimidate them.

Another pro-life project was developed by Reverend Norman Stone and Jerry Horn, of Appleton, Wisconsin, and was launched with a three-month abortion clinic blitz called ''Phase I of the Save the Babies Project''. It was based on the same principle as Project Jericho, but with a limited time span—limited, but intense. This group has as its ultimate goal the closing of an abortion clinic targeted in its area: the Fox Valley Reproductive Health Care Center.

This project began with a rally and sign-up of members, and continued with a monthly rally, banquet, and assembly, always with a new member sign-up program. Their plan is to have protesters at the clinic from the time it opens for business in the morning until it closes in the evening. As long as the clinic is open, there will be pro-lifers protesting outside.

Phase II of Save the Babies Project called for establishment of a pro-life facility next door to the clinic, to offer genuine support to women with problem pregnancies. This was achieved by Appleton pro-lifers on July 30, 1984, when they took possession of the house adjoining the Fox Valley abortion clinic. They opened the counseling center with a party attended by more than two hundred people, and local television, radio, and newspapers. Highlight of the affair was a lease-signing ceremony and blessing of the house, in full view of the enraged abortion clinic personnel.

Similar projects are going on all over the country. It is no longer possible to list the groups that have set out to close down abortion facilities in their communities systematically.

It is encouraging to see the new militancy spreading rapidly within the pro-life movement. Frequently, there is conflict both locally and nationally, between traditional pro-life groups that take less aggressive action and activist groups. However, the activist groups are generally too busy to become embroiled in internecine battles. Activists are convinced that, ultimately, the use of non-violent direct action will cause the abortion clinics to lose so many patients that they will be forced to close their doors. As a matter of fact, it is happening already.

Highlights of *State of Arizona, Plaintiff, v. Henry D. Barton and Mark Drogin, Defendants*, in the Municipal Court of the City of Phoenix,

Maricopa County, dated September 20, 1982, to October 19, 1982, Case
No. 8317339, before the Hon. Judge Ralph G. Smith.

The decision I make is not to be construed as being pro-abortion or
anti-abortion, pro-life or anti-pro-life. That question is certainly not
before us. This is a trespass case.

The crucial matter, in the Court's opinion, is whether or not the
Defendants had a right, under the First Amendment, to be on that
property notwithstanding the fact that it is private property.

I find two very interesting Supreme Court cases. One is *Amalgamated
Food Employees Union v. Logan Valley Plaza*, 391 US 308, a 1968 case.
In Logan Valley the Court held that the employees were permitted, under
the First Amendment, to go in and picket, even though it was on private
property within a shopping center area, because of the fact that their
picketing was aimed at a particular establishment within the shopping
center. Now, as the Court noted there, the picketing carried on by the
petitioners was directed specifically at patrons of the Weiss Market,
located within the shopping center, and the message sought to be
conveyed to the public concerned the manner in which that particular
market was being operated. We are, therefore, not called upon to
consider whether respondent's property rights could, consistently with
the First Amendment, justify a ban on picketing which was not thus
directly related in its purpose to the use to which the shopping center
property was being put, and they noted that the union's picketing was
directed solely at one establishment within the shopping center, and that
the narrow public paths and sidewalks were from 300 to 500 feet away
from the Weiss store, and they noted that this distance made it difficult to
communicate with patrons of Weiss and to limit the effect of the
picketing to Weiss only. There was a further note that all entry onto the
mall premises by customers of Weiss appears to be by vehicle from roads
alongside the narrow paths. Thus, the placards bearing the messsage
which petitioners seek to communicate to patrons of Weiss must be read
by those to whom they are directed either at a distance so great as to
render them virtually indecipherable, or the Weiss customers are already
within the mall, or while the prospective reader is moving by car from the
roads onto the mall parking area by entrance ways cut through the narrow
paths. Likewise, the task of distributing handbills to persons in moving
automobiles is vastly greater and more hazardous than it would be for
petitioners permitted to pass them out within the mall to pedestrians.

In this particular case we have a situation where the Defendants were
attempting to communicate with people who were using the Planned
Parenthood facilities. There was testimony that the so-called clients of
Planned Parenthood were entering by automobile, that they would get out

of their automobiles in the parking lot and go to the facilities there. The Defendants and others of this group would have no direct access to them except insofar as they pass by in their automobiles on their way to the parking lot. I think that under the First Amendment they would be entitled to more than this. I think they were entitled to enter onto the parking lot and enter into these premises for the purpose of communicating with the particular people who were using the Planned Parenthood facilities, that they were directing their efforts at a particular facility. I think this is further bolstered by the fact that, after this picketing occurred, the media were invited into the parking lot, and here we have a situation where some people were being given the right and opportunity to express their views to the media within the confines of this parking lot and the petitioners, or the Defendants in this case, were being denied the opportunity to be present where all of this was going on. I think they were entitled to that and, therefore, it is the holding of the Court that the Defendants, each of the Defendants is not guilty of the offense charged solely by reason of the provisions of the First Amendment of the Constitution.

87 OVERCOME FEAR WITH CONVICTION

Some people in the pro-life movement are afraid. They are afraid of the movement itself and of what it portends. They are afraid of the activists and of being identified with fanatics. They are afraid that their reputation might be damaged. They are even afraid of what they might have to do in the fight against abortion, even though they know that what they are doing is right.

It is not difficult to understand this fear. We all know many people who live in fear, and they are good people. They simply are not accustomed to the kind of activity that they are now called upon to engage in. Nothing prepared them for it. They have never been involved in a life and death struggle like this. They have never faced a moral combat such as we are engaged in today. Fear is natural, and it can be healthy. It can prevent people from doing foolhardy, dangerous things. It can keep them alive.

Fear of being killed slows you down on the highway. Fear of being arrested may prevent you from going through a red light. That is healthy fear. But fear of fighting the critical battle against the killing of children can stifle and paralyze good people, preventing them from doing what is absolutely necessary to save lives.

Pro-life activists have found that the best remedy for paralyzing fear is the development of a strong conviction that what you are doing is absolutely the right thing to be doing. This conviction must be based on the reality of moral absolutes.

When you are going into an abortion clinic to talk with clinic personnel, the doctor, the proprietor, or the women awaiting abortions, you must be absolutely certain that what you are doing is a good thing. You must be convinced that it is better to do it than not to do it. You must be convinced that good will come from it, and that lives will be saved. Your intention must always be to save lives. With a strong conviction and with the motive of saving lives, fear will not prevent you from doing what must be done.

There are going to be times when you may decide that you have to do something that will bring you into conflict with the authorities. You know you will be embarrassed if you are arrested. You are afraid that your arrest will be publicized. To handle this, you need conviction that what you are doing is absolutely good. This conviction will give you the courage you need to do it, and the strength to take the consequences.

During the investigation for the twenty-part "Abortion Profiteers" series in the *Chicago Sun-Times*, our pro-life organization was infiltrated by a newspaper reporter posing as a volunteer. When the series ran, there were articles about our activities. These were embarrassing to some of our members. We were accused of painting out abortion posters at train stations, and although we had never told anyone who actually did it, all of us were ridiculed as being little better than vandals. This was embarrassing to some of our friends. Some church groups and individuals denounced us. They did not want to be identified with an organization that might do something they considered "radical", uncouth, or un-Christian. We also believe it is uncouth to go around with a spray can defacing property. We hate to see grafitti. We are offended by people writing words and names and making drawings on train station walls. We do not endorse or support vandalism.

But we also have strong convictions that when somebody violently attacks our most cherished beliefs, our deep-rooted moral convictions, and offends us by posting advertisements that tell women where they can make arrangements to have their children murdered, this attack on public decency is so offensive that it must be removed, even at personal risk.

A woman who read a newspaper account saying that some abortion ads had been removed at a CTA station called our office to say she could no longer support our efforts. She believed the account without even ascertaining whether it was accurate or not. She called it un-Christian. I asked her if it would be un-Christian to remove a pornographic picture, obscene slogan, or statement damaging someone's good name. I asked her if everything posted in a public place had to remain there, no matter how evil, perverted, or immoral. Wasn't an offer to kill innocent children an attack on morality? Should it not be removed? She could not understand my argument. I did not hear from her again, and she never even knew if the newspaper story was true.

Pro-life activists must do everything with absolute conviction. Demonstrations, blitzes, sit-ins, removing abortion ads, handing out literature, sidewalk counseling, whatever hurts the abortion business and is not itself immoral.

We should support those who carry out these activities even if we cannot do all of them ourselves. They are based on zeal to protect the unborn. While we do not condone any form of violence, we should not condemn without compassion and understanding those whose strong convictions may lead them to illegal activities. We should comfort them and try to help their families. We should assure them that they have a friend, and while we may not condone their actions, we admire the zeal that these actions manifest.

Some pro-lifers would not agree with this. They would turn their backs on a kidnapper or someone who damages a clinic. But without agreeing with these methods, we can admire the zeal that led them to do something we wouldn't do ourselves, and we can stand by them and their families, and we can visit them or at least write them in prison. When Christ said to visit the prisoner he did not add, "But only if he's innocent".

It is easier for me to respect someone who commits an act of violence against an abortion clinic, where no one is injured, than to respect pro-lifers who talk about abortion as murder, but don't do much more to stop it than attend pro-life banquets once or twice a year.

The fear we have of being ridiculed and losing respect can be overcome by knowing that we are right. God sees all things in their proper light, and we need to pray that He will direct all our actions.

What pro-life activist on a mission to stop abortion has *not* become weary and depressed, wanting nothing more than to drop the whole thing and go home? Then a sense of duty tells you there is still more to do. You stick to your project and discover an opportunity to save lives or scuttle an abortion program where you least expected to find it. When your mission is over, you feel peaceful and confident that what you did was God's will. Some people even in the pro-life movement say it is not God who prompts us to do the more controversial things. But we know better.

It is difficult to picture God punishing someone for removing an abortion ad. Jesus himself pushed over tables in the temple and drove out money changers, and Scripture does not record that He paid damages or even apologized for what he did. We should not be afraid to be led by a zeal for God's law.

88 CLASSROOM SPEECHES

This chapter is important for students who might face a classroom project in which they could introduce the subject of abortion. Such an opportunity could come up in almost every class, but the course in which it would most easily fit would be a speech class, especially if the assignment is to give a speech to persuade. The objective would be to convince the class that abortion is wrong.

In debate, the subject of abortion is a natural. The pro-life side should always win. The abortion defenders have a hard time in a debate. It is difficult to sell the idea that abortion is good and that killing babies for convenience is reasonable. When you use abortion in a debate, fight for permission to use visual aids so that you can show pictures or give a slide presentation or show a film that depicts fetal development and abortion methods.

Almost any course, including economics, can be a vehicle to illustrate how abortion is destructive to society. Society depends on people for industry, education, farming, defense, even to support the Social Security system for the elderly.

In giving pragmatic examples you can show, for instance, that when Social Security was first established, there were seventeen workers paying into the system for each retired person on Social Security. Today, that figure is 3.3 workers for each person on Social Security. If this trend continues, either there will not be any Social Security in the future or there will be only one or two laborers supporting each retired individual. That means the payroll deduction for Social Security will have to be increased again and again, leaving less pay to take home.

In almost any school class, the abortion issue can be worked into a discussion. And it should be. A clever pro-life student will use all the resources available to him, such as handouts, slides, films, fetal models. If it is a small class, he might give each student the "Life or Death" flyer, especially if he is not allowed to use slides or films. "Life or Death", or any other publication that is inexpensive and shows the development of the unborn child and what abortion does, should be permitted as a handout as an integral part of the talk. Occasionally, a well-written assignment on abortion will be selected to be read aloud to the class. No student should pass up an opportunity to bring the abortion issue before his classmates.

Classroom presentations have far-reaching effects. Students are sometimes asked to go before other classes with their presentation or debate, if they did an exceptionally good job. They can introduce the issue in the classroom where often adult pro-life speakers cannot get invited. The student is already there to tell the pro-life story, make converts, and become a resource for those who would otherwise not hear pro-life arguments. If there is no right-to-life organization, the students should start one, because even a small pro-life group can have a powerful influence on a school.

Thousands of adults each year take classes in public speaking from Toastmasters, Dale Carnegie, Gabriel Richard, and others. Pro-lifers taking such courses, or who address meetings as public speakers, should bring up the abortion issue often.

There are many occasions on which abortion can be brought up. Colleges and many high schools have a campus radio or television station, eager to have controversial issues debated live on the air. Be on the lookout for biased, one-sided programming on such stations, and make certain it does not go unchallenged.

If a speaker is well informed on the issue, he should not be afraid of the opposition. They make us look good. Sometimes the best spokesmen pro-life has are angry, illogical, mercenary abortionists who appeal to selfishness, self-interest, carnality, and the lowest instincts. Our appeal to the value of human life and the sanctity of motherhood are realities that make the abortionists look monstrous by contrast. Their arguments are weak, being drawn from a stock debate sheet put out by the National Abortion Rights Action League about fifteen years ago.

To get information that will help you with your arguments, call your local pro-life office. Look in the phone book under "right-to-life", or "pro-life", or under the name of your city or state for such names as "Seattle Right-to-Life" or "Illinois Right-to-Life Committee". Find out where the local pro-life office is and then call or visit their office to get background information. An old standby source of basic information on abortion is Dr. and Mrs. Jack Wilke's *Handbook on Abortion*. There are many excellent books, films, and tapes on abortion today. You should have no trouble getting information on every aspect of the abortion controversy. The important project, however, is to put this knowledge to work.

To debate the abortionists it is helpful to analyze *their* arguments. Ask these organizations to send you a model plan for debating pro-life:

WESTCHESTER COALITION FOR
LEGAL ABORTION
    149 Grand St.
    White Plains, NY 10601

NARAL FOUNDATION
    825 15th St., NW
    Washington, DC 20005

89 USE THE HORROR STORIES

The horror of abortion should be conveyed to the public at every opportunity. Do not refrain from using descriptions of the abortion culture that will horrify the public, such as the infants aborted alive and left to die, the horrible methods of abortion being used, the use of live, aborted fetuses for experimentation. There are even documented cases of aborted babies being cut open and their organs taken out for transplants. There is the cosmetic use of fetal tissue, called collagen, which is becoming more common. There is the celebrated case of a shipment of frozen aborted fetuses halted at the Swiss border while on the way to a factory in France to be used in making cosmetics.

In Chicago, there was a firm that offered embryos and other human organs in paperweights. The Turtox Cambosco Company, located near Michael Reese hospital, advertised a sliced fetus, cut down the center, encased in plastic and sold as a paperweight. Their catalogue boasted: "Turtox Cambosco sells biological supplies primarily to schools and colleges, but individuals can also obtain the plastic embedded embryos and organs by sending a check with their orders. Shipment is by United Parcel Service, Parcel Post, or Express." Their catalogue listed embedments of human embryos for $97.80, stating, "These embryos range from three to four months in age. They have been bisected along the median, cleared, and mounted naturally. Specify age or ages desired. *Customers desiring other age embryos are advised that occasionally ages other than those listed can be furnished.* Please write us for current information." (Emphasis added.)

There was a case in Wichita, Kansas, in which a local hospital where abortions were performed was burning bodies of aborted children along with cats and dogs in the Humane Society incinerator. We were given pictures of the incinerators with a baby's body in front of it ready for burning and facts explaining the travesty. All of this material we immediately released to the press. The story got national attention. This was soon stopped as a direct result of all the publicity.

Pro-lifers have distributed leaflets describing the find in Los Angeles, California, of almost seventeen thousand aborted babies in a pathologist's

309

back yard and have described this ''American Holocaust'' on numerous radio and television programs.

Whenever instances arise that describe the inhuman treatment abortionists show toward the remains of aborted babies—fetuses found in sanitary district tunnels, fetal parts clogging garbage disposals, bodies dumped on the streets of New York and Milwaukee—these must be publicized, emphasized, and discussed. They are all part of the American abortion culture.

Most of what went on in the death camps of Europe during World War II did not reach the public at the time, and when it was finally reported it was already too late to do anything about it.

But we *know* what is happening in America's abortion clinics while it is happening. We have to report these atrocities in an effort to turn Americans away from abortion. It can work. People who see these stories on television are moved to do something to stop them. Most Americans are not in favor of such atrocities.

Former abortionists and women who have had abortions have been turned around by hearing that the unborn suffer pain. Descriptions of abortion that may upset squeamish pro-lifers often bring neutrals into the pro-life fold. We should not hesitate to describe in graphic detail the horrors of abortion and infanticide, the misuse of human beings and the exploitation of women.

A powerful letter was sent by Sandy Ressel of Scott City, Missouri, to her local newspaper, the *Bulletin-Journal*, after she attended the 1984 National Right to Life Convention in Kansas City, Missouri. Her letter described a film of a suction abortion she had seen during a lecture by Dr. Bernard Nathanson. Her description exemplifies what we mean by being graphic. Imagine the effect this letter has had on thousands who have read it, introducing them into the horrors of first trimester abortion. Here is an excerpt from Sandy's letter:

. . . The most powerful speaker for me, and I'm sure everyone else who saw him, was Dr. Bernard Nathanson. For those who aren't familiar with him he is one of the founding fathers of NARAL—The National Association for the Repeal of the Abortion Laws. In short, he said he is very much responsible for the unleashing of the abortion monster on this country. Yes, he is a ex-abortionist who once operated the largest abortion clinic in the Western world in New York and presided over 60,000 deaths—7,000 with his own hands. He is now one of our very strong pro-life leaders.

Dr. Nathanson brought with him for the very first public viewing the first ultrasound film of an actual suction abortion. An ultrasound makes an actual moving picture of an unborn child out of the sound waves from the womb. This picture was then enlarged so we could see the images more clearly. "This", he explained to us, "is the first time an actual abortion will ever be shown from the victim's point of view." He also reminded us that this ten-week-old child represented ninety-five percent of all legal abortions—that is at least ninety-five percent of all unborn children being aborted are at least ten weeks after conception. At ten weeks an unborn human being has everything you and I have—fully formed with an active brain, sensitive to pain, and a beating heart.

"This little girl", he said, "is very active." We could see her playing and turning around and around and sucking her thumb. Her little heart we could see beating away at a normal rate of about 120. But when the first instrument touched the uterine wall the baby immediately recoiled and her heart rate rose considerably. The baby had not yet been touched by the instrument but she knew something was trying to invade her sanctuary.

We watched in horror as this innocent human child was literally drawn and quartered, first the spine, then a leg, piece by piece with the child wildly writhing in agony, living through most of the process, thrashing around and trying to escape the menacing instrument. I saw with my own eyes her head throw back and her mouth open in what Doctor Nathanson called "her silent scream". At one point her heart rate was over 200 and we could see on the screen her tiny heart beating frantically because she was so scared. Lastly, of course, we witnessed the ghastly outline of the forceps fishing around to find the head to crush and remove because it is too large to pass through the suction tubing.

This killing process took twelve to fifteen minutes. The abortionist that did this particular abortion filmed the ultra-sound mainly out of curiosity. When he saw the film he left the clinic and didn't return. . . .

Abortion kills a human child in a painful and barbaric way. The only difference between that child and the one you may now be holding in your arms is the unborn child hasn't yet had a birthday. Think about it.

Mrs. Sandy Ressel
Scott City, MO.

90 MAKE APPOINTMENTS

The practice of calling abortion clinics to make appointments designed to load their schedules has divided pro-life activists for years. Some believe it is unethical to make appointments they do not intend to keep. This is a valid consideration.

The way others have dealt with the problem is to plan to keep the appointment at the time it is scheduled and go to the clinic to engage in Truth Team activity, check the layout of the clinic for future action there, or discuss policy with clinic personnel.

Those who are able to reconcile making appointments they do not intend to keep, reason that since what goes on at an abortion clinic is an immoral activity—the destruction of innocent human life—loading the appointment book is a legitimate, life-saving action. The finer ethical rules, they reason, may be waived when dealing with an evil like abortion. For example, you might tell a robber, who asks where your valuables are so that he can take them, that they are not in the house. The full statement is: "They are not in the house (for you to steal. . . .)". Where you keep your valuables is none of his business since he intends to steal them. This is known as use of the mental reservation.

However one resolves this difficulty, when you make an appointment you may be asked to give your name and telephone number. You need give only a first name—abortion clients often do this. But give your real telephone number. If the clinic calls you to confirm the appointment you may confirm or cancel it as you see fit. These appointments confuse clinic routine and cause the operators to prepare for a heavy case load.

Clinics soon get wise to these appointments and will overschedule to meet this threat. But they cannot negate their effectiveness. Clinics operate on a relatively low margin of profit, paying some staff on a per-client basis, while others receive an hourly wage. On heavy days they may call in extra help, open extra operating space and alert the staff to expect a heavy load. If only half the scheduled clients show up the clinic is at a disadvantage. They will adjust their schedule to accommodate these appointments, but they cannot be certain which calls are genuine and which are not. Those who use the appointment device say it is most effective to work in teams.

It is also effective, they point out, to send couples to the clinic on days when these appointments are scheduled. In this way pro-life sidewalk counselors will be able to talk these ''couples'' out of abortion in sight of the abortionists. This will partially allay a suspicion that fake appointments have been made. They will think these are real clients turned away by the sidewalk counselors.

Pro-lifers need to do more ''play acting'' at the abortion clinics. We dealt with a variation on this technique in Chapter 2 on Truth Teams.

91 TELEPHONE CALLING

Abortion clinics are big business and the abortion providers learned long ago that it pays to advertise. What they advertise most is their telephone number, since most appointments are made by phone. They use classified sections of the newspaper, billboards, even match-book covers, and balloons to make their numbers known. They welcome calls of inquiry, so long as those calls lead to an abortion appointment.

Pro-life can use this broad exposure by the clinics to set up effective road blocks to the abortion business, simply by using the phone numbers they so widely advertise. Calls can be made to the clinic at any time, but it is best to have a program of calls, incorporating a team of about twelve callers, each given a specific time to call the clinic within a designated block of time.

For instance, caller A should place a call at 9:00 A.M. and try to engage the clinic personnel in conversation for five minutes. At 9:05, caller B dials the number and again questions someone at the clinic for approximately five minutes. And so on through the next ten callers. This team should shift its calling time, but each member should keep his place in the sequence.

When there is a single clinic targeted, this method will soon be detected and callers may receive short answers on each call, but since the clinic is doing busness it cannot cease answering each call, even if only to hang up. Callers must continue to make their appointed calls at the designated time, no matter what the response. Persistence is the key.

A consequence of these routine calls is that clinic personnel are made suspicious of all incoming calls. Eventually, they omit their ''sweetness and light'' approach to callers, real or pretended.

What do you talk about? The best approach is to ask legitimate questions: How far in advance must a woman make an appointment for a pregnancy test? How much does an abortion cost? Can I bring my boyfriend? It is best not to get into an argument with clinic personnel. The purpose of the call is to tie up the line, not make personnel angry.

In large cities, where there are a number of clinics, telephone teams should trade off clinics with each other from time to time, keeping the

314

same sequence of callers but perhaps varying the time block in which calls are made. If an individual caller will not be able to call at his specified time, it is important for him to trade times with another caller on the team or provide a substitute. Scatter calls are also effective and may be made any time, but the block call has a special purpose and has proven very effective.

These calls are legal. You are not harassing the clinic because you are an individual making a single call to ask legitimate questions about a particular business. It is best not make more than *one call a day* to any individual clinic.

To appraise the effect of this approach, picture yourself in a highly competitive business, spending a great deal of time each day answering calls that are not bringing in new business. Wouldn't that suggest to you that your particular business disturbs many people in the community and that they want you to go away?

92 HOW TO CONTROL THEIR ESCORT TEAMS

A tactic used more and more by the abortionists is to get volunteer groups of feminists, homosexuals, students, or ministers to serve as escorts for women entering the clinic on days abortions are performed and when they expect pro-life sidewalk counselors to be there. We sometimes refer to these escorts as "goon squads".

They are there to make sure the abortions take place. They want to make certain the women do not get to hear both sides of the issue, but go into the clinic uninformed about the humanity of the child and the dangers of abortion.

The abortionists talk about freedom of choice, but they are not in the least interested in letting the woman have a choice. They are interested in her making the decision to abort. If we try to give the woman information about the child and the complications, damages, and regrets that having an abortion will bring, the abortionists become terrified that we may dissuade her from going through with her abortion.

They are in business, and as an abortion counselor said on national television when asked if they ever try to talk women out of abortion or answer their questions honestly, "Are you kidding? That's our paycheck." The woman *is* their paycheck. Doing an abortion on her is the way they make their living. Protecting the paycheck is the reason for goon squads.

Goon squads can be irritating because they try to put a barricade around the woman. But there are several ways to handle this situation.

If you have enough people, you can walk along with the goons and start your own conversation. You can still hand the client literature. You should try to go ahead with your counseling program despite the goon squads, even if this causes confusion and some chaos. Goon squad members will be saying things like, "You don't have to listen to these fanatics; you don't have to take their literature. You have a right to an abortion." They may be carrying signs and handing out literature of their own. On occasion they will seriously interfere with your counseling. This is a fact you must deal with.

On occasion, when we have seen the goon squads at a clinic where we customarily counsel, we simply go to another clinic. Since there are nearly thirty abortion clinics in Chicago and some of them are not covered regularly, we can leave the goons behind and just go to a different clinic. Since they do not have anything to do if you are not there, they will eventually dissipate, and then you can return to that clinic.

Another thing that has been effective is to send decoys, a man and his "girlfriend" to drive up to the clinic, and when the goons come out to escort them, the couple intentionally misinterprets their purpose and tells the goons to leave them alone. They leave the goons with the impression that they drove away because of them. You can also have a couple walk up and tell the goons to leave them alone. They want to talk this over with the sidewalk counselors. It may make the goons question whether or not being there is a good thing.

Also, you can have a series of decoys pull the goons off to escort them so that you can counsel the real clients. These tactics require considerable planning and a squad of young, talented pro-lifers.

Sometimes the goons present an advantage to pro-life efforts, especially when you conduct a media event such as a picket or demonstration. The goons may call the press themselves, and since the media are interested in conflict, they will come more readily than if only pro-life pickets are present. At a January 22nd picket of a Chicago clinic, we had seventy demonstrators present by the time the goons arrived. Fifteen goons marched in front of the clinic. While this caused conflict, it also brought the police and the press. The reporters interviewed both sides. The fact that the goons had come late resulted in their getting less coverage than pro-life, so they called one of the stations and asked them to return to the clinic to interview them. We had been ready to leave, but we stayed a half-hour longer and got some of our best coverage of the day from media the goons had called.

Pro-lifers can expect more of this kind of harassment. In Appleton, Wisconsin, a group of so-called ministers escort women in to have their abortions at the Fox Valley Reproductive Health Care Center. It caused a jolt to some members of the community who counsel outside this clinic to see their own pastors escorting women in to have abortions. This caused so much concern that two church groups called for meetings with the pro-life directors, Reverend Norman Stone and Reverend Jerry Horn, to see if there was any room for a compromise on the abortion question. They could not believe that their own pastors would be doing something that was evil. They had been scandalized.

Speaking in Appleton the evening after this occurred the first time, I discussed pastors who say they believe in God as the author of life, but work on behalf of an abortion clinic. I expressed doubt that a person could really believe in God while using religion as a cover-up for evil. I called it the height of hypocrisy to work for the extermination of God's most helpless creatures while pretending to be on God's side. After the talk the concerned parishioners were able to resolve their dilemma. They decided they had been following false teachers. They would leave the churches that were headed by pro-abortion ministers.

The escorts are more of an aggravation than a threat. One of the best ways to counter any kind of pro-abortion activity outside the clinic is to get *inside* the clinic. If the clinic owner uses goon squads or puts up a fence or builds a private parking lot, pro-lifers will have to reach the customers when they are inside. That is why Chapter 2 on Truth Teams is important.

The best defense against goon squads is the covert program of Truth Teams. We believe this is going to become more effective in stopping abortions in the future.

93 HOW TO GET INTO THE HIGH SCHOOLS

Planned Parenthood, family planning organizations, and even abortion clinic personnel have been active in getting their message to high school students. Pro-life offices constantly get calls from parents saying that their daughters or sons had to listen to a talk on contraception and abortion in a social studies or health class.

When pro-lifers are alerted to a situation like this they should immediately call the high school and offer to come to present the pro-life message. They will often have a difficult time getting an invitation to come because usually someone in authority doesn't want the students to hear the pro-life side of the issue.

If pro-life is the first to call the school to ask to speak, they will frequently be told that if they allow pro-life to present its side, the school will have to allow the opposition in too. It rarely occurs to them that when they have already allowed in the opposition, they should also allow pro-life to present its argument. There is a double standard in many schools regarding the abortion issue and most pro-lifers have had to deal with that.

One thing we found to be effective was getting a list of all the high schools in the area and phoning their administrators, asking to speak to the appropriate person to help us set up a pro-life talk. This always engendered a lot of shifting around from office to office, but we generally ended up with a social studies or health class teacher. When we got someone to listen to us, we made an appeal to them to let us come to the school and talk to their class or a number of classes, to present a lecture and slide presentation or to show a film. There are a number of good films, such as *A Matter of Choice*, a short version of *Assignment: Life*, and the sequel, *Conceived in Liberty*. (See the list of available films at the end of this chapter.)

A Matter of Choice runs a half-hour and leaves time for questions and discussion afterward in a regular fifty minute class period. We prefer to use a color slide presentation since we can run it quickly or slowly, adjusting it to the particular class and the desire for discussion and questions.

Another method of getting in is to send literature. Get a list of high schools in the area and send them all a letter with some material explaining your speaker's program. This may not get as much response as a direct phone call, but your materials may be kept on file for future reference and serve as a preliminary step that can be combined with a phone call follow-up.

You might also contact some of the parents whose children have complained of hearing a pro-abortion presentation. Ask them to contact the school and urge that your organization be invited in to give a pro-life presentation.

There are some schools you will not be able to get into. If they are adamant about not allowing you in, there is always the option of distributing leaflets to the students. In Chicago, we have crews go to the schools in the afternoon to leaflet when the students are leaving the building or in the morning as they are arriving. Three or four of us stand on the sidewalk at strategic locations and rapidly distribute literature.

The leaflet should be comprehensive. It should incorporate photographs of unborn children and photographs of what abortions do to babies. "Life or Death" is an excellent piece, as is the "American Holocaust" or any number of flyers that are effectively graphic in presenting the subject. We have found young people to be receptive. They are interested in the issue and will usually take the literature willingly. They will discuss abortion among themselves and with their teachers. They will take the literature home and talk about it with their parents. The problem comes not from students, but from the teachers or administrators, who often will not allow you to distribute literature. Ignore them.

Young people leaving school move fast, and it may take only fifteen or twenty minutes to reach the majority of them. At some schools they load the buses in the parking lot and many of the students also park there. If you are distributing literature only out on the sidewalk you are going to miss these students. You can make a request to the administrator that on a particular day you be allowed to distribute literature in the parking lot. Chances are slim that you will get permission, but you might on a one-time basis. Some of our workers have simply used their own discretion and gone into the parking lot, made a rapid distribution, and left quickly. If you are asked to leave, you will probably have time to continue distributing leaflets while discussing the consequences of not leaving. Stall for time in order to get as many leaflets as possible into the hands of students.

We have had one or two arrests when our leafleters refused to leave a parking area, but those have in general been settled by an agreement that the pro-lifers not return to the parking lot without explicit permission to do so. We have agreed, since one massive distribution can take care of a school for the entire semester if you use enough volunteers to cover all entrances. There are cases where judges have ruled in favor of pro-lifers entering the parking lots to distribute literature, on the grounds that freedom of speech is such an important freedom that sometimes the only way to reach the majority of people who need to hear a particular view is to use their tax supported, semi-public property to distribute literature. There are others, though, who say it is private property and you cannot walk there.

Perhaps this matter needs to be tested in your community. It doesn't hurt to have in hand copies of cases favoring pro-lifers who have distributed leaflets on parking lots to show to school administrators or the police. A book such as John Whitehead's *The Right to Picket and the Freedom of Public Discourse* is an ideal text to have on hand. These rulings conclude that this activity is not a violation of the trespass law because that law can be set aside in favor of the right to free speech.

It is helpful if you can find someone associated with the school who supports the pro-life position and will speak up for you. The best arrangement is to have someone in the school arrange for you to speak to a class or several classes or even address a general assembly. Sometimes this will be a student who brings up the subject of abortion in class and finds that the students have little knowledge of fetal development, methods of abortion, or the extent of the Supreme Court rulings. The student will recommend you to his teachers.

You will probably be brought in to debate a ''pro-choice'' person. Accept, whatever the offer. It is usually preferable for speakers to come at separate times. The pro-abortionists give their talk, and then you come in on your own to present facts on abortion. A lot of time is wasted in a debate with abortionists. Students often side with whoever has the best personality or looks the nicest. They are impressed by appearance, and tend to let extraneous matters sway their opinions. It is better if you discuss the issue by yourself and present the facts of fetal development and the dangers of abortion without the distractions and shallow arguments pro-abortionists use.

But any way they arrange the program, pro-life has the convincing arguments. The abortionists appeal to convenience, selfishness, and the things that appeal to self-centered young people. But pro-life arguments register with students who respond to objective reality, can discern the truth, and care about justice.

It is not always personally rewarding to talk to high school students. You may give an informative talk and think you have established the value of the unborn child. Then a student will say, "What if there is a deformity?" You will reply, "Doesn't a deformed child have a right to life?" and he will begin talking about the cost to the family and the quality of life. You may argue, "But would you kill a deformed child who is already born?" and he replies, "Why not?" You will often lose a large segment of the class on the question of rape, since rape is an injustice, the pregnancy is not planned, and many young people have not yet grasped the value or uniqueness of an individual life. Many of them have been conditioned through television drama and the movies to get rid of problems in the quickest way, though not always the best way. Almost always in these situations the inconvenient person dies. That is how problems in fiction are solved. On television you rarely reform, convert, or heal; you just kill. That is the easy solution. Young people often get reality and fiction confused.

It is difficult for some people to grasp what we mean by the value of an individual human life. We find students to whom it would never occur that a child conceived through rape is of any consequence at all. Sometimes you will just have to go on with the questions and realize that you will not be able to convince some students that a girl should not have an abortion if she is raped or if the child is deformed. The best you can do in a case like that is to tell them to think about the facts you have given them. Tell them to try to put themselves in the place of the child or ask them to discuss it with some of their classmates who have grasped the argument.

It is best not to address other issues during the question period. If you get into capital punishment, nuclear freeze, or whatever, the students will get distracted and may become more involved in the distraction than in the abortion issue you are discussing. Someone will probably try to get on the subject of contraception, but it is better to hold steadfast to the subject of abortion.

When speaking to high school students, be careful not to use sarcasm or levity. Someone in the group might be sensitive and easily offended. This often happens unintentionally. You may say something like: "What if your mother had been raped, and you are the product of that rape. Wouldn't you still be a valuable human being?" The student will not see that as a reasonable argument. He may see your example as an attack on his mother or himself. If you try to use forceful arguments that involve the students, you may appear to some as being too harsh.

Also, in a high school situation, don't expect a lot of questions or discussion. Most of the questions you will hear are on rape or deformity. Be prepared for those. But you may leave ten minutes for questions and not get any, so be prepared to go on with your presentation and ask questions they should be asking, then answer them. Many young people have not been thinking much about the issue, and they don't know what to ask.

Try to get students motivated to do something useful to fight abortion. Recruit them to come out to the clinics. Look for leaders. Some students will approach you after your talk and say they want to do more. Have a handout with suggestions of things for them to do and someone they can get in touch with. Before your talk, find out if there is a pro-life group at the school, and if there is someone active in pro-life who will help get the interested students involved in the movement. And keep an eye out for hostile teachers. In some schools, there are avid "pro-choice" teachers who have brain-washed some of the students and will even have the students prepared to try to embarrass you and make you look foolish before the class or assembly. They will have the students prepared to find your presentation "tasteless and emotional".

Most talks to high school students will be rewarding, but it is wise to be prepared for any situation that could possibly arise.

Films:

Assignment: Life (52 min./16mm color), *A Matter of Choice* (30 min./16mm), *Conceived in Liberty* (59 min./16mm color), *The Silent Scream* (27 min./16mm color). Purchase from:

AMERICAN PORTRAIT FILMS
1695 W. Crescent Ave.
Suite 500
Anaheim, CA 92801
(714) 535−2189

All are powerful films which feature interviews with abortionists as well as pro-lifers. *Assignment: Life* shows an actual saline abortion and *Conceived in Liberty* has a video-taped sonogram of an actual D & C abortion described and explained by Dr. Bernard Nathanson.

Abortion—A Woman's Decision (23 min./16mm), *The Committee* (21 min.), *The First Days of Life* (28 min.), *Pregnant? Need Help?* (20 min.), *Two is a Crowd* (35 min.). Rent from:

ILLINOIS RIGHT TO LIFE
COMMITTEE
   53 W. Jackson St., Rm. 832
   Chicago, IL 60604
   (312) 922−1918

Who Shall Survive? (20 min.). Purchase from:

LIFE CYCLE BOOKS
   12 Richmond St., East
   Suite 633
   Toronto, Ontario M5C 1N1
   (461) 364−7940 or 532−5037

The Reality of Abortion (26 min.). Rent from:

NATIONAL RIGHT TO LIFE
COMMITTEE
   419 7th St., NW
   Suite 402
   Washington, DC 20004
   (202) 638−4396

The Commitment (25 min.). Purchase from:

THIS IS THE LIFE FILMS
   Box 14572
   St. Louis, MO 63178

94 THE ABORTION HOSPITAL: A SPECIAL PROBLEM

Hospitals where abortions are performed present a special challenge to the pro-life activist. Finding out which hospitals perform abortions is more difficult than discovering the abortion clinics, because hospitals rarely advertise their abortion program.

It is necessary to check with hospital personnel or make phone calls to the OB-GYN department to ascertain if abortions are done, and at what stages of pregnancy they are performed. It is helpful to have an insider keep you informed on numbers of abortions, the names of the doctors who perform them, complications, and even incidents of survival of live-aborted babies.

When you suspect that a hospital is considering allowing abortions, try to arrange a meeting with the board of trustees or hospital governing committee and ask to present arguments against adopting a pro-abortion policy. Occasionally such a request will be granted. If it is, use the time to make a graphic presentation of fetal development, show abortion photographs, and use all the arguments you can muster against abortion. Many on the board will not be acquainted with these facts.

More often than not, your request to meet with the board will be denied and you will have to approach the board members one by one. They are often local businessmen, ministers, or pillars of the community, who may meet with you if you approach them openly and honestly.

When we were trying to keep abortion from being introduced at a suburban hospital, we contacted half the governing board and showed them a slide presentation. Half the board voted against abortion. These were the ones we had talked to. But the split vote allowed the proposal to go through.

Another time, while abortions were being performed at a Chicago hospital, we tried to have the board reconsider its policy. We contacted a powerful member of the board at his office in the Loop. We convinced him that abortion was contrary to good medical practice as well as being immoral. He assured us that he would speak against the hospital's abortion policy. Then he contacted his Episcopal bishop for spiritual advice and was assured that abortion was sometimes justified. Thanks to the bishop, we lost the case.

But in other instances, we have been able to talk governing boards out of making abortion hospital policy or into reversing an existing pro-abortion policy. All of this has been accomplished at the board level.

When it is impossible to influence hospital governing boards, other measures must be taken to try to stop abortion in a place dedicated to healing. The hospital is in a sensitive position from a public relations perspective. It is more sensitive than an abortion clinic. The hospital depends on public support and approval. It is vulnerable to bad publicity.

By alerting hospital administrators to your plans to leaflet, picket, hold demonstrations, and do all of these things with press coverage, you sometimes will force them to meet with you. While these meetings often bear little fruit, they free the activist to begin a more aggressive program with a public statement that every channel of diplomacy has been tried and has failed. Most of our meetings with administrators have been failures, and the media have always been supportive of the hospital. But at least the groundwork was laid for our activist program.

It is more difficult to picket a hospital than to picket an abortion clinic. It is nearly impossible to counsel outside of a hospital, due to the volume of patients, inaccessibility of the abortion area of the hospital, and the coming and going of ambulances, visitors, and staff, most of whom are not involved in the abortion practice. A sit-in in a hospital is rare, and something from which most pro-lifers shy away because of the possibility of interfering with routine hospital activities that might hamper the legitimate operation of the hospital. This does not mean that hospital sit-ins have not taken place, but they must be carefully planned and precautions must be taken to avoid harm to the patients.

The most effective activities against an abortion hospital are marches and public demonstrations, with appropriate signs, caskets, muffled drums, and chants; wide distribution of leaflets, such as that reproduced at the end of this chapter; contacts with patients, visitors, and hospital personnel outside the hospital; gathering of pro-life forces inside the hospital's reception area, with the administrators invited to meet the group to discuss the hospital's abortion policy. In one instance in Chicago, seventy-five pro-lifers with thirty small caskets, signs, and banners, gathered in the hospital reception area where a statement was read. When the administrator did not respond, the statement was read again, slowly and deliberately. The media came inside to televise and record the events.

On another occasion in Madison, Wisconsin, only two people from the pro-life group were allowed to enter the hospital to meet with the administrator. The other pickets stayed at the hospital entrance with signs and other pro-life paraphernalia and continued to chant. Their support helped make the meeting a media event.

At a demonstration in Bloomington, Indiana, following the starvation death of Baby Doe, six members of the pro-life group entered the hospital while a hundred demonstrators lined up outside. Thirty small caskets were placed on a purple cloth on the lawn in front of the hospital. Children opened the caskets and placed roses inside. All of this activity—the meeting as well as the march and the casket display outside—made a good story that received excellent media attention and has been repeated many times on national television.

It has been the ambition of more than one pro-life leader to get people from the community served by the hospital to organize demonstrations, make phone calls, write letters, carry out boycotts, and instigate effective action against the hospital. At one point the Pro-Life Action League organized a series of hospital demonstrations, intending to train local pro-lifers to take up the cause and keep the demonstrations going. This worked for a while in one Chicago suburb, but eventually this died out. Occasional demonstrations are held, but the leadership has to be brought in from outside. When pro-lifers from the community do not organize the demonstrations, the effort inevitably fails. It is nearly impossible for an outside organization to coordinate dozens of hospital demonstrations on an ongoing basis.

The League has tried many programs to close down abortion wings of hospitals in the Chicago area and elsewhere. The most successful was the closing of the V.I.P. (Voluntary Interruption of Pregnancy) ward at Cook County Hospital in 1980. The undertaking required six years of on-again, off-again effort, including attendance at Cook County board meetings, pickets, demonstrations, radio and television debates, infiltration of the hospital with pro-lifers, confrontations with hospital personnel, work on state legislation to cut off tax funding of abortions, and meetings with the Cook County board president.

Outside forces also played a part in that the Hyde Amendment, which cut off federal funds for welfare abortions, had to be found constitutional before the Illinois state law could go into effect. When this happened, the county president decided that the Hyde regulations also applied to tax funded abortions in the county. When all of these efforts came together, Cook County board president George Dunne closed down the abortion ward. He announced that since no specific amount was designated for the performance of abortions, no county money at all could be used to keep the abortion ward open.

The decision triggered a wild outcry from feminists, the American Civil Liberties Union, and other pro-abortionists. But even after public hearings, the Cook County board voted unanimously to uphold Dunne's decision. In 1984, an effort was made to reintroduce abortion at Cook County Hospital, but pro-life efforts and Dunne's determination defeated the recommendation.

Pro-life leaders in Chicago had hoped that the Cook County Hospital pro-life victory would trigger similar action across the country, but we have learned of only one other hospital, in Texas, where abortions were discontinued through use of similar tactics. (If our readers know of other instances of hospital boards discontinuing abortions, please contact our office and relay this information to us.)

When abortion first became legal in Illinois in 1973, we met with the head of the OB-GYN department of Evanston Hospital and listened to a story about how he had to perform abortions against the Hippocratic Oath and his own better judgment. At that time, we asked him what it would take for him to stop performing abortions and his answer was direct, but cowardly: change the law.

The only sure way to get abortion out of America's hospitals is to make abortion illegal. Until then, pro-life activists will work to get hospital boards to change their abortion policy. While this is a difficult and frustrating battle, without it there will be no victory. Someday we will be glad we fought the battle for the American hospitals, because hospitals are for healing, not for killing. It will be to everyone's advantage when this lesson is finally learned.

SPECIAL HANDOUTS FOR HOSPITALS PROVIDING ABORTION

While it is more difficult to get abortion out of a hospital, the notoriety a hospital will get from a leaflet like this can be more effective than a sit-in or picket. Leaflets may be distributed to employees, to staff, to visitors, and throughout the neighborhood. In Chicago thousands of these leaflets have been placed under the windshield wipers of cars parked in the vicinity of the hospital where abortions are performed.

HOSPITALS ARE FOR HEALING. WHY DO THEY KILL HERE?

A hospital is a place where sick people come to be healed. This hospital heals a lot of people. But it violates its pledge to heal each time it treats a pregnancy like a disease and aborts a living human being.
Science is clear about the beginning of human life; it starts at the onset of a woman's pregnancy, at fertilization. Doctors know this. Most of them have taken an oath not to perform abortions. But they break that oath each time they destroy an unborn baby through abortion.

Here are the terrible and inhuman methods used in abortion. This hospital utilizes one or more of them:

The Dilation and Curettage abortion uses a loop shaped, steel knife. The uterus is entered through the vagina. The cervix is stretched open, the surgeon then cuts the tiny body to pieces and slices the placenta from the inside walls of the uterus. The operating nurse then reassembles the parts to make sure the womb is empty. The **D&E(Dilation & Evacuation)** is similar to the D&C except that the baby is large. Special forceps with teeth must be used to tear off the arms and legs.

The suction abortion is like the D&C except that a powerful suction tube is inserted into the womb. This tears apart the body of the developing baby and his placenta, sucking them into a jar. The body parts are easily recognizable.

Saline or Prostaglandin abortion is used when a baby is too large to be cut up and must be aborted by means of chemical injections. Salting out involves injecting a concentrated salt solution into the amniotic sac. This poisons the baby and burns off the outer layers of skin. Prostaglandin is a drug given to the mother to bring on premature labor. Both methods can result in a live birth.

Hysterotomy abortion is a method like a Caesarean Section until after the cord is cut. Instead of the baby's phlegm being sucked out and the baby taken to intensive care where everything is done to save her, in an abortion she is cut free and dropped into a bucket and left to die. At this late stage they move, breathe and some even cry.

IF you want to help us get abortions **stopped** at this hospital, and return it to a place dedicated to healing only, contact us for information and assistance:

PRO·LIFE ACTION LEAGUE

Joseph M. Scheidler, Director   6160 N. Cicero Ave. Chicago, IL 60646   Office (312)777-2900 Newsline (312)777-2525

95 HOLD A TRIAL OF ABORTIONISTS

Several years ago Paul Brown, founder of the Life Amendment Political Action Committee, checked the map of the United States and found a little town in Pennsylvania called Nuremberg. Paul decided the pro-life movement should hold a second Nuremberg Trial.

Nuremberg, Germany, was the seat of the Nazi party. The Nazis held a huge rally there every year. It seemed appropriate when the Allies conquered Germany to make Nuremberg the scene of the trials to judge the crimes against humanity committed during the Third Reich.

Paul thought it would be newsworthy for pro-life leaders to hold a trial in Nuremberg, Pennsylvania, for the U.S. Supreme Court justices who had been responsible for the holocaust of millions of unborn children. He began planning a mock trial of the justices and other leaders of the abortion movement.

Some people thought this was a good idea. Others didn't like it. After some debate, Paul scuttled plans for the Second Nuremberg Trial. But it is a clever idea, and we think it should be revived.

A symbolic event like this could single out the main leaders of the abortion movement: judges, doctors, politicians, philosophers, movie stars—abortion leaders in every walk of life would be singled out by name to represent all those in each profession who support and encourage abortion.

A leaflet put out by The Center for Documentating the American Holocaust in Palm Springs, California, names people behind the abortion industry in California. The authors, Phil and Janette Dreisbach, urge pro-lifers to list the names of local abortion providers and promoters in their own publications.

Some people call this judgmental, and even un-Christian. Certainly we must be charitable. But, sometimes the most charitable thing we can do, in the face of a great evil, is to admonish the evildoers to turn away from that evil. Identifying the abortionists is not evil but may be the best thing for them and for the community. Identifying the abortionists is a reasonable step in dealing with an issue that is badly misunderstood. By identifying them, abortion may get discussed in connection with community members, and the cover of misinformation may begin to dissolve. This might lead them to question whether they want to be identified as the local abortionists. To be Christian is sometimes to do the difficult thing and sometimes the seemingly unkind thing, for the sake of a greater good.

The Nuremberg trial would have to be conducted with the accused *in absentia*, of course, through the device of the empty chair or some form of effigy. The proceedings, the presentation of witnesses, the selection of a jury, a prosecutor, a defender, and the judge would all have to be done in such a way that everything would be dignified. Everything would be done with the understanding that it was serious symbolism, and a way to point out to the public who is guilty of a crime against humanity and against our country.

The mock Nuremberg trial would remind people that abortion is a grave evil and that those who are responsible for it are the enemies of this country. What would an enemy, determined to destroy our nation, attempt to do but destroy our young people and sap the nation of its strength? This is what abortion has been doing to America.

When our plan to hold a mock Nuremberg trial of abortionists in the little town of 1,500 in Pennsylvania appeared in a story in *Newsweek* we began getting phone calls from newspapers in that area. We believe a mock Nuremberg trial could be a significant media event, and we intend to carry it out with the cooperation of other activist pro-life groups who have written to express their interest in taking part in it.

96 BE A PRAYER WARRIOR

The bottom line is this: we must pray and work. *Ora et labora*, pray and work, has been my motto for many years, since I was a Benedictine monk studying for the priesthood. The way to stop abortion is to pray as though everything depends on God and to work as though everything depends on you.

The power of prayer and the need for prayer cannot be stressed enough. Prayer is something that everyone can do to stop abortion. If you cannot be an activist, you can do active praying. And prayer works. I have seen prayer work, and I have received tremendous help from the prayers of others.

We must pray for the perseverance of pro-life activists. It helps them cope with the abuse, rejection, threats, and the ignorance, selfishness, and disregard for life that makes their jobs so difficult. We must pray for mothers, so that they can discover joy in the awesome gift of motherhood and respond positively to its responsibilities. We must pray for abortionists, so that they will come to realize the value of the lives they terminate. We must pray for the unborn—those still living, but threatened with imminent death, and those who have died. We must become Prayer Warriors.

There are countless stories that I could use to illustrate the power of prayer. One stands out. I was addressing a crowd at the conclusion of our First National Activist Convention in a church in Ft. Lauderdale, Florida. The next morning I was going to fly to Los Angeles to spend three days with 600 abortion providers at the National Abortion Federation Convention (NAF). In my talk I mentioned that I could understand how Christ must have felt at the Last Supper when He longed to be with His Apostles because He knew that He was going to face a terrible experience shortly afterwards.

I told the group that I was about to face the most difficult three days I spend each year. The conventioneers give me a bad time, knowing that I am from the Pro-life Action League. I have to suffer through discussions on how they suck out brains and rip off arms and leave parts in the uterus and deal with syphylitic women. It's a hard three days.

I asked the group to pray that I would survive this convention without any spiritual or physical harm, so that I could learn the abortionists' methods and techniques in order to use this information to expose the sordidness of their profession. The group prayed, and I am sure most prayed for me during those next three days. I know because I worked with a sense of inner peace that I have rarely felt, before or since. I was castigated, threatened, put out of meetings, shoved and called names, but I took back with me more valuable information and more horror stories from the abortionists, more quotable quotes than I ever found before in such a short time. I uncovered material that I continue to use to this day. My food and fuel was prayer. It sustained me. It made that hideous meeting a success for the pro-life movement. The experience was another proof to me that we cannot succeed in this work without prayer.

Work and pray. Pro-life meetings start and end with prayer. By the nature of their work, pro-lifers become more prayerful. Before any pro-life event, pray that you will know what is right, and then do it with the knowledge and trust that God has chosen you to preserve and save His children.

On the other hand, I do not recall a single meeting or workshop or even a meal at the abortionists' conventions, where anyone ever stopped to pray. I do recall them holding a moment of silence once when they received word that one of their colleagues had died.

Prayer seems, in fact, to terrify the abortion providers. We held an all night prayer vigil at a clinic in Chicago with pro-lifers coming in shifts and some remaining throughout the night. We were praying and singing. It upset the clinic personnel so much that they hired a security guard to stay all night. That cost them extra money. Around midnight the building owner and his wife arrived. They were furious. They had set up police barricades, and they watched us from the clinic window throughout the night.

We had no picket signs and we did not chant. We had vigil candles and we prayed. We were still praying when the clinic staff began to arrive in the morning to do their grizzly work. They seemed disgusted with our prayer vigil, and when patients began arriving many were intimidated by our prayerful presence there. By midmorning the abortionists had become so enraged that they called the police and made unreasonable and false charges against us. The police began barking orders and eventually arrested one of our group for no apparent reason. Clearly our prayerful presence had greatly disturbed the abortionists.

And clearly they have a reason to be disturbed and to be uneasy. They must surely know that God is on the side of life.

As Dr. Charles Rice, Notre Dame Law Professor, said several years ago, the pro-life movement is a movement of prayer and action. That is the combination that will restore America's Judeo-Christian heritage and belief in the sanctity of life. The battle will be won. Legalized abortion will be stopped, but not just through books about how to stop it or through the activities of those who work to stop it. It will be stopped by the combination of these activities with deep, fervent prayer, with the conviction that God is there and that He wants us to do His will.

97 WHATEVER YOU DO, DO IT WITH LOVE....

Even though some of the things pro-life activists do to stop abortion may seem hostile, we must never lose sight of the fact that what we are trying to do is save lives, while helping preserve women's mental, physical, and spiritual health. We can do these things only if we love the people we confront.

Our concern is manifest in what Fr. John Powell, S.J. calls "tough love". It is not soft, saccharine love, but a love that says, "We want you to do the right thing. But since you don't know what is right, we will make you look at abortion in its ugly reality. If you can't learn through persuasion, we will use pressure." That doesn't mean we don't love the abortionists. The parent who never punishes an unruly child doesn't love his child. A weak parent is concerned about being liked and fails to do the loving thing. What we are doing has to be done, like punishing an unruly child. What the abortionists are doing is evil. Out of love, we do what we must to change their minds.

Franky Schaeffer told pro-lifers that the most loving thing he had done in the past year was to spank his son, who had run into the street and nearly got hit by a truck. To prevent future tragedy, punishment had to be administered. Punishment might save his son's life. It was given because Franky Schaeffer loves his son and wants him around for a few more years.

Those of us who confront the abortionists and debate them on radio and television, do not like them very much. They are selfish and humorless. But occasionally one is likeable, and you feel a genuine concern for him. Sometimes it is hard to realize that to make a living, he kills children and ruins women's lives.

But whatever natural revulsion or even attraction they elicit, the fact remains that everything we do in relation to the abortionists is done because we love them. We do not want anyone to lose his soul. We do not want the abortionists to be punished in hell for eternity. Yet we believe there is reward and punishment after this life, that good will be rewarded and evil punished. Our determination to get the abortionists out of their grizzly business is a greater act of love than they are shown by their colleagues.

To talk a person out of doing abortions or to put him out of business shows greater love than excusing what he does. We tell abortionists that what they do is wrong. Who loved Herod? John the Baptist, who pointed out his evil and told him to repent, or Herodias, who asked for the head of John? John tried to convert Herod. Herodias merely wanted the Baptist silenced. Throughout history, it has been those who really love who try to convert people from evil to good.

We know in advance that love for our enemy will be misconstrued and that we will be made fun of for mentioning it. Many cannot understand what we are talking about. Most of them will not believe us. But some suspect that we may be right. One abortion clinic operator told us she realized that what she was doing would send her to hell, but that was her decision to make and not ours. She was right. But we had to try.

We don't expect most abortionists to understand that what we are trying to do is for their good. It is not important that they understand.

We must be careful not to do any of these things out of hatred. We cannot fight the battle for the unborn with hatred. We do it selflessly for someone who will never know we did it. We do it knowing that the person we save at the clinic door may never realize he was in mortal danger. We do it to bear witness to society, and to the abortionists, that there is a better way to solve problems than by killing children.

Pro-life is a movement based on the highest form of altruism, so there is no room for hatred. We can hate abortion, but we cannot hate the abortionist or we betray our cause. We do everything for the love of God and the children. We are trying to save the parents who, under different circumstances, would not consider abortion. We do it even out of love for the abortion providers, some of whom have been deceived into thinking they are solving a problem. Some may believe that abortion is the lesser of two evils. It is difficult to understand such a deception, but we are not in a position to judge their guilt.

We can base our activities on our hatred of abortion, but not on hatred of the abortionists. Scripture admonishes us to love our enemies and do good to those who hate us. We are told that charity is the greatest virtue and that God loves each of us. If God loves the abortionists, we must love them, too.

The ultimate hatred is that which sends a soul to hell. In *Hamlet*, the prince in planning to murder his step-father, catches him in prayer and decides not to kill him then, because he might send him to heaven. Hamlet wants his step-father to go to hell and decides to murder him in the midst of some debauchery. It is true hatred to wish to see a person eternally lost.

This is not what we want. We want the abortionists to be converted, return to God, and be saved. We bring them to God by loving them, not by hating them.

Many women who have had abortions have repented and are now pro-lifers. Many former supporters of abortion now defend the unborn. A young Chicago couple, Darryl and Debbie Trulson, go to clinics, appear on radio and television to discuss abortion, and fight tirelessly for the unborn. At one time they supported abortion and defended it. Seeing them totally committed to pro-life, it is hard to realize that they were once the enemy. I frequently encounter pro-life people who confess, "Last year at this time I was fighting you." People are fighting us today who will be pro-life leaders tomorrow. We love them when they join us. We should love them before they join us.

As Christians, we must love everyone. We want to change society so that it is not so difficult to love, and someday that may happen. In the meantime, we must love what we've got, pray for the abortionists and, through "tough love", help them realize that what they are doing offends God. Never stop believing that your prayers and efforts to close their clinics will turn them from the evil of killing children.

No matter what anyone says about our activities, and our attitudes, whether it is evident or not, we know that pro-life non-violent direct action is based on love.

98 YOU ARE THE PRO-LIFE MOVEMENT

Many people believe the pro-life movement has to be a national organization, with headquarters in Washington, D.C. They think it must have national leaders whom all pro-lifers look up to and take their orders from. The constant refrain, "Why don't all the pro-life groups get together under one umbrella?" is well meaning, but also trite and unrealistic.

The reason we don't come under one umbrella is that the pro-life cause is a grass roots movement. Abortions are not done only in Washington, D.C., but in cities and towns across America. The battles must be fought on the battlefields, and the battlefields are everywhere. So pro-life has to be organized on the local level to fight local battles.

The pro-life movement probably doesn't need a national leader to take orders from. What it needs, though, are thousands of local leaders who can organize and activate local groups. Effective national leaders are supposed to organize effective national programs that work on the local level and find the leadership in the areas where these programs are needed. Then they stay in touch with local leadership and encourage local groups to do the work that needs to be done where they are. The successful pro-life movement consists of little cells of pro-life activists all over the country closing down the clinics in their locales; stopping women from having abortions in their town or neighborhood; setting up pregnancy help agencies there; educating local high school students; parents, and teachers; getting into the classrooms—and all using the basic, simple story that every life is precious and that abortion is murder and, if allowed to continue, will destroy the country. That is the way the movement should be functioning if it plans on winning. That is the type of program the Pro-Life Action League has been promoting.

This means that the pro-life activist reading this book is the pro-life movement. The movement is everyone who works, suffers, and sacrifices for the unborn. The movement is not any individual. It is not Jack Wilke. It is not Nellie Gray, Judie Brown, or Curtis Young. It is you. You have the power to stop abortion. And that is the way it should be, especially in this country. Every person in America is a sovereign citizen, an important individual with inalienable rights, and with a constitutional guarantee supporting those rights.

Many Americans seem to have lost that traditional belief in their own value and importance. An American citizen is a marvelous and powerful thing to be. It is unlike almost any other citizenship in the world. Our forefathers knew this well, but we seem to have forgotten it.

An American citizen has tremendous power and importance. We should recognize this power and use it for good. That is why it is exciting to see the movement coming back to the people. It can be successful in the hands of the people because the power structure in this country is based on the people. If the people don't want something, they will work successfully against it. If they don't like the laws and regulations or the way things are being decided for them, they will eventually change them. That is what America is about. It is the government of, by, and for the people.

The American people, with some local exceptions, were never allowed to vote on abortion. Abortion-on-demand was handed to Americans by a Supreme Court *fiat*, through a very serious misinterpretation of the Constitution. So if Americans don't want abortion-on-demand, they can change it. They have the power to change their laws. They also have the ability to change their legislators. They can even change their judges, although this is more difficult. They can demand that whatever is ruining their country and destroying its moral fiber be stopped.

The power of the individual in defying a bad law is never exercised more strikingly than when a person goes to an abortion clinic, confronts someone who is going in to deny another human being his guaranteed right to life, talks her out of having an abortion, and preserves the life of her child. That is something each of us can do. In saving a life, we perpetuate decency, morality, righteousness, and the spirit of the Constitution. It is something that every God-fearing, patriotic, pro-life American should experience. It is an on-the-spot reversal of the *Roe v. Wade*, *Doe v. Bolton* abortion decisions at the doorstep of the abortion clinic. This should be done all over the country. It is being done. There are pro-life sidewalk counselors on the streets of America today who have stopped as many as twenty abortions in a single day at a single clinic.

If a few can do it, it would seem that every pro-lifer who wants to can do the same. Such an achievement shows the power of the individual and the strength of the pro-life arguments. It proves that life is stronger than death and that individual initiative is a powerful weapon against all odds: the courts, the media, feminist propaganda, the American Medical Association, the American Civil Liberties Union, Planned Parenthood, and evil leaders. It says the dedicated pro-life activist can defeat the enemy through his ability to convince and persuade. It is a life-saving use of his constitutional rights of free speech and assembly.

These rights need to be protected and strengthened, and that happens by exercising them. The right to free speech and the right to join others in a common pursuit, give pro-life activists the power to save lives and eventually reverse the Supreme Court abortion decisions. This knowledge, reinforced by experience, builds the activist's confidence and appreciation of himself as a free citizen. If you are that kind of person, you are the pro-life movement.

The abortionists must depend on the police, the courts, the media, their own propaganda machine, a steady parade of confused, unhappy women, wimpish boyfriends and spineless spouses, and lots of money to keep their abortion business operating. They depend on resources we don't have, such as money, and many that we don't want, such as lies, greed, and deception, to keep abortion "viable". We depend on the value and integrity of the individual based on the laws of nature and those of God.

Remember that when you are praising or condemning the pro-life movement you are praising or condemning *yourself*. The movement is powerful because it consists of powerful individuals working hand-in-hand with the best traditions of this country, based on the Judeo-Christian ethic and flowing directly from the law of God. The pro-life movement is weak when it is made up of weak, fearful, unreliable people who have high motives but resolutions they can't live up to.

When our actions catch up with our ambition and resolve, the collapse of the abortion industry in America will be only a matter of time.

99 WRITE THE NEXT CHAPTER YOURSELF

The book ends here.

But this may be the most important chapter of all, because the battle against abortion really begins when you adopt these suggestions, recommendations, and clues in your battle against the outrageous crime of abortion in this country. The things we have discussed in this book *will* work. They have worked, and are working today. Some work better than others. Some will work for you but not for other pro-lifers. You have to be selective. There are special circumstances that make your situation unique and call for some of these techniques and rule out others. You have to be the judge of that.

But these chapters do not tell the whole story of how to close the abortion clinics. The best chapters may be waiting to be written. This is why the final chapter of this book is an invitation and urgent recommendation for you to use the kind of inventiveness represented here to think up new programs to close abortion clinics and bring about the collapse of the industry.

It has often surprised me, when discussing techniques described here, how many pro-lifers had not thought of them before. Loading the appointment books, sending coverts into the clinics posing as patients, leaving messages on their tape machines, assisting patients in suing the clinic, checking malpractice suits, getting the doctors' home addresses from their license plates—there is nothing unusual about these ideas. Any pro-life activist can come up with similar or better ones. The more determined you are, the more inventive you will be.

There is a lot of imagination and creativity still untapped in the pro-life ranks. There are effective means of carrying on the guerilla warfare necessary for victories in the battle against abortion. There are many ideas not mentioned here because we haven't thought of them yet.

We have discussed some uses of electronic devices, but there must be many more ways to use audiovisuals to impress on people going into the clinics the horror of the abortions that go on inside. We have considered playing taped recordings of women who have had abortions, appealing to those going in for abortions. We thought of having a shaded screen and behind the screen a projector so people coming to the clinic could see what an abortion procedure looks like or watch a film on fetal development. We have thought of playing a tape of the heartbeat of the baby in the early stage of development. These things and many others can be implemented with a little determination and skill.

Use your imagination and the facilities at your disposal, and study the tactics of those who have successfully achieved social change in the past. It doesn't hurt to find out what has worked for our opponents. Study the techniques and methods of strategists like Saul Alinsky, who have achieved their goals and helped others achieve theirs, even though our goals are different. Be careful to follow moral principles and draw the line between a godless revolution and a God-motivated one.

We must not deceive ourselves into thinking we may do whatever we please. Not everything is permitted. The end does *not* justify any means. But we cannot succumb to pietism and the idea that all that matters is that we preserve our peace of mind, save our souls, and gain respect. We have an obligation to try to change the society we live in. Probably the most serious error in Christian thinking during the last fifty years has been preoccupation with individual spirituality while ignoring what is happening to society. Christ said we are our brother's keeper. There are times when we have to let our brother know what is right and what is wrong.

People often say that we cannot impose our morality on others. That is partly true, but mostly false. It is true that we cannot force others to be moral, but we can certainly show them what morality is. Someone must impose God's morality—genuine, true Judeo-Christian morality—on society soon. Failing that, one of these days this country will be lost. The United States is in grave danger.

We have a God-given obligation to be concerned for each person's well being, and society's well being. We are part of society and part of its history. It is time we understand that and start living according to a philosophy that says we look out for our neighbor because we are our brother's keeper. If our brother doesn't know what is right and wrong, we have to impose a little of our morality on him, whether he likes it or not.

The next chapter, or the next ninety-nine, or whatever it takes to shut down the abortion industry, are yours. I have tried to present some suggestions for putting the abortionists out of business. But the fight belongs to us all. New ideas are forming now in the minds of many. Someone is going to come up with the plan or combination of plans that will bring about the final collapse of the abortion industry, an industry of destruction and death. The abortion industry will ultimately destroy itself. But since it is destroying society along with itself, we must speed up the process of its destruction, in the hope that our society will survive.

There is a footnote in history that says Abraham Lincoln met Harriet Beecher Stowe, the author of "Uncle Tom's Cabin". He addressed her, "So you're the little lady who started the big war." Her story about slavery had to be told, in graphic, emotional terms because she needed to arouse a sleeping nation. The story of abortion must also be told that way.

The solution to slavery was a terrible war. Abortion, the most bloody war in our country's history, is going on now in abortion clinics and hospitals and doctors' offices across the nation. We are witnessing a civil war. There must be an all-out effort to end the tragedy of this century, the murder of our helpless unborn, one every twenty seconds in the abortion industry.

This book is a step in the early phase of the beginning of the collapse of that industry. It is part of a new Activist Manifesto to do something about the outrage of abortion. This is a Manifesto for which you, or perhaps your children, will write the final chapter.

INDEX

Hackell, Nancy: 251
Hah, Ming Kow: 173
Harvard University: 11
Hayes Publishing Co., Inc.: 38, 97, 125, 186
Hekman, Randall: 60
Helms, Jesse: 251
Heritage House '76, Inc.: 39, 96
Hippocratic Oath: 93, 328
Holy Family Society of U.S.A.: 107
Horn, Jerry: 165, 300, 317
Hospital and Medical Services Governing Commission: 86
Human Life and National Family Foundation: 292
Huxley, Aldous: 12
Hyde Amendment: 44, 264, 265, 327
Hyde, Henry: 100, 162, 251, 264, 281

Illinois Pro-Life Coalition: 150
Illinois Right to Life Committee: 125, 150, 324
Illinois Women's Agenda: 72
Infomat-Right to Life: 97
Information from the Dominican Educational Association (IDEA): 97
Institute for Fund-Raising: 130
Internal Revenue Service (IRS): 83, 84, 167, 168, 175

Jakubczyk, John: 9, 165, 297
Jefferson, Mildred: 251, 264
Jones, Sandra: 9
Journal of the American Medical Association: 201

Kasar, Naim: 155, 156
Keaton, Brey: 228
Kelly, John: 85, 86, 165
Kentucky Right to Life: 150

Kennedy, Edward: 142, 266, 267, 283
Kesey, Ken: 39
Kirkbride, Sandy: 246
Kiwanis: 124
Knights of Columbus: 38, 89, 124
Koop, C. Everett: 77

Labor Department: 264
Landwehr, Carl J.: 34
Law, Bernard: 11
Lee, Sam: 251
Lennon, John: 142
Lewis, C. S.: 12
Life Amendment Political Action Committee, Inc.: 285, 330
Life Cycle Books: 38, 77, 96, 125, 324
Lifeline: 137
Lincoln, Abraham: 280, 343
Lions: 124
Luedke, William J.: 292

Mackey, John: 100
MacNeil/Lehrer Report: 238
Madison General Hospital: 204
Maguire, Marjorie: 74
Mann, Nancy Jo: 228
Marzen, Tom: 251
Masella, Marian: 219
Mead Johnson and Company: 202
Menes, Barbara: 9
Merck, Sharp and Dohme: 202
Miles Pharmaceuticals Division: 201
Miller, Jeanne: 136
Mills, Lynn: 254
Monaghan, T. Pat: 237
Montgomery, Marjorie: 148, 150
Moral Majority: 105, 239
Mormon Church: 84
Mormon Tabernacle Choir: 226
Morris, Pat: 228
Morrow, Greg: 179